THE HISTORY OF MANN'S PATENT STEAM CART AND WAGON COMPANY

Eur Ing John Pease BSc CEng MInstMC

Published by

LANDMARK
Publishing Ltd

Landmark Publishing Ltd
Ashbourne Hall, Cokayne Ave, Ashbourne, Derbyshire DE6 1EJ England
Tel: (01335) 347349 Fax: (01335) 347303
e-mail: landmark@clara.net
web site: www.landmarkpublishing.co.uk

ISBN 1 84306 205 4

British Library Cataloguing in Publication Data: a catalogue record for this book is available from the British Library.

Print: Bath Press Ltd, Bath

Design: Mark Titterton

Cover: James Allsopp

Front cover: The revised 5-ton wagon of 1908 was constructed with a rolled steel chassis, to which was bolted the major components. *(David Riley-www.photoarchives.co.uk)*

Title page: This delightful photograph shows one of the agricultural tractors introduced during World War I. *(Martin Hallows collection)*

Back cover top: As title page. *(Martin Hallows collection)*

Bottom: An early Mann undertype lorry owned by brick makers and contractors, Garforth Brothers, of Mirfield. *(Martin Hallows collection)*

All photographs from the authors collection except where stated

LANDMARK COLLECTOR'S LIBRARY

THE HISTORY OF MANN'S PATENT STEAM CART AND WAGON COMPANY

Eur Ing John Pease BSc CEng MInstMC

Landmark Publishing

Contents

Acknowledgments

This book is by necessity a collection of evidence from a multitude of sources, and therefore sincere thanks are given to the many people who assisted in providing information, documents and photographs:

Joan Blakeley, Norman Boyes, Tony Brown, Les Burberry, Philip Calvert, Neil Dowlan, John Goodchild, Peter Griggs, Martin Hallows, Tony Hunt, Ernst Huwyler, Michael Lane, Pierre-Louis Lapointe, Geoff Lumb, Ziegler Markus, Stefan Mattes, John Middlemiss, Richard Morris, Malcolm Parsons, Derek Rayner, Joy Richens, David Riley, Henry Roskilly, Paul Sharpe, Phillip Sheppy, Tim Smith, Sarah Stocks, Frank Strange, John Walker, Michael Walters, Roger West, Robert Whitehead.

I would also like to thank the following organisations that have allowed me access to the documents used to compile this book:

Archives Nationales Quebec, Canada; Armley Mills Industrial Museum, Leeds; Bradford Local Studies Library; Bridlington Local Studies Library; The British Library, Boston Spa; Dampfwalzen-Club Schweiz; Institution of Mechanical Engineers; Leeds and District Traction Engine Society; Leeds Local History Library; Museum of English Rural Life, University of Reading; National Motor Museum, Beaulieu; Patent Information Unit, Leeds; The Probate Registry, York; Public Record Office, Kew; Register of Births, Marriages & Deaths, Dewsbury, Hull, Leeds and Sheffield; Road Locomotive Society; Royal Agricultural Society of England; Society of Antiquaries of London; Society of Motor Manufacturers and Traders; University of Leeds, Brotheron Library; Wakefield Local Studies Department; West Yorkshire Archive, Leeds and Wakefield; Yorkshire Agricultural Society, Harrogate; Yorkshire Archaeological Society, Leeds.

Finally, for their support of my research, and for their help and advice with my draft script, I would like to thank my wife Suzanne, and my sons Tom and Andrew.

Glossary

Ackermann steering. Ackermann steering is the type of steering used on most modern road vehicles. The wheels turn on the ends of the axle beam whilst the axle itself remains stationary. This is in comparison to most traction engines where the wheels are fixed to the axle beam and the whole beam rotates about a central pivot.

b.h.p. brake horse power - is a figure determined by attaching a test machine, the brake or dynamometer, to the engine output shaft and measuring the delivered power under a range of speeds and conditions. This figure is the actual available power from the machine and this measurement superseded the earlier systems because of its practicality

Bevel gear. A system of toothed wheels that connect shafts whose axes are at an angle to one another (usually 90 degrees) but in the same plane.

Compensating or Differential gear. When a vehicle turns a corner, the wheels are operating at different radii and therefore need to rotate at different speeds. The Compensating Gear allows this to occur whilst still providing torque to both wheels.

Compound cylinders. Compounding is a system where the exhaust from a cylinder is used to feed a further cylinder to extract additional energy. To be effective, the second cylinder is made a larger diameter than the first. In effect, the steam is used twice, thereby improving efficiency and reducing fuel consumption.

n.h.p. nominal horse power - is a system devised by the R.A.S.E. based on the diameter of the piston. This system was simply based on piston area, such that 10 square inch of piston area equals one nominal horsepower. In mathematical terms: n.h.p. = D x D/10, where D is the piston diameter in inches. This approach is very inflexible and takes no account of piston speed and boiler pressure, both of which have a significant effect on real power.

Overtype. This is a vehicle where the engine is mounted on top of the boiler, in a similar way to a traditional traction engine.

p.s.i. unit of pressure in pounds per square inch

R.A.S.E. Royal Agricultural Society of England

r.p.m. unit of speed in revolutions per minute

Radius-rod. A method of controlling the movement of an axle. A link or rod is fixed to the axle at one end and pivoted at the other. The result is that when the vehicle rides over a bump in the road the axle follows a circular path, constrained by the radius-rod. If the centres of the two transmission spur wheels are located, one at the axle centre and the other at the pivot centre, then these gears will remain in constant mesh, irrespective of axle movement.

Royal Show. The annual show of the Royal Agricultural Society of England, usually held in the first week of July.

S.M.M.T. The Society of Motor Manufacturers and Traders

Spur gear (or wheel). The simplest form of gear where a pair of toothed wheels connect input and output shafts that are parallel to each other. The smaller wheel in this arrangement is often called the **Pinion gear** or wheel.

Undertype. This is a vehicle where the engine is mounted below the load platform, usually between the front and rear wheels.

Worm and wheel. A gear of high reduction ratio, connecting shafts whose axes are at right-angles but do not intersect. The worm consists of a helical thread, which meshes with a concave faced gear wheel.

Introduction

It is not well recognised that the Mann steam cart and lorry, introduced in 1898 and 1899 respectively, were pioneers of load-carrying road vehicles, indeed, the overtype steam cart was the first successful machine of its type. The full story of Mann's Patent Steam Cart and Wagon Company and its predecessor Mann and Charlesworth has not been well researched before. This is partly because the company ceased trading in 1929, and little primary evidence, in the form of company documents, has survived. This book is a collection of evidence, found from a multitude of sources, assembled into a cohesive order, so that the reader can gain a good perception of the people and products that portray the company over its short, 36 years of existence.

The story of the company starts in June 1893 with the purchase of the small Canning Works on Dewsbury Road, Leeds, and the formation of the company Mann and Charlesworth early in 1894. In the early years, a variety of traditional steam traction engine related products emerged from the works. In addition, Mann and Charlesworth introduced their patent single-eccentric reversing gear in July 1894, which became one of their trademarks.

In parallel with these activities in Leeds, others were actively constructing early steam wagons. In 1896, Thornycroft constructed a 1-ton steam van in Chiswick, and at the same period, the Lancashire Steam Motor Company constructed in Leyland a similar looking vehicle. Meanwhile, back in Leeds, Mann and Charlesworth constructed their first steam cart in 1897. This was a very important development, as it was Britain's first load-carrying overtype machine, a configuration later used by many others, for example, Foden. The Mann vehicle was the catalyst for a new range of road vehicles that would sustain the company for more than thirty years, and make them one of the leading suppliers of steam wagons in Britain.

After what seems to be a difference of opinion, Charlesworth left the partnership in 1898, and James Hutchinson Mann continued trading independently for a short while. In September 1899, the organisation called Mann's Patent Steam Cart and Wagon Company was registered. The success of the patent wagon was such that Mann decided to construct a new works on Pepper Road, Hunslet, Leeds. The land for this was purchased in September 1900, and by December 1901 the company had moved to the new premises. This large, modern, well-equipped works was an ambitious move and was initially very successful. The period up to and including the First World War was the heyday of the company.

During the First World War, the petrol-powered lorry became a mature product and was produced in large numbers, partly as a result of government subsidies. At the cessation of hostilities, many of these petrol lorries became surplus and were sold at modest prices. This created a massive problem for steam lorry manufacturers because their products were not needed in any quantity. In addition, there is no evidence to suggest that Mann's attempted to design or construct an internal combustion powered vehicle. By 1926 Mann's Patent Steam Cart and Wagon Company was in trouble, and despite attempts to introduce modern products and provide additional finance it was not possible to save the company. In 1929 the works closed completely, followed in 1932 by the formal dissolution of the company.

Chapter 1

The People

James Hutchinson Mann was born on 2 May 1860 at 3 St. George's Terrace, Leeds.[1] His parents were William and Elizabeth Mann (née Staniforth). William Mann had previously married Elizabeth Hutchinson, on 4 January 1849 at St George's Church, Leeds, however Elizabeth died on 14 July 1856. William's second marriage, to Elizabeth Staniforth, took place at Norton Parish Church, Sheffield on 3 June 1858. Elizabeth's parents, Thomas and Ann, farmed 170 acres at Herdings Farm, Norton – which is now the south-eastern terminus of the Sheffield tramway. At the time of the wedding, William was 50 years of age, whilst Elizabeth was only 20 years old.[2]

William Mann appears to have been of independent means, for in contemporary local directories and his marriage certificate he is identified as a "Gentleman". In addition, records in the West Riding Land Registry indicate that he owned a portfolio of properties that were rented out.

In addition to James, the couple had three other children:

- William Hutchinson Mann who was born in Leeds, England in 1859
- Annie Elizabeth Mann who was born in Leeds, England in 1862
- George Hutchinson Mann who was born in Montreal, Canada in 1865

William Hutchinson Mann

William Hutchinson Mann, James' elder brother, was born in Leeds on 22 April 1859. He married Alice Jane Hudson, the daughter of Thomas Hudson, Maltster, of Pannal near Harrogate. Alice's brother Thomas Hudson was later to become a shareholder in Mann's Patent Steam Cart and Wagon Company. William also took engineering as a career and became a partner in the business Pullan & Mann, Brick Machinery Makers, Cambrian Works, Holbeck, Leeds. Like his brothers James and George, William was also an inventive engineer and there are numerous patents registered in his name. Over the twenty years 1890 to 1910 he lodged twenty-seven patents, all relating to machinery for making bricks, pipes and sanitary ware. All the patents are in the joint names of William Hutchinson Mann and John Samuel Pullan, with the first three also including John Gill who was a partner in the business at this time. William was one of the founding members of Mann's Patent Steam Cart and Wagon Company, and continued as a director and major shareholder until his death in 1926.

Figure 1: Pullan and Mann, Brick Making Press
James Hutchinson Mann's elder brother, William Hutchinson Mann was a partner with John Samuel Pullan as brick machinery makers in Elland Road, Leeds. This engraving illustrates one of their brick-making presses. *(The Engineer)*

Annie Elizabeth Mann

James' sister, Annie Elizabeth Mann was born in 1862. She married Thomas Loxley Horsfield at Leeds Parish Church on 16 February 1887. On the marriage certificate, Thomas Loxley Horsfield is described as a Pawnbroker. His father, Loxley Horsfield is recorded as being an Engineer. The Horsfield family were partners in the Larchfield Foundry, Hunslet, Leeds.

George Hutchinson Mann

George Hutchinson Mann, James' younger brother, was born in Montreal, Canada, on 4 June 1865.[3] Why he was born in Canada is not clear, but there is tenuous evidence that the family had relatives out there and perhaps William and Elizabeth were visiting. Unfortunately young George never met his father, because he died in Canada on 22 May 1865, aged 57, two weeks before his son's birth. On returning to Leeds, the family lived at Louis Street, which was (and still is) off Roundhay Road in the Potternewton district.[4] On 4 September 1876 Elizabeth was remarried, to William Holgate, a woollen manufacturer of Calverley near Leeds, and the family moved to 2 Eva Villas, close to Louis Street. At this time, George is recorded as being employed as a Mining Engineer's Apprentice.[5] At the age of 23, George married Fanny Tingle at St. Clement's Parish Church, Sheepscar, Leeds, on 22 January 1889. Fanny's father, William Tingle, is described as a Mechanic of 16 Francis Street.[6]

George Hutchinson Mann was also an inventive engineer, and played an important role in the establishment of the original Mann and Charlesworth company. His supporting role in supplying finance to the company allowed the fledgling business to expand and prosper. (See chapter 2 for further details.) In 1900 he lodged a series of patents, all relating to road vehicles:

Patent	Title	Applicants
12,282	Gearing for Motor Road Vehicles	G H Mann
21,608	Improvements in the Construction of Tubular Boilers	G H Mann and Joseph Clayton*
22,191	Improvements in or connected with Motor Propelled Road Vehicles	G H Mann and Joseph Clayton*

*Joseph Clayton's details are given as: Oak Hill, Park Lane, Moortown, Leeds, Gas Engineer. He was the son of Lawrence Clayton the founder of Clayton Son & Co. Ltd., boiler makers and gasholder makers, Hunslet, Leeds.

The second of these patents, lodged on 29 November 1900, *Improvements in the Construction of Tubular Boilers*, describes what was to become the 'Yorkshire' boiler. In Ronald Clarke's book, *The Development of the English Steam Wagon*, he says that this boiler was initially offered to Mann's Patent Steam Cart and Wagon Company, however James Mann rejected the idea. This sequence of events is probably accurate, since Ronald Clarke interviewed James Mann during the preparation of his book. The first practical machine using this boiler was built by the Yorkshire Steam Motor Company, of Ingham Street, Hunslet, Leeds in 1901. This was a 4-ton flat wagon with a compound undertype engine.[7] The cylinders were mounted external to the frame, one either side, for easy accessibility, and the transmission was by spur gears. Two-speed gearing was provided to give road speeds of 5½ and 2½ miles per hour. Subsequently Joseph Clayton went on to form the Yorkshire Patent Steam Wagon

Company, and the double-ended return-flue boiler, which George H. Mann had invented, became synonymous with this company. In retrospect, it is rather ironic that two brothers should create similar products that were in direct competition with each other. In addition, a further twist of fate determined that the two companies were located side by side on Pepper Road, Hunslet, Leeds. The evidence indicates that the relationship between George H. Mann and the Yorkshire Patent Steam Wagon Company continued for some time. In 1903, patent 21,109 was lodged in the names of George H. Mann and Deighton's Patent Flue and Tube Company Limited. This design concerned a method of meshing spur gears together so that if there was misalignment, for example, when going over a bump in the road, one of the gears could operate 'off centre' thereby preventing damage to the gears. Another joint patent was number 21,412 of 1902, which relates to *Improvements in Grease Lubricators*. Deighton's Patent Flue and Tube Company Limited was one of the partners in the formation of the Yorkshire Patent Steam Wagon Company.

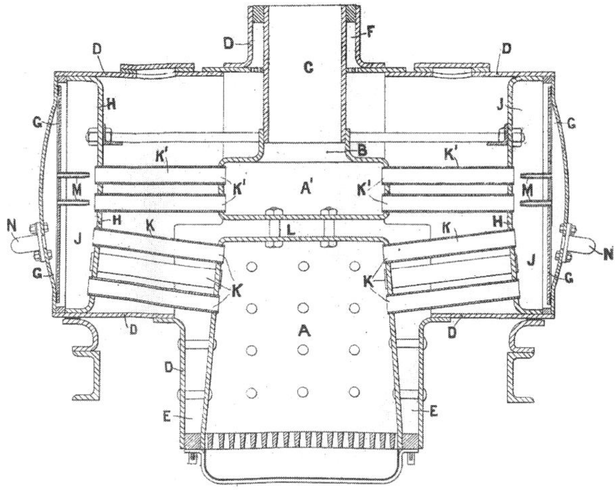

Figure 2: Patent Drawing 21,608, The 'Yorkshire' Boiler George Hutchinson Mann along with Joseph Clayton lodged this patent on 29 November 1900. The boiler was later to be taken up by the Yorkshire Patent Steam Wagon Company and became synonymous with their wagons.

In the following years, George continued to be active in steam road vehicles as evidenced by the following patents:

Patent	Year	Title
25,125	1903	Improvements in the Construction of Vertical Fire-tube Boilers
115	1905	Improvements in the Construction of Wheels for Road Vehicles
9738	1906	Improvements in or relating to Power Driving or Transmission Gear for Motor Road Vehicles
1975	1906	Improvements in or relating to the Disposal of the Exhaust of Steam Engines
27,587	1906	Improvements in or relating to Liquid-fuel Apparatus for Steam-generator Furnaces
6254	1906	Improvements in and relating to Elastic Tyres for Road Vehicle Wheels
16,420	1909	Improvements in Valves and Valve Gear for Internal-combustion Engines*
1105	1915	Improvements in Tubular Steam Boilers.**

*Patent 16,420 of 1909 was registered jointly with Henry Berry of Croydon Works, Hunslet, Leeds. This company made hydraulic machinery (and still do), so why they had an interest in internal-combustion engines is outside the scope of this book, and needs further research.

** In patent 1105 of 1915, George Hutchinson Mann's address is given as Neithrop Villa, Banbury, Oxfordshire. Why he was living in this part of England is unclear.

Figure 3: An early 'Yorkshire' Wagon
This view illustrates an early 'Yorkshire' wagon with undertype engine. The characteristic double return-flue boiler is self evident. The wagon is in service with the brewers Bellamy Bros. Ltd., Grimsby, Louth and Skegness, and is probably engine number 66, delivered in May 1904. *(David Riley – www.photoarchives.co.uk)*

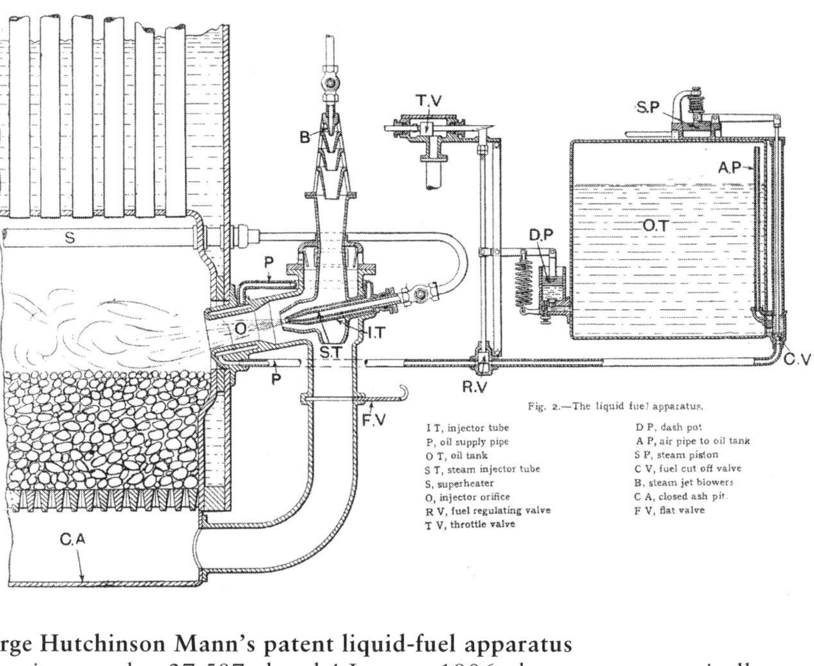

Figure 4: George Hutchinson Mann's patent liquid-fuel apparatus
This patent drawing, number 27,587, dated 4 January 1906, shows an automatically controlled steam boiler fuelled by oil. The fuel control system was automatic with the fuel-valve responding to the throttle position, and a secondary fuel-valve being controlled by boiler pressure. *(Motor Traction)*

In 1907 the Yorkshire Patent Steam Wagon Company constructed a wagonette on behalf of and to the design of George Hutchinson Mann. This was a very advanced machine with an undertype engine and a vertical boiler. The boiler operated at 250 p.s.i. and was fired with creosote as the fuel onto a bed of coke. The fuel control system was automatic, with the fuel-valve responding to the throttle position, and a secondary fuel-valve being controlled by boiler pressure. A steam injector generated the air pressure to spray the oil into the furnace. A ring-shaped chamber in the burner-casting preheated the fuel and the burner-casting was fitted through the firebox door. The heated fuel was forced out of the nozzle by superheated steam, so that the fuel blown into the furnace was in a gaseous state. George Hutchinson Mann, Joseph Clayton and John Robert Pickering, jointly patented this system in 1906. John Robert Pickering of The Beeches, Harehills, Leeds, also held patents for a corrugated construction of road wheels (1902) and gasholder construction (1907), the latter in conjunction with Clayton, Son & Co.

A radiator was fitted to the front of the wagon and was able to condense the exhaust steam, except when operating at full power. The engine developed 35 b.h.p. at 400 r.p.m. and had compound cylinders of $4\frac{1}{2}$in. and 7in. diameter with a $7\frac{1}{2}$in. stroke.[8] Each of the rear wheels was individually shaft driven by its own bevel gear; a rather complicated arrangement. Over an undulating surface this allowed each wheel to rise and fall, with the enclosed drive-shaft behaving like a radius rod. The two drive shafts were themselves driven by a transverse shaft, each side of this being the outputs of the differential gear and two-speed gear. This mechanism provided a fully enclosed drive system that was continually lubricated. In October 1907 the wagon was photographed on trial between Leeds and Wakefield,[9] and by the following summer the vehicle was operating successfully on pleasure trips around the Yorkshire Dales carrying up to 25 passengers. Commencing at Ilkley, the wagonette travelled along the picturesque Wharfe Valley offering a circular route of around forty miles and visited such places as Harrogate and Bolton Abbey. It was stated that in one place, a gradient of 1 in 15 extended for a distance of some two miles, and this was taken in eleven minutes, which gives a speed of about eleven miles per hour.[10]

Rather curiously, an article in the journal *Motor Transport* describes a similar wagon built in 1908 by Mann's Patent Steam Cart and Wagon

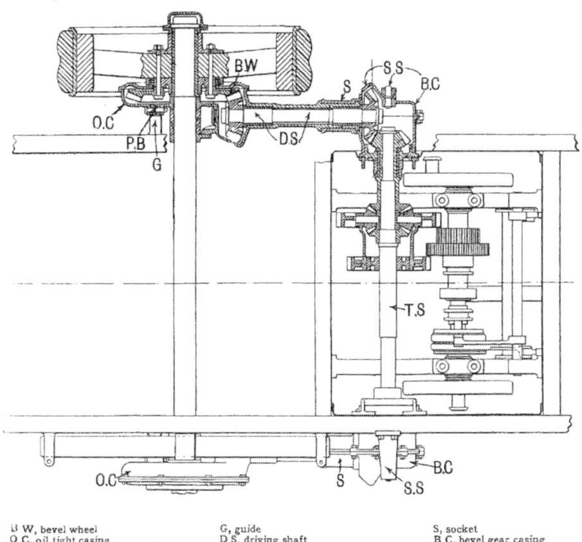

Figure 5: George Hutchinson Mann's patent independent transmission design
Patent 9738 was filed on 26 April 1906, and this drawing illustrates the arrangement. This complicated design provided independent shaft-drive to each rear wheel, using enclosed bevel gears, thereby allowing flooded lubrication. *(Motor Traction)*

Company, and fitted with a vertical fire-tube boiler.[11] The boiler was fired by burning creosote oil sprayed onto a bed of coke in the firebox. The article goes on to say, "This latter machine was designed for carrying either passengers or goods, and a novel feature was the side propeller-shaft, driven by bevel gearing from the countershaft and driving through bevel gear the near-side back wheel, the arrangement eliminating the necessity for propeller-shaft universal-joints." The similarity with the 'Yorkshire' built wagon, and the corresponding date is too great a coincidence and suggests that perhaps this machine was a joint affair between the two brothers James and George H. Mann.

Figure 6: George Hutchinson Mann's design of steam wagonette
This vehicle, designed by George Hutchinson Mann, was very advanced for the time. It included an exhaust steam-condensing radiator and a fully automatic fuel control system. *(Motor Traction)*

George H. Mann was associated in the early 1920s with Peter Brotherhood Limited, Engineers, of Peterborough, Northampton, to design a steam wagon. During this period George's address is listed as "Stanmore", Abbey Road, Llandudno, Caernarvon,[12] and judging by the remoteness from Peterborough, it appears that George was acting purely in a consultant role. The three patents taken out in the joint names of Peter Brotherhood Limited and George Hutchinson Mann are:

Patent	Date	Title
152,512	8 Oct 1919	Improvements in or relating to Slide Valves
158,303	8 Oct 1919	Improvement in Tipping Gear for Road Vehicles
180,100	4 Mar 1921	Improvements in or relating to Steam Boilers

According to Ronald Clark, in the years immediately after the end of the First World War, Peter Brotherhood were looking for additional products to manufacture after the termination of war work. To this end they commissioned George Hutchinson Mann to design a wagon for them.[13] The resulting machine was rather like a 'Yorkshire' wagon, particularly with its double-ended return-flue boiler. This operated at 200 p.s.i. and had a total heating surface of 75 sq. ft. The vehicle was an undertype, with all gear transmission, similar to his earlier wagonette, with twin drive shafts. The compound engine had cylinders 4½in. and 7in. by 8in. stroke. The cast-steel twin rear wheels were fitted with rubber tyres of 1050 mm. diameter, whilst the front wheels, which used Ackermann steering, were fitted with rubber tyres of 900 mm. diameter. For carrying goods, a body 13ft. long by 6ft. 6in. wide was fitted and this accommodated a load of five tons. A tipping version was also available. Ronald Clark suggests that the Yorkshire Patent Steam Wagon Company objected to the similarity, although legally they had no recourse, as the original patent had expired in 1915. It appears that George H. Mann attempted to circumvent the resemblance in the boiler by lodging a further design, patent 180,100, but to no avail. Peter Brotherhood were part of the Agricultural and General Engineers Group (A.G.E.). A.G.E. were formed in 1919 as a result of financial difficulties caused by the denial of debts by the Russian Government. The A.G.E. Group comprised 14 companies, which as well as Peter Brotherhood included the well known names of Aveling & Porter Ltd., Charles Burrell and Sons Ltd. and Richard Garrett and Sons Ltd. This latter company was well known for their high quality wagons and it may be that the A.G.E. Group did not want Peter Brotherhood developing a new product that would compete with Garrett.[14] As a result Peter Brotherhood only made three steam wagons.

James Hutchinson Mann

James Hutchinson Mann commenced his formal education at the age of 7, attending the Leeds Collegiate School from 1867 to 1875. His initial technical instruction was carried out as an apprentice at the Leeds works of J. & H. McLaren. This company was formed in 1876 by John and Henry McLaren to manufacture traction engines and agricultural implements. James Mann was one of their first employees, and perhaps their first apprentice, commencing his training in 1876. James, who was living at 2 Eva Villas, Potternewton, Leeds,[15] became Principal Draughtsman at J. & H. McLaren in 1881, a position he retained for four years, until being appointed Works Manager in 1885.[16]

James Mann's inventiveness first appears publicly in 1885, when on 16 May of that year he lodged a patent, number 6046, entitled *Improvements in Spring Wheels for Traction Engines or for other purposes.* His address at this time is identified as 123 Roundhay Road, Leeds. The opening phrase reads: "My invention has for its object to provide simple efficient and durable spring wheels for traction engines or other purposes." This invention defines a wheel with curved spring spokes made from steel, not unlike similar products patented by his employer J. & H. McLaren in 1882 and 1883. It would seem that James Mann had ideas that differed from his employers and as a result he patented them independently.

On 29 October 1885, James married Georgina Ball at St Nicholas Church, Pendoylan, Glamorgan, Wales. Pendoylan is a small village mid-way between Bridgend and Cardiff, approximately 200 miles from Leeds. James and some work-mates had delivered an engine to a customer in the locality and were putting it into service and training the driver. James struck up a friendship with Georgina and later they were married.[17] The couple had two sons, Sidney and Arthur. Sidney was born 28 July 1893,[18] and Arthur, 12 January 1895.[19]

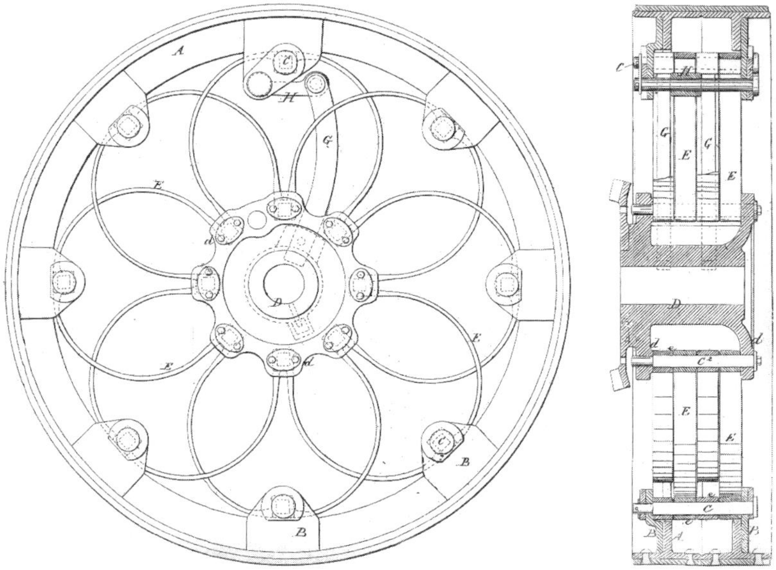

Figure 7: Patent Drawing, Spring Wheel
This drawing is taken from patent number 6046, lodged on 16 May 1885. The torque arm, which transmitted power from the hub to the rim, can be seen at the top half of the wheel. Whether the wheel was ever manufactured as a commercial product is uncertain.

Figure 8: James and Georgina Mann at Foscote, Weeton, near Leeds
This photograph, taken in the 1930s, shows James Hutchinson Mann and his wife Georgina outside their bungalow, Foscote, at Weeton, near Leeds. *(Joy Richens collection)*

James Mann is named in patent number 7349 of 1886. This application was for a chaff cutter and the co-inventors are named as Samuel Burlingham and George Harding Innes. These two gentlemen are described as Agricultural Engineers, of the Exchange Iron Works, Hitchin in the County of Hertfordshire. Unfortunately the Patent Office did not accept the proposal, and therefore the detail of its contents are not recorded.

In 1887 James Mann resigned his position at the Midland Engine Works of J. & H. McLaren and was employed as a draughtsman in Gainsborough at the Britannia Iron Works of William Marshall, Sons & Company. He was later put in charge of the traction engine department.[20] Marshalls was formed in 1848 and began by making threshing machines. In later years the company expanded its product range to include stationary engines, portable engines, traction engines and road rollers. Curiously, James' brother, William Hutchinson Mann is also recorded as living near Gainsborough, and it seems likely that they were both employed at Marshalls. James was evidently impressed by the quality of Marshall engines for in later years when he was equipping the new Pepper Road Works, the main driving engine was supplied by Marshalls. During 1888 and 1889, James Mann is recorded as living at Morton, which is approximately one mile north of Gainsborough.[21] This substantiates other reports that he was employed by William Marshall, Sons & Company, Gainsborough.

In 1890 he must have had "second thoughts" about working for Marshalls, for he returned to Leeds and was appointed Chief Draughtsman with his original employer J. & H. McLaren. Four years later, in 1894, he again left the employment of J. & H. McLaren and set up in partnership with Sidney Charlesworth under the title Mann and Charlesworth. This new association was evidently amenable to Henry McLaren for it was he who sponsored Mann's application to join the Institution of Mechanical Engineers in 1894.[22] In this membership application, James Hutchinson Mann recorded that he had recently set up a partnership, Mann and Charlesworth as "Engine and Boiler Makers", and this confirms other evidence that 1894 was the commencement of this association.

James Mann was an active member of the Leeds Association of Engineers and on Thursday, 27 May 1897 he gave a lecture entitled 'Autocars'. In his lecture he discussed the Locomotives on Highways Act of 1896 and suggested that this would provide the impetus to advance the use of road vehicles, although he was critical of the slow progress in the development of motor cars at that time. One of the major influences on potential purchasers was the cheap price of horses. To counter this, he suggested that any motor vehicle needed to be simple and reliable in order to keep the price cheaper than horses. In a review of different forms of propulsion he thought that steam engines were the most promising prime-movers for road vehicles. He particularly praised the Serpollet** boiler for providing an "instantaneous steam-generator". James Mann described some experiments that he had conducted on the use of liquid fuels and commented that, "the most successful he had tried being to burn it with an injector over a slow-combustion coke fire, but he thought the use of coke alone better still." [23] In his conclusion he made the following statement, "He looked forward with keen anticipation to a great future for autocars, but at the present time, from a manufacturer's point of view, he should not care to put into inexperienced hands a complicated machine, especially with a guarantee for any considerable time."

(** Leon Serpollet, was a well-known French engineer, who produced in 1888 an oil-fired multi-tube flash boiler. This boiler raised steam relatively quickly by means of heated tubes. Serpollet's invention was so successful that in 1902 he was able to break the world land speed record, by driving at Nice, the 'Oeuf de Paques' (Easter Egg), a steam-powered car at 75.06 mph.)

In the following year, James Mann gave another lecture to the Leeds Association of Engineers, on Thursday, 24 February 1898, entitled "Conveyance of Goods by Steam on Highways". That he was prepared to give a public lecture on the subject indicates his confidence in this topic at this early period of his career as a company leader. The following summary of his talk is taken from a local newspaper, the *Leeds Mercury*.[24]

> "If our roads were used to the best advantage of steam or other mechanical haulage, which was possible, he said, at a cost considerably under existing railway rates, every factory, warehouse, coal pit, and farm would practically have a siding on the premises. County Councils and boroughs (of which there were 150) had the right to make their own bye-laws for the working of traction engines in their respective districts. With one or two exceptions, they all charged £10 for a licence, and did not issue a permit at a reduced price for only one journey into their district. In order to go over the boundary for a mile or two a full £10 licence must be taken out. To take an engine anywhere within a radius of 100 miles from Leeds would cost about £120 in county licences alone without reckoning borough costs. Some prohibited engines running during the day, and others during the night. For long journeys especially, it was a great tax to be compelled to have a man always walking in front of the engine. Closing bridges against traction engines on main turnpike roads, and liability to be sued under the extraordinary traffic clauses were other serious drawbacks. However, things in this respect were looking much brighter now. The Government had recently appointed a Select Parliamentary Committee to enquire into the working of traction engines on roads, and this body had issued a very favourable report – amongst other things, recommending - That every engine having a £10 licence be authorised to pass through any county or borough on payment of an annual registration fee of 2s 6d. The commonly called flagman need not necessarily be in advance, or on foot, so long as he accompanies the engine, and is available for assisting horses past when required. Local authorities shall have no general powers of prohibiting the use of engines for specified hours within their district as a whole. In cases where a bridge is closed against traction engines an appeal may be lodged with the Local Government Board. They had also recommended that the extraordinary traffic clause be amended, and several other things advantageous to the use of traction engines. For long-distance hauling, Mr Mann recommended engines capable of pulling a net load of twenty tons, and suggested attaching a light sleeping van behind the ordinary wagons, so that the men could stop the night at any convenient spot on the road-side. He estimated the working expense of a traction engine including interest on capital, depreciation, repairs, wagons, food, &c. at about £10 per week, or £1 13s. 4d. per day, and showed how much cheaper goods could be hauled on the high roads than on the railways. A traction engine, he said, could pull twenty tons a distance of 40 miles in one day, making 800 ton miles, which, at only 1d. per mile, would amount to £3 6s. 8d. He referred to the growing demand for a combined engine and wagon, capable of hauling about five tons. The great advantage of a combined engine and wagon was that the load got a better adhesion to the road, and wheels with smooth tires were possible, instead of cross strips. Smooth wheels would roll the roads, instead of damaging them, and their use ought to be encouraged by the authorities allowing them to be in charge of two men. The Motor Car Act for the conveyance of goods was spoiled by limiting the weight to three tons. It was almost impossible to get an engine into this weight capable of hauling a paying load, and sufficiently strong to withstand the rough usage on the roads."

Some impression of James Mann's personality may be gathered from an interview with him for the magazine *Commercial Motor*.[25] The reporter writes, "I found it most difficult to get much biographical information from Mr. Mann, because he would appear to have the natural shrinking modesty of the Yorkshireman abnormally developed." He goes on to say that he was, "much impressed by Mann's infinite capacity for taking pains, and by the absorbing interest he evinces in his work. Withal, you have the kindly, brusque, keen, business man, ready with a good story to illustrate, or a Yorkshire aphorism to force home his points, and just a suggestion of the Leeds dialect in his tones which does the exiles heart good to hear."

Figure 9: James Hutchinson Mann, caricature
This 1908 sketch of James Hutchinson Mann, by G. A. Stevens, is a fair representation of the leader of Mann's Patent Steam Cart and Wagon Company. In the associated interview he is described as a modest Yorkshireman and a, "kindly, brusque, keen, business man, ready with a good story". *(Commercial Motor)*

Over the next 30 years or so, James Hutchinson Mann provided the leadership for the companies that bear his name. Initially for the Mann and Charlesworth partnership, and subsequently, following the formation of Mann's Patent Steam Cart and Wagon Company Limited in September 1899, he was Chairman of that company until the business was sold in February 1929. His eldest son Sidney became a farmer, living at Bewholme near Hornsea, and later at Gembling House, Foston-on-the-Wolds, which is approximately eight miles south-west of Bridlington on the Yorkshire coast.[26] Arthur, the youngest son, became a director of Mann's Patent Steam Cart and Wagon Company Limited in 1922, however it has not been possible to trace his career after the company closed.

James Hutchinson Mann was a dedicated, lifelong steam engineer, with a distrust of internal combustion engines. Throughout his 96-year life, he never owned a motor car, preferring to travel by train from nearby Weeton Station to his workplace. In retirement, James enjoyed his walks around Weeton village and his routine was so regular that locals could set their watches by his appearance. His walk was also very recognisable, for he had fallen badly down some steps in Weeton Institute, and ever after walked with a very distinct rhythm.[27] He died at his home, Foscote, on 22 November 1956, and is buried in the peaceful Wharfe valley at Weeton churchyard, alongside his wife Georgina, who had died on 26 February 1940. In James' will, his estate was valued at £3034 11s 2d, a very small sum for such an industrious engineer.[28] James lived longer than both his wife and his two sons, and as a result the residue of his estate went to his two daughters-in-law, Millicent and Mabel, together with his sister Annie's two sons, Loxley Horsfield and Claude Horsfield. The other beneficiary was his housekeeper Audrey Evans. She had looked after him for over twenty years, and in recompense she was gifted £900 plus some furniture from his house.

Figure 10: Mann Family Tree

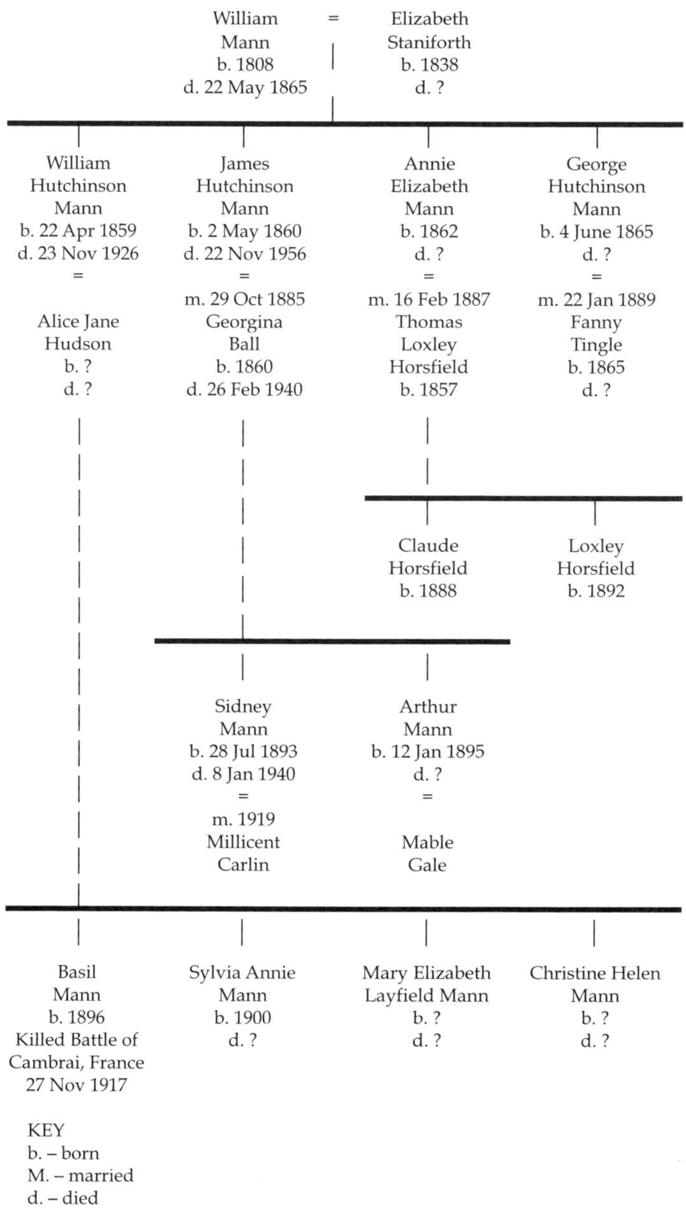

The Charlesworth Family

Sidney Charlesworth was born in Thornhill Lees, Dewsbury on 31 August 1862.[29] His father John Charlesworth was a farmer, living at Headfield, and he had married his cousin, Judith Ann Charlesworth on 28 October 1858. As well as Sidney the couple had two other children, an older son Matthew Henry, born 18 August 1860, and a younger son John, born 9 May 1865.

John Charlesworth

John Charlesworth is perhaps the most celebrated member of the family. He was articled to the Wakefield firm of solicitors, Wainright, Mason and Fernandes and set up his own practice in 1887, a business that continued for over 60 years. However, it is for his spare time activities that he is best remembered, as a historian and antiquary. At the time of his death he was a life member and Vice-President of the Yorkshire Archaeological Society, with which he was associated for well over 50 years. His principal contribution was the transcription and publication of more than a dozen Parish Registers, from the original Latin. Some examples include the registers of Wakefield Cathedral, Emley, Flockton, Hemsworth, Horbury, Swillington, Thornhill, Whitby, and Wragby. These books are still to be found in many Yorkshire public and private libraries as the definitive record of births, deaths and marriages. He was a member of the Yorkshire Parish Register Society and for many years its secretary. In recognition of his work on parish registers, he was appointed a Fellow of the Society of Antiquaries. John Charlesworth practised from his house Lydgate, Horbury, which still survives. Latterly he lived at The Crofts, Horbury. He was also active in his local community, serving on the Horbury Common Lands Trust, the Horbury Public Library Committee, the Wakefield Historical Society, the Horbury and District Golf Club, and the Horbury Conservative Club. He died in 1952 at a Leeds nursing home, at the age of 87, and is buried in Horbury Cemetery.[30]

Sidney Charlesworth

Little is known about Sidney Charlesworth's early life, but he was employed at the Midland Engine Works of J. & H. McLaren.[31] McLaren's works, on Jack Lane, was approximately 500 yards from Mann and Charlesworth's Canning Works off Dewsbury Road. It would appear that it was at McLaren's works that the partnership between Mann and Charlesworth first arose, with both men being employed there. The 1881 national census records Sidney's occupation as Engine Fitter Apprentice. According to Robert Whitehead, Sidney Charlesworth was employed from January 1885 to April 1888 at the Richard Garrett works at Leiston in Suffolk,[32] as deputy to John Sherwood the Works Manager. In Sidney Charlesworth's obituary it is recorded that he spent many years in Australia, however it is not defined in whose employment this took place.[33] Fortunately, some research by Robert Whitehead has revealed that Sidney Charlesworth was employed as manager of the Rous Sugar Mill, Wardell, New South Wales, in 1892. This mill was part of the Richmond River Sugar Company and it appears that Charlesworth was employed for a number of years with this company.[34] This is reinforced by Dr Peter Griggs of the James Cook University, Australia, who has identified that Charlesworth was the Chief Engineer of the Richmond River Sugar Company in December 1889.[35] A further newspaper extract about the Rous sugar mill is worth quoting, "The large iron chimney, 120ft high and weighing 16 tons, forms a prominent land mark in the district, in passing, it may be worth mentioning that it was raised and fixed on its foundation in eight hours, and reflects great credit on the skill of Mr. S. Charlesworth, the company's engineer."[36]

At the age of 31, Sidney married Annie Horsfield, at Isles Lane Chapel, Holbeck, Leeds, on 5 December 1893. Sidney is recorded on the marriage certificate as living at Lydgate House,

Horbury, near Wakefield, which was his brother John's house. Annie was one of five children. Her father was John Napoleon Horsfield, a self employed chemist & druggist of 81 Sweet Street, Holbeck, Leeds, although he is recorded as being deceased at the time of Annie's wedding. Annie's mother was Ellen Horsfield, originally from Halifax.

When the partnership between James Hutchinson Mann and Sidney Charlesworth dissolved, Sidney Charlesworth is recorded as residing at "Leiston, County of Suffolk, Manager of Engineering Works".[37] The 1901 census records also substantiate this, where he is recorded as living at 2 Works House, Leiston cum Sizewell. It seems almost certain, given his background, that this was in the employ of Richard Garrett & Sons, traction engine manufacturers. This is confirmed by Robert Whitehead in his book on Garrett traction engines, where he states that Sidney Charlesworth was the Works Manager from 1899 to 1901.[38] Richard Garrett established his business in Leiston in 1755 for the manufacture of sickles and scythes. Subsequently, other agricultural equipment was produced, for example, ploughs, harrows and threshing machines. In 1848 portable engines were introduced, and in succeeding years a whole range of steam machinery was constructed, including traction engines, stationary engines, and steam wagons. At its peak, around 2000 people were employed on a site exceeding 20 acres.

In subsequent years Sidney Charlesworth was resident in Bridlington, Yorkshire, where he operated as a consulting engineer. In the Wakefield land registry there are numerous records of another of his activities - loaning money for land and property purchases. In 1909 he was elected onto Bridlington Town Council, and was re-elected to the council in 1912 and 1919. One of his roles as a councillor was as deputy-chairman of the Waterworks Committee. In this position, his engineering background was put to good use when new waterworks machinery was purchased, and he personally supervised the installation.[39] The supply of the pumping equipment was contracted to Hathorn Davey of Dewsbury Road, Leeds, whose works was opposite the original Mann and Charlesworth, Canning Street Works. Sidney Charlesworth was also a long-serving member of the Bridlington Harbour Commissioners.[40] In his spare time he was a member of the Yorkshire Archaeological Society and was the founder of the Bridlington Augustinian Society. He died at his home, Headfield, Park Avenue, Bridlington on 2 February 1939. His estate was valued at £21,175 13s 2d, a considerable sum at that time.[41] The main beneficiary was his wife Annie, however smaller sums went to:

Figure 11: Sidney Charlesworth
This rare view of Sidney Charlesworth was included in a brochure promoting his election to Bridlington Town Council in 1909. He was 47 years of age. *(Bridlington Local Studies Library)*

- Joseph Charlesworth, farmer, of Netherton, Wakefield, Sidney's cousin
- Mary (Molly) Charlesworth, daughter of Joseph Charlesworth
- Donald Haldane } sons of Henry Charlesworth Haldane,
- Duncan Haldane } of Clarke Hall, Wakefield,
- John Charlesworth Haldane } Sidney's cousin

In addition, he bequeathed books, prints, pictures and papers to the Bridlington School (boys), the High School for Girls, Bridlington, the Bridlington Augustinian Society and Bridlington Public Library.

Figure 12: Charlesworth Family Tree

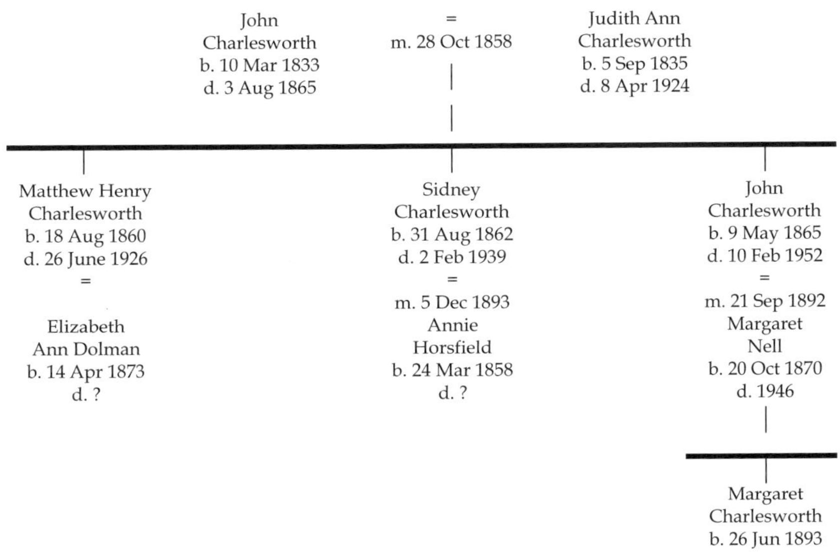

KEY
b. – born
M. – married
d. – died

References

1 *Birth Certificate,* James Hutchinson Mann, Leeds Register Office.
2 *Marriage Certificate,* William Mann, Elizabeth Staniforth, Sheffield Register Office
3 *Birth Certificate,* George Hutchinson Mann, Centre d'archives de Québec.
4 *National Census Records 1871,* RG11, 4576/21
5 *National Census Records 1881,* RG11, 4542/56
6 *Marriage Certificate,* George Hutchinson Mann and Fanny Tingle, Leeds Register Office
7 *Engineering,* September 6, 1901, p324
8 *Motor Traction,* August 1, 1908, p107
9 *Commercial Motor,* 24 October 1907, p174
10 *Motor Traction,* August 1, 1908, p105
11 *Motor Transport,* December 31, 1928, p791
12 *British Patent 152,512,* 1919
13 Clark, R. H. *The Development of the English Steam Wagon,* Goose & Son, 1963 p151
14 Kelly, M. A. *The Undertype Steam Road Waggon,* Goose & Son, 1975, p35
15 *National Census Records 1881,* RG11, 4542/56
16 Mann, James H. *Membership Application,* Institution of Mechanical Engineers, May 11, 1894
17 Walker, John. meeting with author, Weeton, 10 October 2003
18 *Birth Certificate,* Sidney Mann, Leeds Register Office
19 *Birth Certificate,* Arthur Mann, Leeds Register Office
20 *Commercial Motor,* January 10, 1907
21 West Riding Registry of Deeds, Wakefield, *Book 1888, volume 126, page 165*
22 Mann, James H. *Membership Application,* Institution of Mechanical Engineers, May 11, 1894
23 *The Automotor and Horseless Vehicle Journal,* May 1897, p313
24 *Leeds Mercury,* February 26, 1898, p9
25 *Commercial Motor,* 30 April 1908, p230
26 *Kelly's Directory, East and West Yorkshire,* 1939, p464
27 Walker, John. meeting with author, Weeton, 10 October 2003
28 *James Hutchinson Mann's Will,* Probate Registry, York
29 Walker, J. W. *Yorkshire Pedigrees,* The Harleian Society, 1942
30 *Wakefield Express Newspaper,* 16 February 1952, p6
31 Clark, R. H. *The Development of the English Traction Engine,* Goose & Son, 1960, p100
32 Whitehead R. A, *Personal notes taken from Garrett's Staff Register,* c1960
33 *The Bridlington Free Press,* February 4, 1939
34 Whitehead R. A, *Personal notes taken from Garrett Archive, Suffolk Record Office, HC30/B30/44*
35 *The Northern Star,* Lismore, NSW, Australia, 7 December 1889, p2
36 *The Town and Country Journal,* Sydney, Australia, 22 November 1890, p27
37 West Riding Registry of Deeds, Wakefield, *Book 1901, volume 43, p 174*
38 Whitehead R. A, *Garrett Traction & Ploughing Engines,* Tonbridge, 1997, p30
39 *The Bridlington Chronicle,* February 10, 1939
40 *The Bridlington Free Press,* February 4, 1939
41 *Sidney Charlesworth's Will,* Probate Registry, York

Chapter 2

The Company

The formation of a new company in the 1890s to produce steam traction engines and related products was a bold and somewhat risky venture. The long established companies, for example, Ransome, Sims and Jefferies (1789), Marshall & Sons (1848), Aveling (1850), and Fowler (1850), were producing large quantities of well-established products. Despite these obstacles, the new company was able, after a few years, to establish itself as a significant producer of road vehicles, mainly in the expanding market of steam wagons and carts.

The first recorded evidence of the company that became Mann's Patent Steam Cart and Wagon Company Limited, is the purchase by James Hutchinson Mann and his younger brother George Hutchinson Mann of the Canning Street Works on 7 June 1893. The Canning Works had previously been used as a Brass Foundry under the name of Chadwick, Smith & Co. In the few years before being purchased by the Mann brothers, Walter Foster, a Machine Broker used it, and as a result of its previous owners, it came complete with "steam engine, boiler, shafting, going gear, piers and beams for a Goliath (crane) and other fixtures". [1] The works occupied a total area of 2,012 square yards, and was located off Dewsbury Road, one of the main arterial roads of Leeds.

As an interesting aside, the building opposite the Canning Works was Hathorn Davey's Sun Foundry where very large steam driven water pumps were constructed, mainly for public water supplies and sewage works. The Sun Foundry was originally constructed by Charles Todd, a little-known engineer, but who was one of the most influential figures in the Leeds railway locomotive industry. Todd played an important formative role in the development of Kitson's Airedale Foundry and E. B. Wilson's Railway Foundry. The Sun Foundry was sold by Todd, who was in failing health, in 1852 to Carrett Marshall & Co., who were also active in the construction of railway locomotives, amongst other things. In 1861 the Royal Agricultural Show was held at Kirkstall, Leeds and one of the exhibits was a fascinating steam passenger carriage, built by Carrett Marshall & Co. The carriage had been constructed for George Salt, the son of Titus Salt, the mill owner and philanthropist of Saltaire near Bradford. The machine weighed 3 tons empty and 4½ tons loaded with up to 12 persons, including attendants. The engine was placed horizontally beneath the passenger seats and consisted of a pair of cylinders 6 in. diameter by 8 in. stroke, with valves operated by link motion. Two gear ratios of 1 to 5 or 1 to 2½ could be selected to suit the gradient. The fully sprung driving wheels were 4ft. diameter by 6in. wide, and this combination was reported to provide a maximum speed of 25 miles per hour! The steering was achieved by a single leading wheel of 3ft. diameter.[4] The horizontal boiler, located over the driving wheels, was 2ft. 6in. long and contained 58 solid-drawn copper tubes, each 2in. diameter. The boiler was tested to 350 p.s.i. but its normal working pressure was 150 p.s.i. The firebox was said to contain Clark's steam jets for preventing smoke. A water tank of 140 gallons capacity was fitted. The catalogue price of this machine was £400. In the following year, 1862, Carrett Marshall & Co. showed this same machine alongside their 2-cwt steam-hammer at the International Exhibition held at

Figure 13: Carrett Marshall & Company's steam passenger carriage, 1861
Carrett Marshall & Co. occupied the Sun Foundry opposite the Canning Works. This 5-ton steam pleasure carriage was capable of carrying twelve passengers and was constructed for George Salt of Saltaire near Bradford. *(Hathorn Davey Catalogue, 1931)*

Based on Ordnance Survey map CCXV111.6 dated 1908

Figure 14: Map of the Canning Street Works
The Canning Street Works (shown hatched) was purchased in June 1893 and became the workshops of the Mann and Charlesworth company. The property was sold in June 1901 for use by Oil & Grease Merchants, T. H. Newsome & Co.

South Kensington, London, where the magazine *The Engineer* rather glamorously described it as a 5-ton steam pleasure carriage.[2]

On 2 January 1894, the ownership of the Canning Works is recorded as being transferred from James Hutchinson Mann and George Hutchinson Mann to James Hutchinson Mann and Sidney Charlesworth, trading as Mann and Charlesworth.[3] January 1894 appears to be the formal start of the company Mann and Charlesworth, this date being corroborated by evidence from James Hutchinson Mann's membership application to the Institution of Mechanical Engineers (see chapter 1 for further details). Paradoxically, on 5 June 1897, the entire property was transferred back to George Hutchinson Mann, in the form of a mortgage, presumably to raise additional capital for the benefit of the business.[5] Unfortunately, following the introduction of the first steam cart in 1898, the partnership between James Hutchinson Mann and Sidney Charlesworth appeared to falter. This is evidenced by the fact that patent 13,236, lodged on 14 June 1898, defining the Mann steam cart, omits Charlesworth's name completely. (The reason for this is discussed more fully in chapter 3.) As a result of this personal conflict, the partnership between James Hutchinson Mann and Sidney Charlesworth was dissolved by mutual consent on 30 June 1899. In the journal *The Implement and Machinery Review* the following statement was made regarding the company Mann and Charlesworth; "The debts due to the late firm will be received by Messrs. Pickard, Crossland & Smith, 43, Albion Street, Leeds, Chartered Accountants to whom particulars of all claims against the firm should be sent." [6]

For a brief period James Hutchinson Mann operated independently under the title J. H. Mann & Company, having purchased the Mann and Charlesworth business outright. James Hutchinson Mann was obviously a very determined character with grand aspirations, as very quickly he formed a limited liability company with sufficient capital to develop his ideas. Mann's Patent Steam Cart and Wagon Company Limited was incorporated on 29 September 1899, with a nominal capital of £25,000 divided into 2,500 shares of £10 each.[7] In the Articles of Association, the objects of the company are stated as:

> "1) To acquire by purchase lands, works, patents, stock-in-trade, plant, machinery, buildings, furnaces, warehouses, and all trade premises, and the requisite machinery and plant suitable for carrying on machine-making and engineering, or manufacturing works of whatever description, and to acquire the business and undertaking carried out by James Hutchinson Mann, trading as 'J. H. Mann & Co.', at the Canning Works, Canning Street, Leeds; and to acquire and undertake the whole of the said J. H. Mann in connection therewith; and with a view thereto to enter into and carry into effect, with or without modification, the agreement referred to in Clause 3 of the Articles of Association of this Company.
>
> 2) To carry on the business of Steam Cart, Wagon and Motor Car Manufacturers, Engineers, and Boiler Makers in all its branches.
>
> 3) To carry on all or any of the businesses of mechanical engineers, machinist, smiths, iron, brass and steel founders, boiler makers, and steam haulage contractors; and to buy, sell, manufacture, equip, repair, let out on hire, and deal in articles of all kinds in the manufacture of which steel, iron, tin, brass, aluminium, and other metals and metallic substances, and wood and timber, or any of them are used; and also in any material or other commodity in connection with any business hereby authorised to be carried on."

The solicitor acting for the company was George Denison Lumb, and he was later to take an interest in the company as a shareholder.

The subscribers to the company, initially taking one share each, were:

James Hutchinson Mann	Engineer	34 Dewsbury Road, Leeds
William Hutchinson Mann	Engineer	Pullan & Mann, Elland Road, Leeds
John Edward Davenport	Iron Merchant	55 Black Bull Street, Leeds
Edward Crossley	Iron Merchant	55 Black Bull Street, Leeds
Richard Longden Hattersley	Machine Maker	Northbrook Works, Keighley
Alfred Smith	Machine Maker	Woodworth, Keighley
George Henry Ibbetson	Cashier	34 Dewsbury Road, Leeds

A further clause in the Articles of Association defines the conditions of employment of the Managing Director:

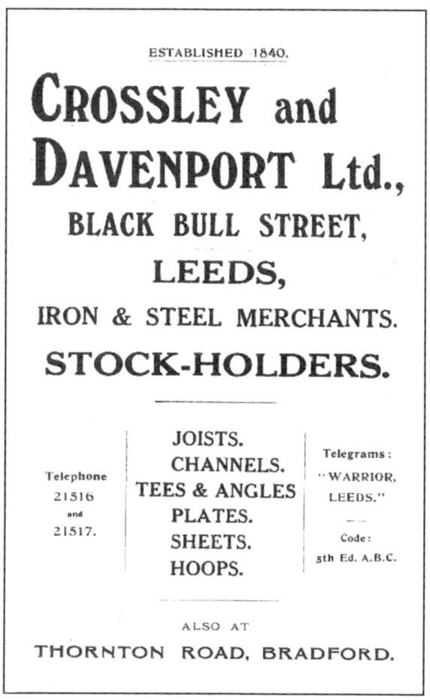

Figure 15: Advertisement for Crossley and Davenport John Edward Davenport and Edward Crossley were both shareholders of Mann's Patent Steam Cart and Wagon Company Limited. In addition, John Edward Davenport was a Director of the company. *(Journal of the Leeds Association of Engineers, 1923)*

"The said James Hutchinson Mann shall be the first Managing Director of the Company, for the period of seven years, at the remuneration of £300 for the first year, with an increase of £50 for every succeeding year until the sum of £500 is reached, together with five per cent. of the profits of the Company or any other Company in whom the business of this Company may hereafter become vested, after allowing for five percent. interest on the whole of the paid-up capital of this Company."

In addition, the Articles of Association also names the first list of Directors, these being:

- James Hutchinson Mann
- William Hutchinson Mann (James' brother)
- Richard Longden Hattersley
- Alfred Smith
- John Edward Davenport

Along with the formation of the Joint Stock Company there was also the legal transfer of ownership of the existing business to the new company. In an agreement dated 25 September 1899, the following statements are included: [8]

"The vendor shall sell and the company when incorporated shall purchase:

Firstly. All the freehold hereditaments specified in the first schedule hereto.

Secondly. All that Patent (No. 13236) A.D. 1898 for 'Improvements in or in connection with road traction engines and draught road vehicles adapted to be used therewith' and all that Patent (No. 13958) A.D. 1894 for 'Improvements in Reversing gear for steam and other engines'.

Thirdly. All the plant, machinery, office furniture, wagons, carts, work in progress, stock in trade, implements, and utensils, models and drawings to which the vendor is entitled under Mr Lambert's valuation or which have been purchased by the vendor at Messieurs Mann & Charlesworth's sale and enumerated in the vendor's stock book and the benefit of all future inventions which shall be made by the vendor during such time as the vendor shall either be the Managing Director or in the employment of the Company in connection with the manufacture or working of steam carts of wagons only."

The agreement states that the value of this transfer was £3,697, consisting of:

- £1,100 for the patents
- £597 for the property and land
- £2,000 for the goods, chattels and plant

This was paid to James Hutchinson Mann as 200 shares (worth £2000) plus £1,697 in cash.

The declaration of shareholders for February 1900 reveals that the company had managed to sell 1,066 shares in the business, with a value of £10,600. In addition to the original seven subscribers, another three individuals had invested in the company, these being; John Samuel Pullan, William Hutchinson Mann's partner; George Dennison Lumb, the company solicitor; and Thomas Hudson, Maltster. Thomas Hudson was the brother of Alice Jane Mann, William Hutchinson Mann's wife. The ownership of shares is tabulated below:

James Hutchinson Mann	Engineer	34 Dewsbury Road, Leeds	200
George Henry Ibbetson	Cashier	34 Dewsbury Road, Leeds	6
William Hutchinson Mann	Engineer	Pullan & Mann, Elland Road, Leeds	140
John Samuel Pullan	Engineer	Pullan & Mann, Elland Road, Leeds	20
John Edward Davenport**	Iron Merchant	55 Black Bull Street, Leeds	} 160
Edward Crossley**	Iron Merchant	55 Black Bull Street, Leeds	}
Richard Longden Hattersley*	Machine Maker	Northbrook Works, Keighley	400
Alfred Smith	Machine Maker	Woodworth, Keighley	100
Thomas Hudson	Maltster	Pannal via Leeds	20
George Dennison Lumb	Solicitor	65 Albion Street, Leeds	20

* Richard Longden Hattersley died on 3 August 1900 and his shares were subsequently transferred to Fanny Hattersley and Clara Hattersley of Springfield, Keighley. These ladies were presumably Richard Longden Hattersley's daughters.

** Edward Crossley and John Edward Davenport were in business together as Crossley & Davenport Ltd., Iron & Steel Merchants, Yorkshire Foundry, Black Bull Street, Leeds. A branch works was at Thornton Road, Bradford.

In the spring of 1900, James Mann approached the John Fowler Company of Hunslet, Leeds, with a proposal for the Mann patent wagon to be manufactured at Fowler's Steam Plough Works.[9] This offer appears to indicate that James Mann realised that the Canning

Works on Dewsbury Road, Leeds, was inadequate to meet the demand for his wagons. Negotiations were held with Robert Eddison, one of Fowler's principals, and J. T. Marshall, one of Fowler's leading designers. However, the head of the company, Robert Henry Fowler, did not support the proposal, with the result that the John Fowler Company rejected Mann's offer. It seems likely that this rejection was the catalyst that initiated the plans to construct a new works. Records held at the West Riding Land Registry reveal that on 29 September 1900, Mann's Steam Cart and Wagon Company Limited purchased land on Pepper Road, Hunslet, Leeds. The sellers were Graham, Morton, and Company Limited, Colliery Engineers, Black Bull Street, Leeds. The area of land amounted to 4,693 square yards, however, no buildings are recorded in the deeds, and so the implication is that the area was virgin land. Incidentally, the Graham, Morton company built their own works in Pepper Road in 1903.[10]

The mortgage document[11] for the Pepper Road factory identifies two transactions, one dated 27 September 1900, almost certainly for the land, and a second, dated 19 March 1901, probably for the buildings and plant. Curiously the area of land quoted in the mortgage is 17,201 square yards, which is much larger than that purchased from the Graham, Morton company mentioned earlier, which perhaps implies that the land was purchased from two or more individuals. The financing of the mortgage was not done through a financial organisation but as a private transaction through the sale of debentures worth £100 each. The total value of the mortgage was £10,000. The two individuals who purchased the debentures are identified as:

Robert Newsholme	Worsted Manufacturer	Belgrave Mount, Keighley
Samuel Clough	Worsted Manufacturer	Barrows House, Steeton, Nr. Keighley

The construction of the new works took about one year, such that on 6 December 1901 the registered office of the company was officially notified, to Somerset House, as the Pepper Road Works, Hunslet, Leeds.

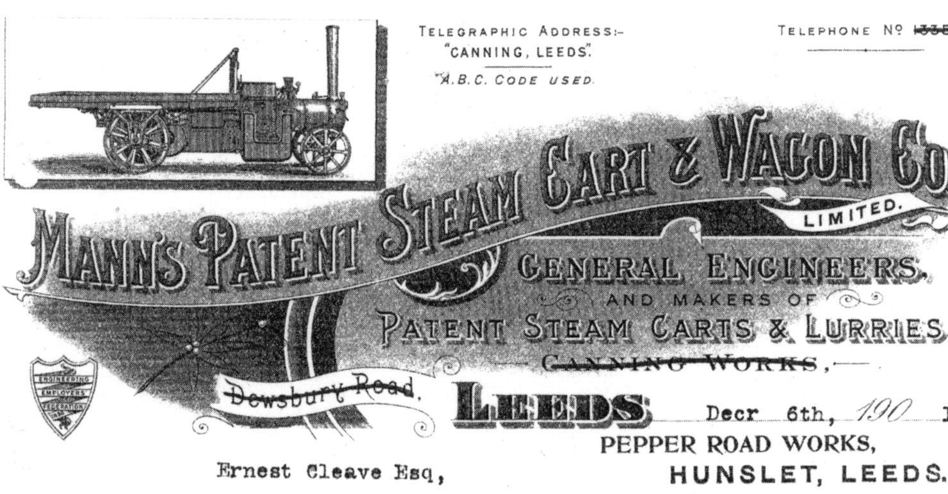

Figure 16: Letter, Mann's Patent Steam Cart and Wagon Company
By the end of 1901 Mann's Patent Steam Cart and Wagon Company Limited had moved to their new works at Pepper Road. Note the deletion of Canning Works, Dewsbury Road.

The Canning Works was sold on 12 June 1901 to Theophilus Hanson Newsome, of Dewsbury Road, Leeds, Oil Merchant.[12] This business traded as T. H. Newsome & Co., Oil & Grease Merchants for many years. Listings in trade directories indicate that the business closed in the early 1940s.

In the October 1901 returns, another individual is identified as purchasing a share of the Mann company. This was Herbert Haggas of Bracken Bank, Keighley, manufacturer. Herbert Haggas purchased 200 shares, with a value of £2,000. A visit to Mann's Steam Cart and Wagon Works in 1903 by staff from *The Engineer* reported that the 285 men were employed, and that, "The land on which the premises are situated... measures four acres, and already the buildings cover two acres, leaving ample space for extension in the future." [13]

The workshops were all arranged under one roof, divided into five well-lighted bays, comprising the following departments:

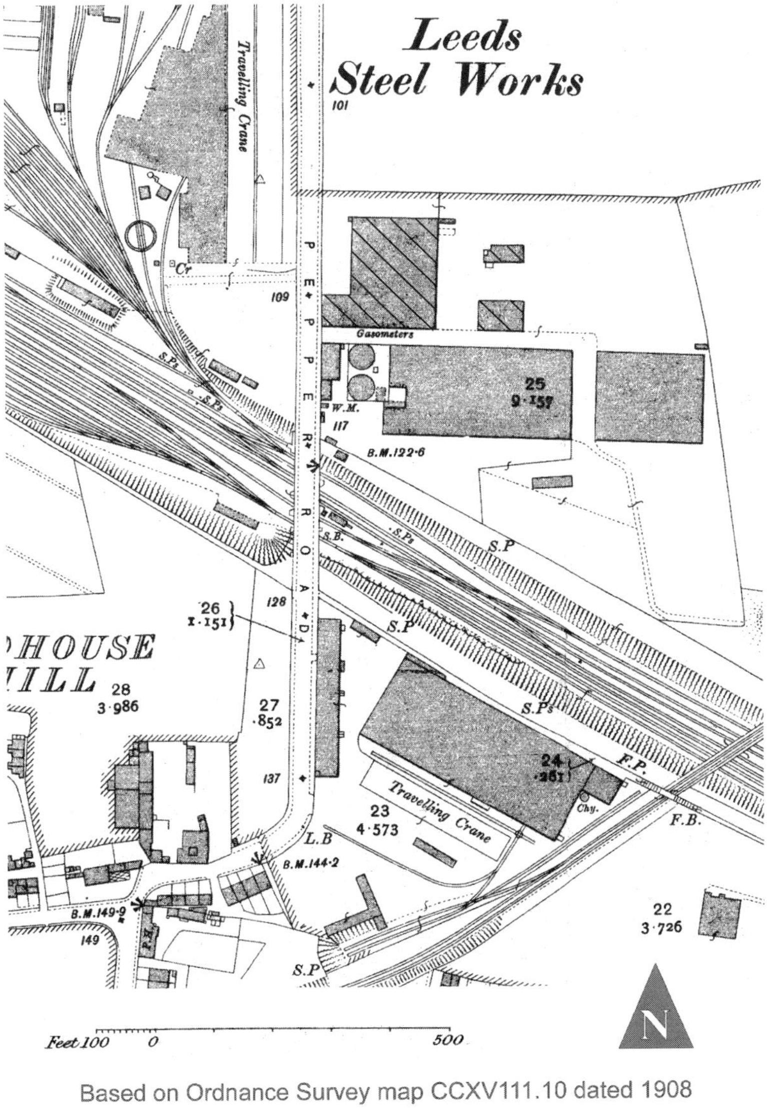

Figure 17: Location Map, Pepper Road Works
Mann's Pepper Road Works is shown in hatched lines on the eastern side of Pepper Road. The building immediately to the south was the Vulcan Works of the Yorkshire Patent Steam Wagon Company.

- Boiler department
- Smith's shop
- Tank and cart body department
- Erecting bay
- Main machine shop

A mezzanine gallery running nearly the whole length of the building accommodated the light machine tools and fitting shop. Two overhead electrically operated travelling cranes were provided, one for the boiler shop and the other for the erecting department.

The Pepper Road building was not a mean industrial building; rather it was constructed to a very high quality with much architectural detail in the brickwork. The offices were at the front of the building with the general and private offices on the ground floor. The drawing office and manager's office was on the top floor, with the latter overlooking the whole of the building.

The engine and boiler-house formed a separate building. A Lancashire boiler, fitted with a Green's economiser, supplied steam at 140 p.s.i. pressure. The steam was delivered to a 200 horsepower Marshall's cross-compound horizontal engine. This drove, by means of ropes, a Wilson-Hartnell four-pole dynamo giving 220 volts at 450 revolutions per minute. The dynamo provided sufficient current to drive four lines of shop shafting at 150 revolutions per minute by means of separate 20 horsepower motors. Electric power was also provided for the overhead cranes, besides providing current for lighting and for operating a small electric motor used in conjunction with the economiser.

Figure 18: Pepper Road Works, Boiler Shop
The Pepper Road boiler shop was spacious and well-equipped. In the foreground can be seen an upturned boiler, with the extended side plates on the firebox clearly visible. *(Mann Catalogue)*

Figure 19: Pepper Road Works, Erecting Shop
The Pepper Road erecting shop has a clean and orderly appearance in this photograph, with a neat row of steam carts and their wheel-sets in the process of assembly. The sprockets on the axles indicate that this view was taken after 1910, the year that chain-driven wagons were introduced. *(Mann Catalogue)*

Figure 20: Pepper Road Works, Architectural Detail
The Pepper Road Works was a high-quality building with detailed features in the brickwork. The circular feature in the gable was originally a glazed window. The date of 1901 over the original main entrance indicates the year the works was opened.

In regard to the boiler house, *The Engineer* reported: "In connection with the power-house it may be mentioned that a considerable saving in lubricant is effected by filtering all the oil used in the main engine and using it for oiling the machinery in the shops."

In addition, *The Engineer* also offered a view on the machine tools used at the works:

> "It is satisfactory to learn that a large majority of the machine tools are of English manufacture, and in selecting these the proprietors have avoided as far as possible the more complex and expensive types. There is some reason in their argument that although the more costly and complicated machines may turn out work at a price fractionally less than their simpler and cheaper brethren, the cost of upkeep, added to the interest of larger capital involved, in many cases counterbalances the savings affected. We are not disposed to take up the argument here one way or the other, but it cannot be gainsaid that the workmanship displayed in the engines turned out from these works leaves little to be desired."

The same article reveals a little about the materials used for manufacture at this time: "A glance round the well-kept stores shows that little other than steel is used in the Mann vehicles. The steam cylinders form the chief exception, these being of cast iron in one piece. The eccentrics are also of cast iron. For other parts where the use of steel is unnecessary malleable cast iron is utilised. When the castings come in from the foundry the storekeeper checks them against his own orders, and puts labels on them giving the vehicle number for which they are intended, the drawing number, maker's name, and also order number to which the work has to be charged. The labour in this connection is greatly lightened by the fact that practically all vehicles are built to one or two standard patterns." According to Wilf Cole, the iron castings were supplied by Hill Brothers, Nevin's Foundry, Goodman Street, Hunslet, Leeds, whilst the steel castings were supplied by Jessop's of Sheffield and latterly by Cattons of Black Bull Street, Hunslet, Leeds.[14]

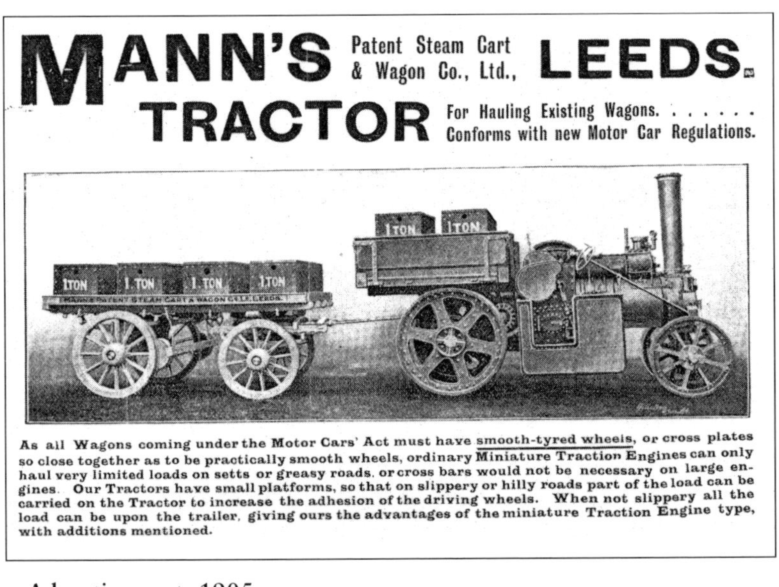

Figure 21: Mann Advertisement, 1905

This advertisement illustrates the new road tractor introduced in 1905. This adaptation of the steam cart had a fixed load-carrying platform, able to carry 2 tons. *(Commercial Motor)*

In 1907, the journal *Commercial Motor* published a short article on James Mann, and in this article they report that the works was giving employment to upwards of 300 hands, exclusively in the manufacture of the Mann carts and wagons, of which nearly 500 had been sold.[15] In the following year, the same journal gave a little more information on James Mann and the Pepper Road Works, "...his own company is turning out wagons second to none, and one only requires to walk round his establishment with him to see the numerous vehicles going through for all parts of the world, to note the organisation of his works, and to be much impressed by Mann's infinite capacity for taking pains, and by the absorbing interest he evinces in his work. Withal, you have the kindly, brusque, keen business man, ready with a good story to illustrate, or a Yorkshire aphorism to force home his points..." [16]

A report of a visit by the Iron and Steel Institute in 1912 indicates that some rearrangement of the factory had occurred, presumably to increase capacity in the main works: "There are five bays all under one roof, viz. Fitting, machine, erecting, smith's, and boiler shops, forming one large shed. There is also a separate joiners' shop for making trailers, steam wagon bodies, &c."[17]

Prior to the First World War, the works manager at the Pepper Road Works was John Thomas Ridealgh. During the war, food shortages were badly affecting the country, and agriculture was high on the government's agenda. As a result, Ridealgh was directed to the firm, Summerscales, of Parkside Works, Keighley, Yorkshire, to design an agricultural tractor.[18] Quite why Summerscales was chosen for this activity is rather curious, as their normal products were commercial laundry equipment, e.g. washing, wringing and mangling machines. The result of Ridealgh's efforts was a fully-sprung three-wheeled steam tractor that weighed 65 cwt. A four-cylinder single-acting vee-engine provided the power, and this was fitted with cam-operated poppet valves.[19] The cylinders were 4 in. diameter with a 7 in. stroke and these provided an engine power of 25 b.h.p. at 350 r.p.m.[20] The engine was fully enclosed and fitted with an oilbath to provide lubrication to crankshaft, tappets, etc. A vertical boiler, fitted with a superheater coil, was located at the side of the driver, in the middle of the vehicle, and the operating pressure was 200 p.s.i. The tractor design was lodged with the Patent Office on 12 Jan 1918 and given number 116,855. Interestingly, the patent shows a 4-wheeled tractor, presumably as a result of poor experience with the 3-wheeled prototype tractor. The patent also suggests that a roller could replace the front wheels if desired. The machine was entered in the South Carlton tractor trials of September 1919, however, it did not take part. The evidence indicates that despite the designer's best intentions, the machine was not a success. After the war, Ridealgh operated a small repair shop in Bradford, Yorkshire, and built a conventional 4-wheeled steam wagon using the vertical boiler and vee-engine developed for the steam tractor. A chain drive was used for the transmission and this gave a road speed of 14 m.p.h. Ridealgh subsequently joined the Yorkshire Patent Steam Wagon Company and was responsible for the design of their WG type of wagon. He also holds a number of patents in conjunction with Deighton's Patent Flue & Tube Company (Yorkshire's parent company) regarding gully-emptying wagons.

In the years leading up to the First World War, little change in the status of the business occurred. A few other individuals invested in the business, namely: Alice Jane Mann, William's wife; Ann E. Smith, of the same address as Alfred Smith, one of the original investors, and probably his wife; and Hemingway Whitfield, who is described as an accountant. The other change was the appointment of Joseph Capel Cornock of Collingham near Leeds, as company

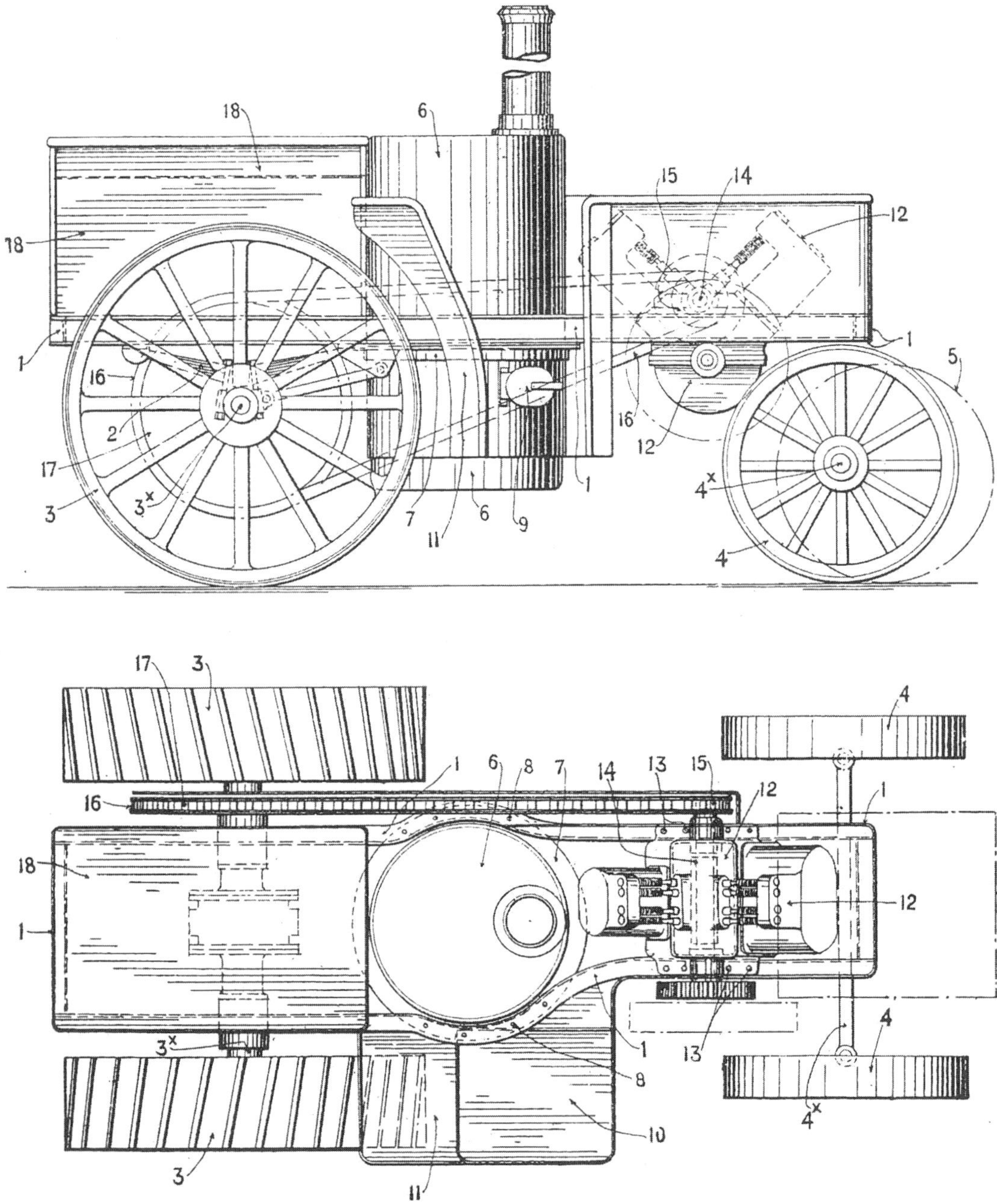

Figure 22: Ridealgh's Steam Tractor
This patent drawing, number 116,855, dated 12 January 1918, shows a chain-driven vertical-boilered steam tractor designed by John Thomas Ridealgh. The appearance of the tractor was rather dated in 1918, and it is difficult to see what novel features it offered. Ridealgh had been Mann's works' manager prior to the First World War.

Figure 23: Pepper Road Works, Stores
This posed view of a very tidy Pepper Road stores shows some of the transmission components on the floor, together with compound cylinders and lifting gear. *(Mann Catalogue)*

secretary, his name first appearing in 1906, the same year that George Ibbetson relinquished his shares in the company. At the 1909 Royal Show, Cornock along with James Mann and James M. Dallas (Mann's London agent) represented the company,[21] however in 1910 he is identified as the works' manager.[22] It would appear that Cornock was a very versatile member of the team and obviously played an important role at Pepper Road.

Business was evidently prosperous during this period, as in December 1912 the £10,000 mortgage, used to fund the purchase and construction of the Pepper Road Works, was repaid in full.

One of the departments that became an important contributor to the company's finances was the service department. Like modern road vehicle suppliers, the servicing and spares activity often plays an important contribution to the profitability of the organisation. In Catalogue C, the company made the following statement:

> "We maintain a large stock of finished parts and a special staff to deal with the prompt despatch of duplicate parts, which is greatly facilitated by the numerous adjacent Main Line Railways with their extensive and direct train services to all parts of the country.
>
> For the convenience of our customers we have a large repair shop entirely devoted to the

overhauling or repairs of their wagons by specially experienced mechanics, under a foreman who is an expert in this service. We can undertake urgent repairs promptly, and if application for space is made in advance for a general overhaul, we will notify the owner the time to send in his wagon, so that it is not off the road for a day longer that is absolutely necessary.

It will be seen that we endeavour to give our customers the fullest consideration, and to assist them to the utmost of our ability.

For the London district and the south of England, arrangements have been made with Messrs. Beck and Pollitzer, of 133/7, Queen Victoria Street, E.C.4, to hold extensive stocks of spare parts; by this means we are able to expedite delivery to our customers.

The services of our London Manager and outside staff are freely available to give advice and assistance to customers on all subjects affecting the running of their wagons and their transport problems.

For customers' further convenience, we have a special staff of highly-trained, competent mechanics, always ready for urgent service, to attend at the customers' premises, and to execute any adjustment and repairs which their investigation may prove necessary." [23]

An article written in 1908 gives an example of this activity.[24] "I was going through the works, (Pepper Road) and happened to observe a hybrid sort of wagon just having the finishing touches applied, and, in reply to my enquiries, I learnt that a Coulthard* wagon was brought in on the Wednesday, at mid-day, and it required a new Mann's boiler, all the brake gear altering to suit, and new brackets forging for same, besides numerous small alterations, all repainted spick and span, and ready to be fetched on Saturday at noon. This is about a record - and it shows what can be done by good organisation and working with a good will." Quite a remarkable achievement!

* Coulthard of Preston, Lancashire, were one of the early producers of steam wagons and were taken over by the Lancashire Steam Motor Company in 1907 to form Leyland Motors Limited.

On 12 January 1914 the board passed a resolution authorising and doubling the nominal capital of the company from its original £25,000 to £50,000.[25] Presumably this was to expand the business and invest in new equipment for the Pepper Road Works.

During the First World War the works became a Government-controlled establishment, however no records have been discovered that reveal the products made during this period. What is clear is that the production of wagons continued unabated, with approximately 400 machines being produced over the years 1914 to 1918. A small number of wagons were produced for the War Department, however the bulk were for civilian purposes. Some vehicles that were used by the War Department include engine numbers 1085, 1086 and possibly 1257. An article covering the Royal Agricultural Society's Show at Nottingham gives a snippet of information: "Mann's Patent Steam Cart and Wagon Company showed one of their standard 5-ton wagons, of which many have been supplied to the War Department." [26]

The list of directors up to this time had been consistent, with the five original members of the board retaining control - James Hutchinson Mann, William Hutchinson Mann, Richard Longden Hattersley, Alfred Smith and John Edward Davenport. In February 1917 Alfred Smith's name is not included, however no explanation is given. In his place is a new member, Captain Stanley Davenport of the Central Flying School, Upavon, Wiltshire, who was probably the son of John Davenport, one of the original directors.

Figure 24: War Department Wagons
Little hard evidence has survived about Mann's involvement in the war effort, however this photograph illustrates that the War Department had at least three wagons, a 3-ton model and two 5-ton models. *(Mann Catalogue)*

During the First World War the government offered incentives for companies to invest in petrol powered wagons to boost the transport capabilities of the nation and to assist in national and military related activity. At the cessation of hostilities, many of these vehicles were to assist in the start of a major shift to road haulage in Britain, a business that had previously been dominated by the railways. This created a major problem for steam wagon builders, such as Mann's Patent Steam Cart and Wagon Company, because their principal products, on which their business depended, were not needed in any quantity, particularly at the lighter end of the road transport business where petrol powered wagons were particularly suited. There was some comfort in this period, because at the heavier end of the market petrol wagons had not been developed to cope with the demands of heavy haulage, and so there was still business to be had for the steam wagon builder, but in an increasingly smaller market place.[27] It was these difficult trading conditions that Mann's encountered at the start of the 1920s.

Figure 25: Advertising, 1923
The petrol wagon was an increasing threat to the steam wagon at this time and the very bold statements included in this advert demonstrate that the company was trying its best to counter this threat. *(Commercial Motor)*

The next surviving business record is the returns for 1922, and in these documents Stanley Davenport is listed again, but in his civilian capacity. He is recorded as living at 18 Earls Terrace, Kensington, London, W8, a prestigious address near Holland Park. It is possible that Stanley was involved with the London office, situated at 9 Fenchurch Avenue, EC3, on the opposite side of London to his home.

Another director appointed at this time was Arthur Mann, James' son, and he is listed as living at the same address as James, i.e. Aldersyde, Huby, near Leeds. Little change is identified in the list of shareholders at this time, however the major shareholders still held a considerable proportion, almost 80%, of the 5000 shares.

- John Edward Davenport 1562
- James Hutchinson Mann 1250
- William Hutchinson Mann 1120

In the following year, 1923, the Register of Directors shows Stanley Davenport to have been replaced by Harold Davenport. He is listed as an Iron Merchant, and his home address is identified as The Arches, Bolling Road, Ben Rhydding.

The 1923 catalogue includes a comprehensive section on the manufacture, materials and workmanship of the Mann steam wagon, as this following extract illustrates:

> "As the knowledge of steel manufacture has progressed, we have kept in touch with the advance of modern metallurgy, taking advantage of every improvement to keep our specifications in line. We use the best grades of High Tensile Carbon and Nickel steels for our shafts and axles according to their functions. Special Case Hardening Steel is used where a glass-hard outer surface and soft core are necessary. Electrically Melted Steel Castings are used where forgings are unsuitable.
>
> The boiler is of the best quality of Siemens Martin Steel conforming with the Insurance Companies' requirements, and all boiler tubes, feed pipes, etc., are of solid drawn Weldless Steel.
>
> The stays are of best brand of Yorkshire Special Stay Iron. The bearings throughout are made from best quality Phosphor Bronze of selected hardness, varying in Hardness No. between 80 and 200 Brinell according to their position and functions.
>
> Paints are specially selected for their suitability to resist the heat of the boiler and general outdoor atmospheric conditions. From the body coat of double boiled linseed oil and upwards, the colour coats are high grade enamels finished with best quality copal varnish.
>
> All important working surfaces, flat, cylindrical and internal, are accurately ground to a mirror-like surface on the very latest pattern of precision grinding machines. This is done after the parts have been subjected to the case-hardening and heat treatment process.
>
> All case-hardening or heat treatments are carried out in the most up-to-date type of gas fired furnace, controlled by electric pyrometers giving an autographic record of time and temperature for the whole operation, to ensure that each batch of work receives the treatment appropriate to the class of steel employed and the final result desired.
>
> All Gear Wheels throughout the wagon are machine-cut on modern gear-generators, giving the involute type of tooth by means of which, in 'The Mann Steam Wagon', the gears retain their quietness of running, even when bearings are beginning to wear.
>
> The workmanship throughout is of the highest possible standard of accuracy and finish.
>
> Special attention is given to the employment of jigs and fixtures in the machine shops to

ensure the maximum accuracy of interchangeability, and all finished parts are passed into a central store of inspection, in order to reduce the chance of accidental faults of workmanship and material to a minimum.

After each engine had been assembled, the valves are correctly adjusted so as to give a correct indicator diagram.

The wagon then undergoes a series of road tests, the final one being over a specially selected route, having some very steep gradients, and generally more severe conditions than are met with by the average user. Accurate records are kept of the time taken and the fuel and water consumption, to see that these are within certain defined limits. After this the machine goes to the paint shop, and when it finally reaches the purchaser, it is as smart and attractive in appearance as it is economical in running." [28]

The Society of Motor Manufacturers and Traders represented a wide range of road vehicle interests, having been formed in 1902. In 1918 they decided to have a steam vehicle section, and representatives of the industry were invited to take office.[29] At the council meeting on 19 June 1924, Mr G. Hoare resigned the Chairmanship of the Steam Vehicle Committee through reasons of ill health. This left a vacancy in the steam vehicle section and Mr James M. Dallas of Mann's Patent Steam Cart and Wagon Company was elected as Associate Member. His companion is recorded as Mr Victor R. Garrett of the well-known company, Richard Garrett & Sons Ltd., Leiston, Suffolk. Mr James M. Dallas was Mann's London representative, based at their offices in Fenchurch Avenue.

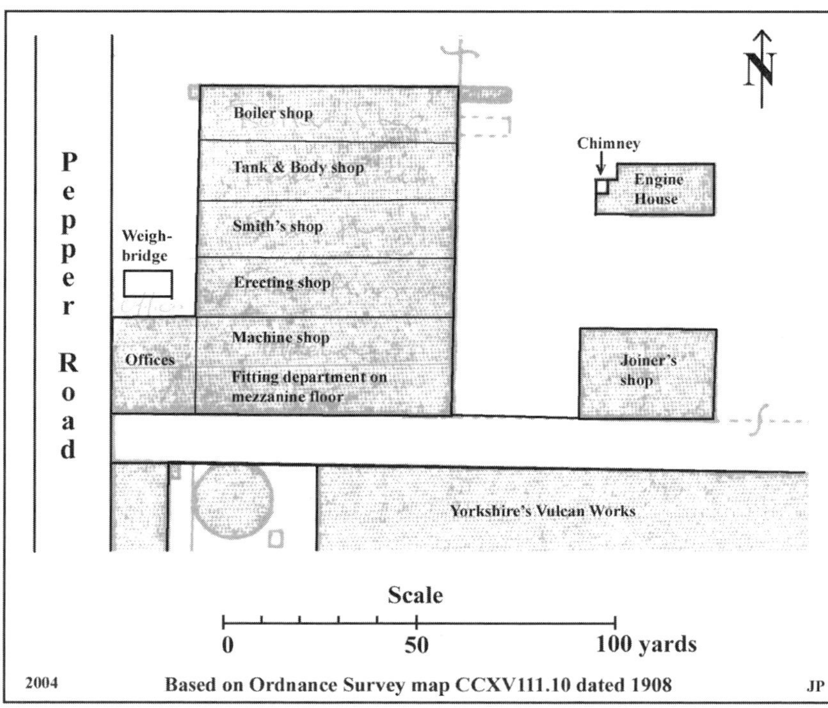

Figure 26: Pepper Road Works, Plan
The Pepper Road Works survive to this day and largely unaltered from this plan based on the 1908 Ordnance Survey. The only casualty is the Engine House, which has been demolished. The separate small Joiner's Shop, where trailers and wagon bodies were constructed, still exists.

Figure 27: Pepper Road Works, Engraving
This idealised view of the Pepper Road Works contains some detail inaccuracies, in that the northernmost bay (on the left of the view) did not extend to the Pepper Road boundary (see plan above). Similarly the length of the workshops was not as long as depicted, although this may have been the long-term aim. *(Mann Catalogue)*

At the beginning of the 1920s, Mann's Patent Steam Cart and Wagon Company embarked on a major development to design and build a new wagon to compete with the petrol wagon. In 1922 patents were filed and by the summer of 1924 the new wagon made its first public appearance. This new machine was named the Express Wagon, and it was a radical departure from previous Mann vehicles. (See chapter 6 for further details.) It is obvious from surviving business records that the introduction of the Express Wagon required substantial investment by the company. In the first instance, the corrugated boiler required large ovens to pre-heat the blank boilerplates. Secondly, hydraulic pressing equipment was needed to create the complex shape of the boiler shell. Whilst this type of equipment would have been used for their traditional boilers, for instance, to form the throat plate, the size of the new boilerplates was considerably greater than previous and probably outside the capacity of the existing ovens and presses. In addition, the new engine was more like an internal combustion engine than a steam engine. To manufacture this engine would need a whole range of patterns making, together with specialist machine tools to create the range of components. To fund this expenditure, a mortgage of £20,000 was obtained in August 1924 from the Westminster Bank. Unfortunately the Mann Express wagon was not the commercial success the company had expected and as a result, the return on this investment was very poor. The repayments on the £20,000 loan proved to be too great a burden for the business, and the company was unable to meet its commitments, for in January 1926, the Westminster Bank appointed James Alexander Couper, a partner in the accountants Lee & Whitfield, 17 East Parade, Leeds, as receiver to manage the company on their behalf.

One of the sacrifices made whilst the receiver was involved with the business, was the loss of Joseph Capel Cornock as Company Secretary. After the end of 1926, the official documents are signed by Harold Davenport as Company Secretary.

To overcome the debt, Debenture Stock was issued to raise additional funds. By December 1926 £9,232 5s 5d had been raised, and this appears to have been sufficient to satisfy the Westminster Bank, for on 2 March 1927 the receiver relinquished his duties. Despite this, Couper was retained as a Director of the company, as can be seen in the List of Directors for May 1927, shown below:

James Hutchinson Mann	Engineer	Aldersyde, Weeton, Nr. Leeds
Arthur Mann	Engineer	Hewenden,Weeton, Nr. Leeds
John Edward Davenport	Iron Merchant	Wells House Hotel, Ilkley
Harold Davenport	Iron Merchant	8 North Hill Court, Headingley, Leeds
James Alexander Couper	Chartered Accountant	Cardigan Court, Cardigan Road, Leeds

This period must have been extremely difficult for James Mann, for as well as all the problems with the business, one of his most ardent supporters, his elder brother William Hutchinson Mann, died at his home in Harrogate on 23 November 1926. His estate had a net value of £7513 8s 4d, and was divided between his wife Alice Jane Mann and his three daughters, Sylvia Annie Mann, Mary Elizabeth Layfield Mann and Christine Helen Mann.

Unlike many of their competitors, Mann's Patent Steam Cart and Wagon Company did not attempt to embrace the internal-combustion engine, which was proving to be a reliable alternative to steam power. Many users found the internal-combustion powered wagons easier to operate as there was no waiting for steam in the morning, no coaling up, no tube sweeping, no boiler examination and repairs, no stopping for water every 30 miles or so. Despite the robustness and unbeatable pulling power of steam, the internal-combustion wagon was taking over, and because Mann's failed to acknowledge this, their fate was inevitable.

In December 1927 Mann's accountants, Lee & Whitfield, made approaches to the Directors of the Yorkshire Patent Steam Wagon Company regarding the possibility of a merger of the two companies. The intention was that the two 'brands' i.e. Mann and Yorkshire, would be retained, as these were both well-established companies with their own distinctive products and loyal customers. The key features of the merger were:

- Only one factory would be retained, with the surplus site and all its equipment being sold off to the benefit of the partnership.
- The drawings, patterns and stock-in-trade of the two partners would pass to the new company.
- A new board of directors would be formed, consisting of two members from "York shire", two members from "Mann" and a fifth independent director.
- The share ownership would consist of £20,000 by Mann's and £40,000 by Yorkshire – representing their existing capitalisation.
- The new Managing Director would be offered a salary of £650 per annum plus commission on profits, and this position would have a five-year agreement of service.

It is not clear if the directors of Mann's Patent Steam Cart and Wagon Company originated this proposal or if the accountants Lee & Whitfield were responsible, however, the 'Yorkshire' board were initially favourable to the idea, with some reservations. Yorkshire's company secretary J. J. Baines suggested that the proposal required "careful consideration". [30] This was not perhaps surprising as they were experiencing the same downturn in sales as all steam wagon manufacturers. Indeed, the notes by the board indicate that at this time they had twenty-four wagons in stock – representing around £20,000 of sales value.

In a second surviving letter, Mr R. G. Thompson, a director of Clayton, Son & Co. suggested: "Because of the position of the Yorkshire, I am predisposed to give favourable consideration to any scheme that has in it possibilities for relieving the situation." [31] Despite these encouraging remarks, ultimately the merger of the two companies did not take place. This was not unexpected given the strong identity of the two organisations and the practicality of the compromises necessary to produce a successful united new company.

In a separate proposal, Marshall's of Gainsborough were approached in 1928 with the objective of some form of amalgamation.[32] This was the company where James Hutchinson Mann had spent some of his early career, specifically from 1887 to 1890. The talks took place between Lee & Whitfield and Arthur Colegate, Marshall's Joint Managing Director, however, Marshall's were similarly in a poor financial position.[33] After some deliberation the Marshall's board of directors rejected the offer.

The last list of directors of Mann's Patent Steam Cart and Wagon Company is dated 31 January 1929. The list contains four directors, namely James Hutchinson Mann, John Edward Davenport, Harold Davenport and Arthur Mann. Curiously, Arthur Mann's address is given as Punda Milia, Makuyu, Kenya Colony. Why Arthur was out in Africa is unclear, however, George Wright states that he was told by one of Mann's fitters that the company was involved in a contract to supply machinery for rope-making to Africa and it may be that these two facts are related.[34] It seems likely that this was in partnership with the Leeds Company, Fairbairn, Lawson, Combe Barbour of Wellington Foundry, who were internationally renowned suppliers and manufacturers of textile and rope-making machinery.

Despite the lack of unequivocal evidence, the surviving balance sheets in the Public Record Office indicate that Mann's Patent Steam Cart and Wagon Company was closed down voluntarily on 31 January 1929. On the following day, 1 February 1929, the goodwill of the business passed to Atkinson Walker Wagons Limited, of Preston. A paragraph in the press announced: [35]

> "An announcement of considerable importance is that Atkinson Walker Wagons Ltd,. Frenchwood Works, Preston, have acquired from the 1st ult. the goodwill and the stock of duplicate parts, patterns and drawings of Mann's Patent Steam Cart & Wagon Co. Ltd. Pepper Road Works, Hunslet, Leeds. We learn it is the intention of the purchasers to give adequate service in the supply of spare parts for all the Mann machines in use and also to continue building new machines of the Mann design. Mann's Patent Steam Cart & Wagon Co. Ltd. will best be known to many of our readers as the makers of the Mann steam tractor, which was awarded a first prize gold medal and £20 at the Royal Agricultural Society's tractor trials in 1920 in Class 4 for direct traction steam engine plant, suitable for ploughing four furrows 10 in. wide by 8in. deep, the engines to comply with the Light Road Locomotives Act."

It appears that James Mann (who was approaching his sixty-ninth birthday) had decided that the end of his business was inevitable and that he should close the company down in an orderly fashion. According to Wilf Cole (who served his apprenticeship at Mann's) the remaining wagons were sold in May 1929, at which a 6-ton overtype tipping wagon was sold to George Armitage & Sons, Robin Hood Brickworks, near Wakefield. In addition, three shaft-drive (Mann Express) wagons were sold, two to Wales, and one to Buxton.[36] This was followed, on 10 July 1929, by the sale of the land and property to H Braithwaite & Co. Ltd. of Swinegate Leeds.[37] Braithwaite & Co. were heating engineers, and the Pepper Road Works became their head office and works. Listings in trade directories indicate that Braithwaite & Co. closed in the early 1940s. After various legal processes were carried through, Mann's Patent Steam Cart and Wagon Company was officially dissolved on 12 January 1932.

The transfer of the goodwill to Atkinson Walker Wagons Limited must have appeared to the users of Mann wagons a fair compromise in the circumstances, as the Lancashire firm had a good track record in the steam wagon trade. Atkinson Walker were an amalgamation of Atkinson & Co. and Walker Bros. (Wigan) Ltd. Previously, Atkinson had taken over the Leyland Steam Wagon Company of Chorley, and in 1929 were still in business as steam wagon builders. The company had originally started as Atkinson & Co. around 1908 as a wagon maintenance and repair business, however they brought out in 1916 their own wagon.[38] This was a relatively advanced design featuring a duplex engine with poppet type valves, fed from a vertical boiler. In 1918 Atkinson introduced an even more advanced wagon that used a uniflow engine.[39] This type of engine produced improved thermal efficiency, which was achieved by having dedicated ports for admission and exhaust, so that the surfaces of the engine remained at relatively constant temperature.

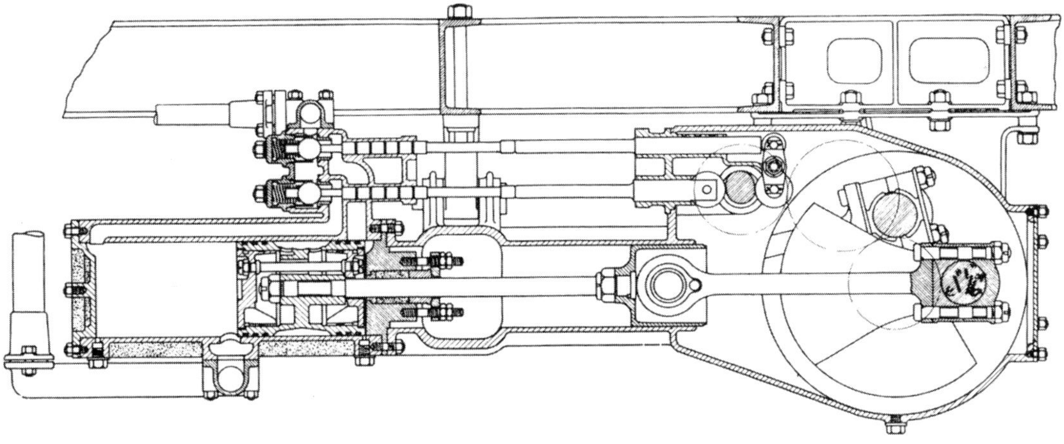

Figure 28: The Atkinson Uniflow Engine Diagram
Atkinson & Co. introduced this advanced efficient engine in 1918. The uniflow engine was in principle simpler than a conventional engine as the self-venting exhaust system removed the need for exhaust valves. *(Atkinson Catalogue)*

The formation of Atkinson Walker Wagons Ltd. took place on 10 July 1925 with a nominal capital of £75,000.[40] The original directors were:

Edward Atkinson	Engineer	Frenchwood House, Preston
James Scarlett Ascroft Walker	Engineer	71 Leyland Road, Preston
William Bates	Co. Secretary	11 Park Road, Wigan

The sale of the original Atkinson business to the new Atkinson Walker Company included the main Frenchwood Works at Preston, plus the Kendal Street Engineering Works, Preston and the woodworking depot, High Street, Preston, together with the 'stock in trade' located at the spares' departments in London, Glasgow, Birmingham, Liverpool, Bradford, Perth, and Johannesburg.

As well as steam wagons, Atkinson Walker also produced 4-wheeled and 6-wheeled chain-driven railway locomotives, using essentially the same engine and boiler as the road wagons.[41] It is thought that around twenty were constructed, with four examples being exported to Singapore. One of the Atkinson Walker locomotives has survived, albeit fitted with a Gardner diesel engine. Its current resting place is the Ulster Folk and Transport Museum, Cultra, County Down.

Atkinson Walker saw an opportunity to increase business and their share of the steam wagon market out of the remains of Mann's Patent Steam Cart & Wagon Company. Unfortunately the fortunes of Atkinson Walker Wagons Ltd. declined, and by October 1929 Mr W. H. Ainsworth was acting as receiver for the company. It appears that the Mann business was seen as a saleable item and a buyer was sought to help to ease the finances of Atkinson Walker. In June 1930 a new limited company was created; Mann Steam & Motor Wagon Company Limited, with its registered offices at Frenchwood House, Frenchwood, Preston, Lancashire. The new company was capitalised at £5,000 with the 5000 shares being valued at £1 each.[42] The articles of association, dated 20 June 1930, declare that the company was established:

To carry on business as manufacturers and repairs of, and dealing in, steam wagons, traction engines, motor lorries, motor cars, omnibuses, coaches, tramcars, locomotives, railway carriages and trucks, and other vehicles, forgings, castings, boilers, engines, screws, nails, machinery, presses, implements, gears, tools, spare parts and accessories.

The first subscribers are recorded as being:

John Thomas Harvey*	Director	Lynwood, Moss Road, Orrell near Wigan
Ernest Mallett	Engineer	1152 Chorley Old Road, Bolton
Edward Atkinson	Engineer	Frenchwood House, Preston

*John Thomas Harvey was owner of the Manley Street Bakery, Lower Ince, Wigan.

Similarly, the list of directors reads:

John Thomas Harvey	Managing Director, J. T. Harvey Ltd., Wigan
Ernest Mallett	Managing Director, Atkinson Walker Wagons Ltd.
Edward Atkinson	Director, Atkinson Walker Wagons Ltd.
William Bates*	Company Secretary

*William Bates address is given as 20 Trafalgar Road, Wigan

On 26 June 1930 the goodwill of the Mann business was legally transferred from Atkinson Walker to the new organisation, Mann Steam & Motor Wagon Company Limited. The vendors of the goodwill are the same people named above, plus William Caldwell, of 171 Warrington Road, Lower Ince, Wigan.[43] The memorandum of agreement states:

> "Whereas the vendors are the owners of the duplicate stock and stores, steel bins, boiler blocks and jigs and the goodwill of the Mann's Patent Steam Cart and Wagon Company Limited, Leeds, together with all drawings, patterns, engine registers, general office books, catalogue blocks, and other stock in trade of the business, and are desirous of selling and transferring the same to the company. The company having as its objects amongst other things the carrying out of the supply of such parts etc."

It has long been rumoured that James Hutchinson Mann insisted on destroying the records of his company when the Leeds business closed, but the paragraph above demonstrates that this was not the case. The fact is, that the business records were taken by Atkinson Walker when they acquired the goodwill in February 1929.

Figure 29: Scammell and Nephew Poster, 1920
Scammell and Nephew purchased Mann Steam & Motor Wagon Company Limited in 1930 from Atkinson Walker Wagons Ltd., who were themselves in financial difficulty. Scammell and Nephew were also agents for Foden steam wagons as this poster indicates. *(Motor Transport)*

This transfer of ownership was transacted for the sum of £3797, and this was paid in shares of the following proportion:

John Thomas Harvey	2299
Edward Atkinson	469
Ernest Mallett	529
William Bates	250
William Caldwell	250
	3797

Very shortly afterwards, the entire company was sold to Scammell and Nephew, although it remained a separate business, still with the same title, Mann Steam & Motor Wagon Company Limited. Scammell and Nephew were also in the business of vehicle maintenance and repair, and their offices were at Fashion Street, Spitalfields, London, E1. They had a long standing relationship with Foden for the sale and servicing of their steam wagons in the south of England.

The sale of Mann Steam & Motor Wagon Company Limited took place on 13 August 1930 and the new directors, all board members of Scammell and Nephew, are recorded as:

Henry Rupert Hood Barrs	The Brewhouse, Cookham, Berks.
Richard Percival England	8a Bruton Street, Mayfair
John Grant Scott	10 Rosenthal Road, Catford

According to Alan Duke, the Scammell and Nephew company assembled a few new Mann vehicles, although it is likely that most of the components were from stock parts. The only one which has been positively identified was given the works number 3001 and was assigned registration number GP7059 around June 1931. This was a roller wagon (patching roller), and was delivered to the Metropolitan Borough of Wandsworth, London.[44]

The next ten years of Mann Steam & Motor Wagon Company Limited are not known, however, on 30 June 1942, the company was renamed Hood Engineering Company Limited and the connection with Mann's steam wagons disappeared.[45] Atkinson Walker Wagons Limited lingered on after the sale of the Mann business but was legally dissolved on 23 September 1938.[46] Following the death of Edward Atkinson in January 1932, W. G. Allen formed a new company Atkinson Lorries (1933) Ltd, and this became the well known builder of modern diesel wagons.[47]

References

1 West Riding Registry of Deeds, Wakefield, *Book 1893, volume 19, p766*
2 *The Engineer*, 19 June 1861, p29
3 *The Engineer*, 13 June 1862, p357
4 West Riding Registry of Deeds, Wakefield, *Book 1894, volume 2, p416*
5 West Riding Registry of Deeds, Wakefield, *Book 1897, volume 24, p97*
6 *The Implement and Machinery Review*, 2 August 1899, p24350
7 Public Record Office, document BT31/16268/63718 Memorandum of Association.
8 Public Record Office, document BT31/16268/63718 Agreement, 25 September 1899
9 Lane. M. R. *The Story of the Steam Plough Works*. Northgate Publishing Co. 1980, p212
10 *The Engineer,* 26 February 1904, p206
11 Public Record Office, document BT31/16268/63718
12 West Riding Registry of Deeds, Wakefield, *Book 1901, volume 25, p369*
13 *The Engineer,* 29 May 1903, p539
14 Cole, W., *Steaming*, Volume 18, National Traction Engine Trust, p162.
15 *Commercial Motor,* 10 January 1907, p415
16 *Commercial Motor,* 30 April 1908, p230
17 The Iron and Steel Institute, *Programme - Leeds Meeting*, October 1912.
18 Cole, W., *Steaming*, Volume 19, National Traction Engine Trust, p134
19 *Commercial Motor*, 12 September 1918, p56
20 Love, W. S., *Portfolio number 113,* Road Locomotive Society, 1969
21 *Commercial Motor*, 24 June 1909, p328A
22 *Commercial Motor*, 23 June 1910, p335
23 Mann's Patent Steam Cart and Wagon Company, *Catalogue C*, p63
24 *Commercial Motor*, 10 September 1908, p12
25 Public Record Office, document BT31/16268/63718 Notice of Increase in the Nominal Capital
26 *Engineering*, 9 July 1915, p41
27 Kidner, R. W., *The Steam Lorry, Locomotion Papers No.3*, Oakwood Press, 1956, p24
28 Mann's Patent Steam Cart and Wagon Company, *Catalogue C*, p57
29 *The Engineer,* 20 December 1918, p531
30 Baines J. J., Letter to Lee & Whitfield, 20 December 1927 (Michael Walters collection)
31 Thompson, R. G., Letter to Clayton Son & Co., 12 January 1928 (Michael Walters collection)
32 Lane. M. R., *The Story of the Britannia Iron Works*, Quiller Press, 1993, p104
33 Lane. M. R., *Correspondence with author*, 25 March 2005
34 Wright, George, *Portfolio number 18*, Road Locomotive Society, 1949
35 *The Implement and Machinery Review*, 1 March 1929, p1170
36 Cole, Wilf, *Portfolio number 27,* Road Locomotive Society
37 West Riding Registry of Deeds, Wakefield, *Book 1929, volume 83, p 538*
38 Abbott, R. A. S. and Lowe, J. W., *Vertical Boiler Locomotives*, Oakwood Press, 1989
39 Clark, R. H., *The Development of the English Steam Wagon*, Goose & Son, 1963, p7
40 Public Record Office, document BT31/32698/207167
41 Lowe, J. W., *British Steam Locomotive Builders*, Goose, 1975
42 Companies House, Archive Record, 248905 Memorandum of Agreement, para 3
43 Companies House, Archive Record, 248905 Memorandum of Agreement, para 1
44 Duke, Alan, *Mann Engine List*, Road Locomotive Society, 1988
45 Companies House, Archive Record, 248905 Special Resolution, 4 Jul 1942
46 Public Record Office, document BT31/32698/207167
47 Kelly, M. A., *The Undertype Steam Road Waggon*, Goose & Son, 1975, p10

Chapter 3

Mann and Charlesworth's Products, 1894–1899

The combined experience of nearly forty years in related companies gave Mann and Charlesworth a powerful starting point for their new venture. In 1894 James Hutchinson Mann was 34 years of age and Sidney Charlesworth 32 years. The important factors that they appear to have considered in the design of their road vehicles are robustness and simplicity. Robustness was absolutely vital because the roads of the day were of very poor quality with bumps, potholes and cobbled surfaces. Any machine not able to take the constant hammering caused by running over these dreadful surfaces was likely to meet a premature end. As today, once a customer has had a bad experience, it takes a lot of persuasion to get him to try a similar product, and so it was essential that Mann and Charlesworth's machines were built to the toughest standards with ample bearing surfaces and with easy access for maintenance. Simplicity was also paramount, since the road vehicle was often owned and maintained by unskilled hands, unlike its close relation the railway locomotive, which generally speaking, was routinely overhauled and adjusted by skilled mechanics in specialist depots, fitted with appropriate equipment. Sophisticated steam vehicles may look attractive at trials and competitions when efficiency of fuel consumption is the deciding factor, but when hauling loads day after day, perhaps in poor weather, the practical haulier and farmer demands reliability, otherwise his business suffers. At the end of the nineteenth century there were many well-established manufacturers of traction engines, and so the new company had plenty of competition. Being late to enter the steam vehicle business, Mann and Charlesworth had a big hurdle to climb in order to be accepted as a serious contender. There can be no doubt that the company built good quality, robust and simple machines, as their success in the marketplace gives testimony.

Figure 30: Mann and Charlesworth Brass Plate
This unrestored brass plate is a rare relic of the little-known company of Mann and Charlesworth. Its origins are uncertain, however, given its large size, it would appear to have come from a stationary engine.

First Products

As with most new companies, Mann and Charlesworth had to be flexible with their range of products and services in order to attract sufficient work to keep the business healthy. The 1898 trade directory[1] defines the company as "Engineers and makers of traction engines", which suggests that they were willing to undertake general engineering work in addition to their primary trade as traction engine builders. The best available evidence indicates that Mann and Charlesworth's first traction engine was supplied to Philip Hardcastle of Follifoot near Harrogate.[2] The following testimonial indicates that this engine was purchased in 1894: [3]

> Follifoot, near Harrogate
> May 18th, 1896
>
> Messrs. Mann & Charlesworth
> Dear Sirs, In answer to your letter asking what I now think of the Patent Reversing Gear after two years experience with it, all I can say is that it still does as well as ever. It has not been repaired, nor does it want anything doing to it now. If I buy another engine I should like to have your gear fitted to it, no matter who makes it. The Engine, although light, is strong, and the best puller I have had to do with in my 19 years' experience of Traction engines.
>
> **Yours truly, P HARDCASTLE.**

Single Eccentric Reversing Gear

The earliest dated document referring to Mann and Charlesworth equipment is the patent application for the Single Eccentric Reversing Gear in 1894. Sidney Charlesworth would have been familiar with this type of gear when he was working at Richard Garrett's works at Leiston in Suffolk (see Chapter 1). They employed a similar device on their portable engines. This was the invention of Ernest Boutard, a Danish engineer who was employed at Leiston over the years 1881 to 1884. Boutard's gear was much simpler than Mann and Charlesworth's in that it only provided two fixed gears, forward and reverse, with no variable cut-off of the valve.[4] This was achieved by having a semi-loose eccentric that was located by a tapered pin in either of two holes.

Mann and Charlesworth's first patent, number 13,958, is dated 20 July 1894, and was their ingenious single eccentric reversing gear.[5] Stephenson's link motion was the conventional form of reversing gear used by most companies for road and rail applications at this period. Stephenson's valve gear used two eccentrics, one to create the forward valve movement and the other to create the reverse valve movement. The two eccentrics were connected via rods to a slotted link, and a die block, which moved along this slot to provide the correct motion for the valve.

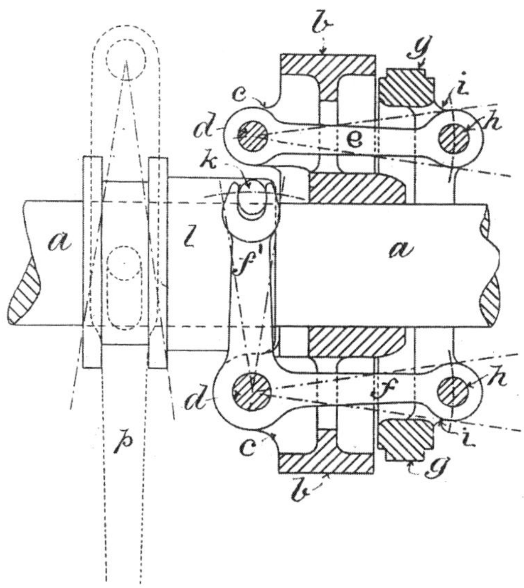

Figure 31: Patent Drawing and Engraving, Single Eccentric Reversing Gear
Mann and Charlesworth's first patent, number 13,958, was submitted on 20 July 1894, and was their ingenious single eccentric reversing gear. Whilst in principle the idea was very simple, it required a number of accurately made components and this must have been relatively costly. It also occupied a good proportion of the crankshaft, which could be a problem with inside valve compound engines.

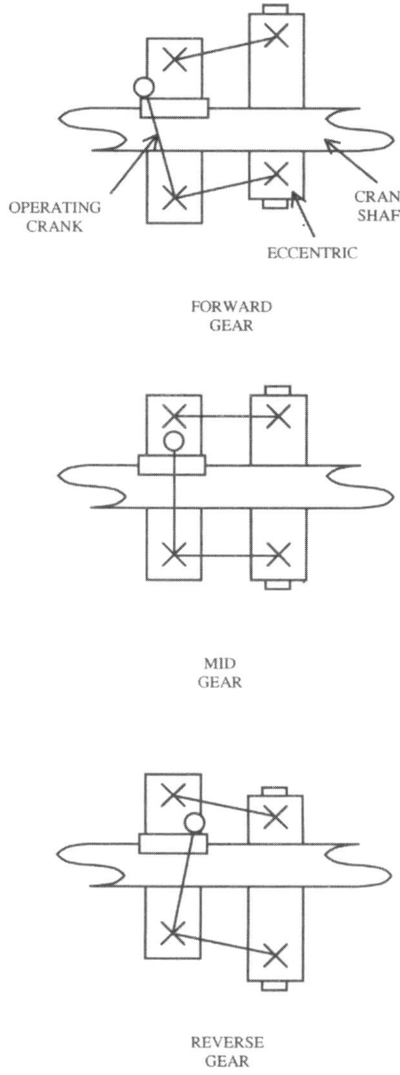

Figure 32: Explanatory Diagram, Single Eccentric Reversing Gear
See description below.

The single eccentric reversing gear does away with the need for the link and die block, with the intermediate valve rod being connected directly to the eccentric sleeve. To achieve the reversing action, the eccentric was fixed to the crankshaft by four links, which acted as a parallel motion (see image above). By this means, the eccentric could be moved radially about the crankshaft. In the centre position, the eccentric was concentric with the crankshaft, which produced no radial movement and hence the steam valve was stationary. In the two extreme positions, the eccentric was offset to the crankshaft, one at 180 degrees to the other, thereby providing the forward and reverse action of the steam valve. A hand lever was located in a groove of a loose sleeve fitted around the crankshaft. This sleeve moved the crank to provide the necessary gear. One of the principal advantages of this type of gear is that once a cut-off is selected, the moving parts remain static in relation to each other, and simply rotate around the crankshaft. This results in reduced wear in the bushes and pins. This is in contrast to Stephenson's valve gear, where the various links and pivots are in constant motion.

The wording of the original Mann and Charlesworth patent is shown below:

Improved Arrangement of Reversing Gear for Steam and other Engines

JAMES HUTCHINSON MANN Mechanical Engineer and SIDNEY CHARLESWORTH Mechanical Engineer trading as Mann & Charlesworth, Canning Works, Dewsbury Road, Leeds, do hereby declare the nature of this invention to be as follows :

Instead of using ordinary link motion reversing gear, we employ the following arrangement; which consists of a disc wheel or boss (which for convenience we use as a governor pulley) keyed on to the crank shaft of the engine, on which are attached two pins forming fulcrums for two levers or arms, one being a bell crank lever. The eccentric is attached to the other ends of the levers or arms by pins, and has a slot hole through it, allowing it to be moved across the crank shaft by the bell crank lever to the backwards or forward positions as required (the levers being of equal lengths insure the eccentric being kept perfectly at right angle to the crank shaft & parallel to the centre line of the engine in any position). The other end of the bell crank lever is connected by a die to a loose sleeve, which is moved along the crank shaft by a hand lever working between notch plates for holding it in the required position for causing the engine either to run backwards or forwards, and also for varying the expansion of steam in the cylinder.

The Yorkshire Agricultural Society's 1894 show was held at Beverley on the 1st, 2nd and 3rd of August. Stand 7 was taken by Mann and Charlesworth and this was their first public show. The company only had one exhibit, and the show catalogue describes this as a 7 h.p. special light agricultural locomotive, suitable for flat, soft districts, with bridges of insufficient strength for ordinary traction engines. The traction engine was keenly priced at £340.[6] In comparison, William Allchin, Globe Works, Northampton, were exhibiting a similar 7 h.p. traction engine on Stand 4 and this was priced at £432. Similarly, E. Foden. Sons & Co., Elworth Works, Sandbach, occupied Stand 11, where they exhibited a 6 h.p. single cylinder traction engine, this being priced at £430.

A brief article in *The Engineer* of March 1895[7] showed a series of drawings and a brief description, from which the following extract is taken: " Messrs. Mann and Charlesworth of Leeds, have brought out and patented a very simple single excentric *(sic)* reversing gear for steam engines. .... The makers sold their first engine with this gear on from the Yorkshire Show at Beverley last year. It has been in regular work since without a hitch."

Mann and Charlesworth offered their single eccentric reversing gear to other manufacturers to incorporate into their own equipment. In the Mann and Charlesworth catalogue they state, "In consequence of several applications, we are prepared to grant permission to a number of leading firms to make it for themselves under a small royalty... Besides Agricultural Engines, it lends itself equally well for Locomotives (with outside cylinders), Marine Launch, Rolling and Winding Engines, Steam Cranes, Winches, &c." [8] One example of this was an unusual three-wheeled traction engine fitted with a 7 n.h.p. tandem compound engine. This machine was built by Brown and May of Devizes, Wiltshire, and exhibited at Leicester in 1896. In this application the valve rod divided alongside the trunk crosshead guide to serve each valve chest.[9] An article in *The Engineer* from 1896 relates: "We learn that the makers' patent single eccentric reversing gear - also illustrated in our columns - has been fitted to a number of traction engines, and in every case it has given great satisfaction, some of them having been in use now for two years. The same gear is being made for a small locomotive, and for a pair of diagonal engines for a Belfast firm." [10] Another user of the Mann and Charlesworth single eccentric reversing gear was the Suffolk firm of Richard Garrett, who produced a traction engine fitted with the product. This engine, number 20485, was supplied to Henninger & Co., Darmstadt, Germany in 1895.[11]

Similarly, the technique was later used by a number of other wagon manufacturers; for example, Savage, of St Nicholas Iron Works, King's Lynn, produced in 1908 their class C wagon. This used a single eccentric gear mounted on a hollow shaft. The operating block ran in slots cut at an angle to the shaft, thus causing the eccentric to displace.[12] A similar gear was used by Clayton Wagons Ltd. of Lincoln, in their 1920 undertype wagon, but in this case an angled rod operating in a slot inside the shaft controlled the movement of the eccentric.[13]

Automatic Expansion Governor

Following quickly after the patent submission for the single eccentric reversing gear, was the automatic expansion governor, filed on 6 February 1895.[14] This patent, number 2571, defines a crankshaft mounted governor, where the two pivoted and linked weights acted against springs, moving radially in response to the rotational speed of the engine. This movement was conveyed to the valve eccentric by a radius piece mounted on one weight acting on a die formed in the eccentric casting. The text, taken verbatim from the original patent, is shown below:

Improvements in Shaft or Automatic Expansion Governors for Steam Engines

JAMES HUTCHINSON MANN Mechanical Engineer Canning Works, Dewsbury Road, Leeds, SIDNEY CHARLESWORTH Mechanical Engineer Canning Works, Dewsbury Road, Leeds, do hereby declare the nature of this invention to be as follows:

In our shaft or automatic expansion governor, instead of pivoting the eccentric by an arm or tail piece, upon a stud in the governor wheel, we employ the following arrangement, which consists of a governor or flywheel keyed upon the crank shaft, having lugs upon it, receiving pins, which form fulcrums for two distance levers or arms, which pass through and carry at their other ends the eccentric, the attachment being made by similar lugs and pins to those on the wheel. The eccentric has a slot hole through it, allowing it to be moved straight across the crank, thereby altering the travel of the valve (or reversing the engine, if necessary), without practically, altering the 'lead'. The distance levers being of equal length insure the eccentric being always parallel to the centre line of the engine in any position. We employ two weights (acting against. springs) pivoted on studs in the usual manner. A radius piece is bolted upon one of the weights which gives the required movement to the eccentric through a die which is taken through the body or that part of the eccentric, encircled by the strap (instead of through an arm or lug cast on it) thereby enabling us to get a much longer bearing. The die arm is further supported by 2 jaws on side of eccentric, made adjustable for taking up wear.

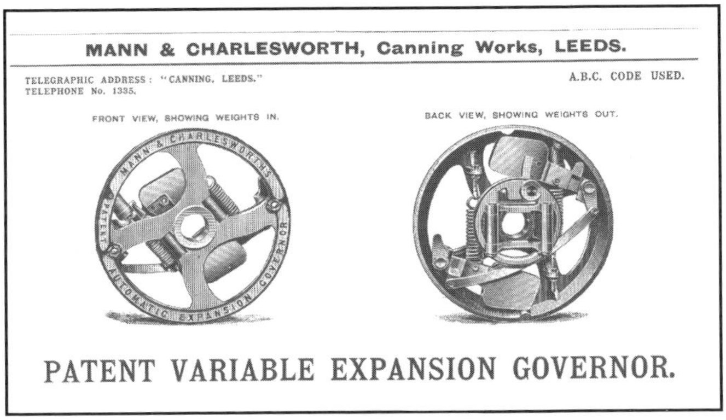

Figure 33: Engraving, Automatic Expansion Governor
The automatic expansion governor was registered at the Patent Office on 6 February 1895. This device can be seen on some of the stationary engines illustrated later in the chapter. *(Mann and Charlesworth Catalogue)*

Double Crank-Shaft Bearing Patent

A refinement of the bearing for the two-speed gear arrangement was the subject of a patent registered on 14 June 1895. This patent, number 11,578, was titled *Improved Double Crank Shaft Bracket for Traction Engines and Road Rollers*. This design proposed a U or trough shaped carrier that was bolted to the horn plate at one side and carried two bearings, one on either side of the trough. Between the two bearings was located the two-speed gear, fixed to a sleeve, so that it could slide laterally by the use of a lever acting in a groove. This lever provided the means to select the two speeds, or alternatively, in the centre position, the engine was out of gear. The benefits of this arrangement were stated as, "this brings the pinions between bearings and obtains the advantages of an inside gear engine, without the addition of the extra intermediate shaft, gear wheels, etc."

The Royal Show of 1895 was held at Darlington, commencing 22 June, and this was Mann and Charlesworth's first showing at a national exhibition. The company occupied Stand number 317, and the show catalogue[15] contains the following detail of their products:

> *Article* **4996** – (*New Implement*) – Traction Engine, 7-Horse Power, Light. Price £390. With two speeds, winding drum, rope, brake, water-lifter, &c., complete; fitted with Exhibitors' patent single eccentric reversing gear (which is much simpler, and quite as efficient as link motion), and their improved double crank shaft bracket, which obtains all the advantages of an 'inside gear' engine, without the disadvantage of an extra shaft, gear wheels, bearings, &c. This engine is specially designed to drive a threshing machine in combination with either a chaff-cutter, elevator, or trusser, and the extreme simplicity of its construction and fewness of parts allows the production of a powerful engine with a minimum amount of weight and cost.

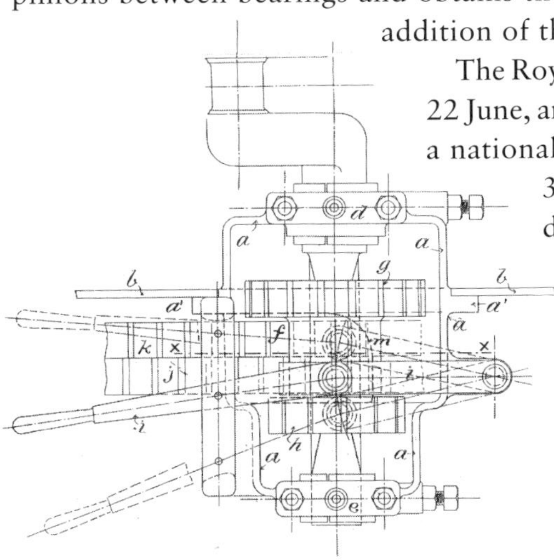

Figure 34: Patent Drawing, Double Crank Shaft Bearing
Patent number 11,578, *Improved Double Crank Shaft Bracket for Traction Engines and Road Rollers*, was registered by Mann and Charlesworth on 14 June 1895. The arrangement provided a mechanically robust support for the gears, without the need for an intermediate shaft.

4997 – Tandem Compound Engine, 10-Horse Power, Price £300 with boiler. For mounting upon a "Loco" boiler fitted with exhibitors' patent shaft governor.

4998 – Pump. Price £4. For washing out boilers, &c.

4999 – Brick Press; mfd. by Pullan and Mann, Elland Road, Leeds. Price £50. For bricks and tiles, with patent power driving gear.

Pullan and Mann was the company of which James' elder brother, William Hutchinson Mann, was a senior partner.

The press were enthusiastic about the company's products at the show, as the following extract from *Engineering*[16] illustrates: "Among the makers of engines Messrs. Mann and Charlesworth of Dewsbury Road, Leeds, hold the leading position on the score of novelty, as they are quite a young firm, and appear for the first time at a Royal Show. They exhibit both traction and fixed engines. In the former, in view of the keen competition that awaits all beginners, they have studied the question of economy as far as it can be done without sacrificing efficiency. As an example, they have substituted for the link motion, with its expensive rods and pins, a single shifting eccentric, ..." Little detail is given about the engines, however the traction engine is described as a light 7 horse-power type, with two-speed gearing. The fast and slow pinions slid on the squared end of the crankshaft, with bearings at each side of them. The main axle also contained a squared portion, fitted with the bevel wheel and winding drum. The engine shown at Darlington appears to have been sold to John Hoyle of Monk Fryston, Yorkshire, as the following testimonial verifies:[17]

Monk Fryston
May 5th 1896

Messrs. Mann & Charlesworth
Gentlemen, The engine I bought from you at the Darlington Show has gone very well. The Patent Reversing Gear acts all right. I have not driven an engine with link motion, so cannot compare the two.

Yours truly, JOHN HOYLE.

7 H.P. LIGHT TRACTION ENGINE.

Figure 35: Mann and Charlesworth Light Traction Engine
This elegant, well-proportioned light traction engine was influenced by the designers' previous experience, for example, the use of the trunk crosshead guide is similar to both Garrett and Marshall examples. *(Mann and Charlesworth Catalogue)*

A more detailed description of the 7-horse-power light traction engine was given in the Mann and Charlesworth catalogue dated circa 1897.[18] The single cylinder was $8\frac{3}{8}$in diameter by 12in stroke, and steam was fed from the boiler through the cylinder jacket to a dome at the top, from where dry steam fed the piston through ample ports. Attached directly to the cylinder was the trunk crosshead guide, and this contained a foot, which attached it to the boiler. Furthermore, this foot took some of the strain of the engine from the cylinder mounting and thereby distributed the forces over a larger area of the boiler top. Reversing gear of the Mann and Charlesworth patent type was used to control steam admission into the cylinder. The governor was set at 150 r.p.m. and worked directly over the equilibrium throttle valve. A mild-steel forging formed the connecting rod and this held phosphor-bronze bearings, which were adjustable by wedges. The 6-spoked flywheel was 4 foot 6in diameter, with a $6\frac{1}{2}$in face. This was attached to a mild-steel crankshaft, bent from a solid bar of $3\frac{1}{4}$in diameter. This shaft was made square where sliding pinions were used, thereby avoiding the need for keyways, which were a source of weakness. The right-hand crankshaft bracket was made double, with two sets of brasses, as defined in their earlier patent, 11,578. A pipe bearing supported the intermediate shaft and this ran across the back of the boiler, with the pipe bearing tying and staying both horn plates together and forming a rigid assembly. A steel forging of 5-inch diameter was used for the main axle, and like the intermediate shaft, used square sections to receive the bevel wheel and winding drum. On these major components, the supporting brackets had turned bosses that fitted accurately into their mating holes in the horn plates, thus relieving the fixing bolts from the strain and vibration of the engine. Crucible cast-steel was used for the major components, such as the two speed gears and the compensating gear. The road wheels were riveted using hydraulic machinery and were constructed of wrought iron. The main wheels were 5 foot $7\frac{1}{2}$in diameter by 16in wide, whilst the front wheels were 3ft 8in diameter by 9in wide. For braking, in addition to engine braking, a screw brake was provided and this operated a wood lined strap.

The boiler was constructed from mild-steel plates, which were edge planed, and then riveted. To give additional strength, the longitudinal seams were double riveted. The smokebox was separate from the boiler barrel and was of the same diameter as the outside lagging. Thirty-five 2-inch tubes were fitted, and, with a grate area of $5\frac{1}{2}$ square feet, this provided a total of 127 square feet of heating surface. To provide water to the boiler, a feed pump was fitted with gun-metal valve boxes and phosphor-bronze valves. The engine was delivered complete with a pair of lamps, tarpaulin cover, spanners, moving spanner, firing tools, bucket, oil can and kettle, extra gauge glasses and fusible plug, spuds and frost studs.

Whilst the catalogue specification is focussed on the 7 horse-power light traction engine, the associated price list gives a number of variations on this. For instance the engine was offered in a range of engine size i.e. 5, 7, 8, and 10 n.h.p. Similarly the three larger sizes of traction engine were also offered with various cylinder configurations, i.e. single cylinder, tandem compound (two cylinders in-line), and double crank compound (two cylinders side by side). According to Ronald Clark, the 7-n.h.p.tandem compound machine had a 10in low-pressure cylinder, a 6in high-pressure cylinder, both with a stroke of 10in.[19] A further option on the traction engine was the addition of a crane, presumably smokebox mounted, although no details are given.

Figure 36: Mann and Charlesworth 7 horse-power light traction engine
This delightful rural scene includes Mann and Charlesworth 7 h.p. traction engine, number 54, being set up to drive a Foster threshing machine. The engine was owned by John Croft of Naburn near York. *(Martin Hallows collection)*

Semi-Portable Tandem Compound Engine and Boiler

In 1896 an article[20] in *The Engineer* describes a semi-portable tandem compound engine and boiler made by Mann and Charlesworth. The engine was mounted on a locomotive type boiler, however, if desired, the engine could be bolted to a stone or concrete foundation as a separate horizontal engine.

The engine was of the tandem compound arrangement, i.e. the 7in. diameter high-pressure cylinder and the 11in. diameter low-pressure cylinder were in line sharing a common piston rod, having a stroke of 12in. The high-pressure cylinder was steam jacketed, and both cylinders were insulated and cased with steel sheeting. The high-pressure cylinder and low-pressure cylinder were connected together by a single casting, which had turned projections at each end, thus providing accurate fitting into the end of each cylinder. The bedplate was of the double girder type, and was self-contained, relieving the boiler from all the working strain of the engine. The crankshaft bearings were bolted to an extension of the firebox shell sides. The crankshaft brasses, adjustable by wedges, were of gunmetal, with large wearing surfaces. The crankshaft was 4in. diameter, bent out of a round steel bar, and was of sufficient length for the flywheel to be put on either side. The patent variable expansion governor, acting directly on the slide valve of the high-pressure cylinder, controlled the speed of the engine. The eccentric was carried in a very similar manner to the single eccentric reversing gear, and automatically cut off steam from nil to five-eighths of the stroke without any alteration of lead. The eccentric was moved by a radius quadrant bolted to one of the weights, and the latter was pivoted in such a position as to form a locking gear. The connecting-rod was a steel forging, with adjustable phosphor-bronze bushes at each end. Gunmetal valve boxes and phosphor-bronze valves were fitted to the feed pump. This pumped water through a feed-water heater that used the exhaust steam to raise the temperature of the water entering the boiler to a few degrees under boiling point. The boiler was constructed of steel plates, and strongly stayed for a working pressure of 140 p.s.i. It contained 164ft. of heating surface and 7.5ft. of grate area.

Figure 37: Engraving Semi-portable Engine
This semi-portable engine was of the tandem compound arrangement with in-line 7in. diameter high-pressure cylinder and 11in. diameter low-pressure cylinder sharing a common piston rod, having a stroke of 12in. *(The Engineer)*

The Royal Show of 1896 was held at Leicester. Mann and Charlesworth's stand was very similar to their previous year's exhibit, with the light 7-horse power traction engine forming the centre-piece.[21] Other articles shown were the wash-out pump and the shaft governor. This latter item could be bought separately for £15 and fitted to other makes of engines. In the following year the Royal Show was located at Manchester and Mann and Charlesworth's products were a repeat of their previous examples.[22]

Stationary Steam Engines

In addition to the semi-portable engines, Mann and Charlesworth also offered in their catalogue a range of horizontal and vertical stationary engines. The horizontal compound engines were available with powers ranging from 9 n.h.p. to 25 n.h.p. and these were priced at £145 and £290 respectively. Additionally, the horizontal machine was built as a single cylinder type, and three sizes were offered over the range of 6 n.h.p to 12 n.h.p., these being priced at £64 and £120 respectively. Feed-water heaters could be supplied at additional cost. The patent variable expansion governor was fitted as standard.[23]

Similarly, a range of less expensive single cylinder vertical engines was produced at the Canning Works. The vertical engines were available with powers ranging from 3 n.h.p. to 10 n.h.p. and these cost £32 and £80 respectively. A simple governor acting on the throttle valve controlled the speed, or alternatively, the patent variable expansion governor could be supplied, and this was said to be more economical in the consumption of steam. This range of engines could be supplied with a separate vertical boiler, or alternatively as a combined engine-boiler unit, with wheels fitted as an option.[24]

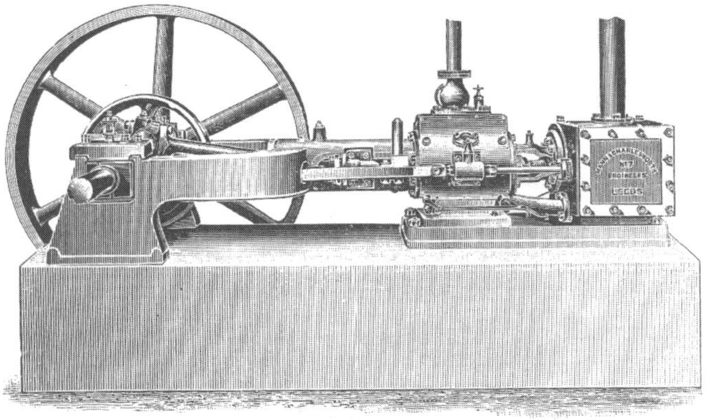

Figure 38: Mann and Charlesworth Horizontal Tandem Compound Engine
This horizontal tandem compound engine had a low-pressure cylinder cover, cast with No.7 on it, presumably its works number. Lack of evidence does not allow further discussion on the number of these engines produced. *(Mann and Charlesworth Catalogue)*

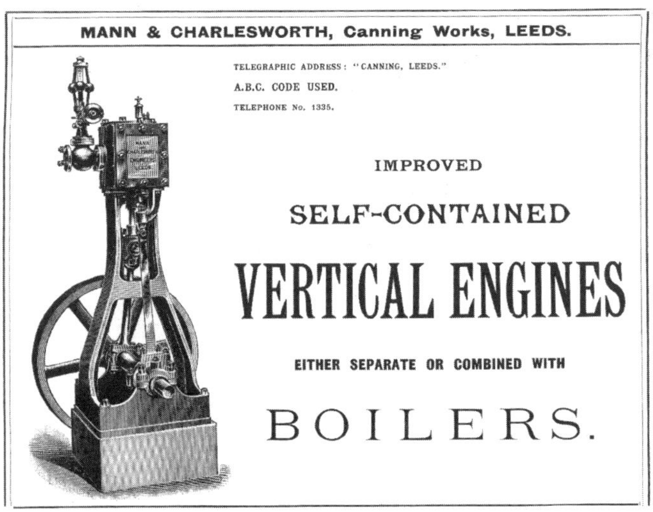

Figure 39: Mann and Charlesworth Vertical Engine
This neat-looking single cylinder vertical engine was offered with powers ranging from 3 n.h.p. to 10 n.h.p. and these cost £32 and £80 respectively. They could be supplied as a combined engine-boiler unit, with wheels fitted as an option. *(Mann and Charlesworth Catalogue)*

Other Products of Mann and Charlesworth

Electric light engines were another of the products made at the Canning Works. A catalogue reference relating to the vertical engine states, "At a slightly advanced price, we supply them with increased wearing surfaces, and improved lubricating arrangements, suitable for running at a high speed for electric lighting purposes." Similarly the same catalogue, when describing the semi-portable engine and boiler, includes the sentence, "Will run steadily under varying loads, and consequently suitable for Electric Lighting." This is further supported by verbal evidence given by James Mann to his young friend John Walker, that an electric lighting engine was supplied for a political meeting on Woodhouse Moor, Leeds.[25] At the end of the nineteenth century, public power supplies were in their infancy and as a result were often of limited capacity and unreliable. In anticipation of this unreliability, the Mann and Charlesworth electric lighting engine was brought to the evening meeting and, in the event, the public supply failed and the standby steam engine was put into service.

In the Mann and Charlesworth catalogue, circa 1897, the cover includes the phrase, DESCRIPTIVE CATALOGUE, PATENT TRACTION ENGINES, ROAD ROLLERS, SEMI-PORTABLES. There is little surviving evidence of road rollers produced at the Canning

MANN & CHARLESWORTH,

Engineers & Boilermakers,

CANNING WORKS, DEWSBURY ROAD,

LEEDS.

DESCRIPTIVE CATALOGUE

OF

Patent Traction Engines,

ROAD ROLLERS, SEMI-PORTABLES,

COMPOUND HORIZONTAL,

VERTICAL & ELECTRIC LIGHTING ENGINES, BOILERS, &c.

PATENT SINGLE ECCENTRIC REVERSING GEAR,

AND

AUTOMATIC EXPANSION SHAFT GOVERNORS.

Telegrams: "CANNING, LEEDS." TELEPHONE 1335.

Figure 40: Mann and Charlesworth Catalogue Cover, circa 1897
This rare catalogue shows on the cover the wide range of products offered by Mann and Charlesworth at this early period.

Works, however, a fascinating photograph in the Swiss archives has been brought to the attention of Derek Rayner by Ernst Huwyler. This illustrates engine number 28, a 14-ton roller made by Mann and Charlesworth in 1898.[26] The boiler was rated 12 Atmospheres (approximately 175 p.s.i.). The machine was originally delivered to the well-known German road contractor Heinrich Reifenrath of Niederlahnstein, and was their number 37. By 1908, Reifenrath had transferred the machine to Mülhausen, and in 1916 the well-known locomotive builder, Henschel & Sohn, Cassel, fitted a new firebox. In 1920 the machine was sold to Schweizerische Strassenbau - Unternehmung A. G. Bern, Switzerland. It was in this ownership that the boiler details were registered and from which these records were obtained. Further tube replacement is recorded in 1925, 1946 and 1952 until in 1961 the roller was scrapped – a remarkably long life for such a rare machine.

According to Ronald Clark, the Mann and Charlesworth road rollers were, perhaps not surprisingly, an adaptation of their range of traction engines, and were available with the same sizes and types of cylinder.[27] The conversion was simply achieved by replacing the pair of rear wheels by a pair of rollers. The front wheel conversion was somewhat more complicated and required a cast forecarriage attaching to the smokebox, with a single wide roller replacing the front wheels. Another minor change was the use of a solid flywheel, as opposed to the spoked-type used on traction engines.

A related article made by the company was a hand force pump for washing out boilers. These were said to throw a strong continuous stream of water for a considerable distance. In addition to their primary purposes of washing out boilers, they were also promoted for filling the boiler

Figure 41: Mann and Charlesworth Road Roller
This superb photograph shows Mann and Charlesworth road roller, engine number 28, delivered to Germany in 1898. At the time of this photograph, the roller was in service with Schweizerische Strassenbau – Unternehmung A. G. Bern. After more that sixty years of active service, the roller was scrapped in 1961. *(Archive Dampfwalzen-Club Schweiz)*

when empty, watering gardens, washing carriages, putting our fires and many similar purposes. This same design of hand pump was still included in catalogues thirty years later, which indicates the robustness of the product.

Traction wagons were another item included in the Mann and Charlesworth price list. These were supplied with wrought-iron wheels, draw-bar, brake and springs. The 4-ton version was priced £63, the 6-ton £73, and the 8-ton £83.[28] It is not known if these were bought in from another manufacturer or built at the Canning Works to complete their range of products.

Finally, as with most new companies, Mann and Charlesworth had to adopt a flexible approach to business. The catalogue referred to previously contains footnotes with the following phrases, ‘TRACTION AND PORTABLE ENGINE REPAIRS A SPECIALITÉ’ and ‘RE-BOXING BOILERS A SPECIALITÉ’. This type of work, the repair of engines and boilers, whilst not promoting their primary business, helped to fill their order books and keep the finances of the company healthy.

An article in *The Engineer*, dated 25 March 1898, is entitled "A NOVEL STEAM CART". The cart was produced by Mann and Charlesworth to the designs of its patentee, Mr Philip Joseph Parmiter, of Tisbury, Wiltshire.[29] The basis for this machine was embodied in patent number 5282, filed on 22 March 1884 by P. J. Parmiter, and titled *Improved Combined Traction Engine and Truck for Travelling on Common Roads or on Land*. The central feature of this patent was the wide rear roller, which would allow the wagon onto a field without sinking in or damaging the land.

A machine of this type was built by Messrs Elliot & Garrood of Beccles and exhibited at the Norfolk Agricultural Show at Great Yarmouth in 1890. According to Ronald Clarke, this cart had small duplex cylinders rated at 5 n.h.p. and was fitted with a vertical boiler.[30] Its list price was £150, but the cart was never sold, instead it was used by Elliot & Garrood to transport materials between Beccles, Yarmouth and Lowestoft.

The patent drawing that follows, illustrates the key features of Parmiter's design that became part of the 'Mann Cart', these being the tipping wagon, with its powered lifting device immediately behind the firebox, and secondly the driving position on the side of the boiler and the associated firebox door located on the side of the vehicle. One aspect of Parmiter's proposal that was mechanically a poor idea was the ratchet drive arrangement. Mann and Charlesworth's machine did not incorporate this latter mechanism, as there were easier and more proven techniques available. Nevertheless, it is absolutely clear that Parmiter was the originator of what was to become the Mann Cart.

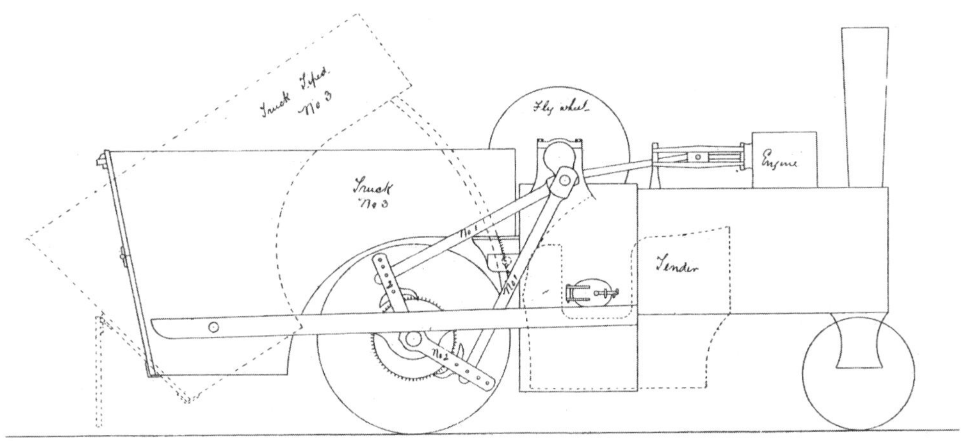

Figure 42: Patent Drawing, Parmiter Cart of 1884
Philip Joseph Parmiter, of Tisbury, Wiltshire, registered this design in March 1884. Mann and Charlesworth built a similar machine for Parmiter in 1897. Whilst the details vary, the basic origins of the Mann Steam Cart are clear to see.

In the machine produced by Mann and Charlesworth in 1897, the rear of the wagon was carried on a single broad drum or roller, in place of the normal twin rear wheels. External to the roller but on the same axle, there was attached two wheels of smaller diameter, but which did not under ordinary circumstances touch the ground – except where it was very soft or uneven. The advantage claimed for this arrangement was that the exceptionally wide wheel surface was obtained without increasing the width of the engine. This spread the load and thereby prevented the formation of twin ruts, as was normal on farm tracks. As well as its use for haulage, the wagon could also carry other loads e.g. manure, chalk, etc., if the land was not wet. A winding drum could be provided on the end of the axle for land cultivation on the double-engine system. The front part of the wagon was a conventional overtype, 4-horse-power single cylinder traction engine and boiler, having the fire-door, tank, and coal bunker on the right-hand side. The valve gear was the Mann and Charlesworth patent, single eccentric reversing gear. Direct gearing between the engine and the axle provided two speeds, of four miles per hour and two miles per hour. The wagon had a capacity of about six tons, and was tipped by a screw. After it had been tipped, the wagon could be detached, and the engine could be moved forward without it, and be used for agricultural work on the land. Before leaving Leeds the machine was tested, taking a load of six tons up an incline of 1 in 9, and owing to its wide wheel it did not sink into even the softest ground. The report states that the advantage of combining the wagon with the engine was that the load gives the roller such a great adhesion that it is possible to dispense with cross strips, so that the roads should be rather improved than damaged by its use, as it practically becomes a road roller. The final statement in *The Engineer* reads: "It is intended, however, to fit this wagon with two hind wheels fitted with differential gear instead of the wide central roller keeping the combined width of the tires the same as that of the roller." [31] Three months later, in June 1898, this machine had been built.

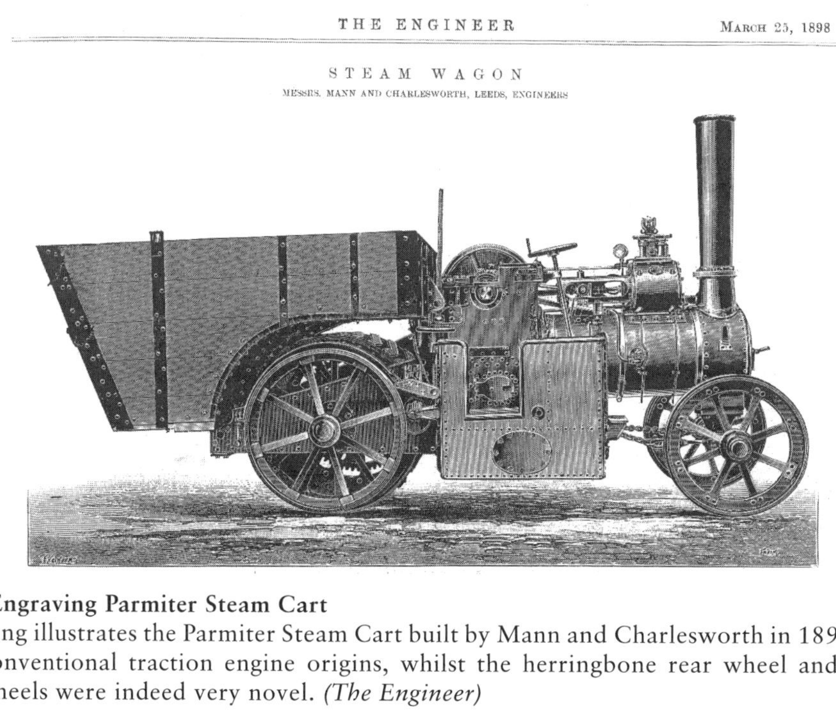

Figure 43: Engraving Parmiter Steam Cart
This engraving illustrates the Parmiter Steam Cart built by Mann and Charlesworth in 1897. The front end is of conventional traction engine origins, whilst the herringbone rear wheel and the pair of outrigger wheels were indeed very novel. *(The Engineer)*

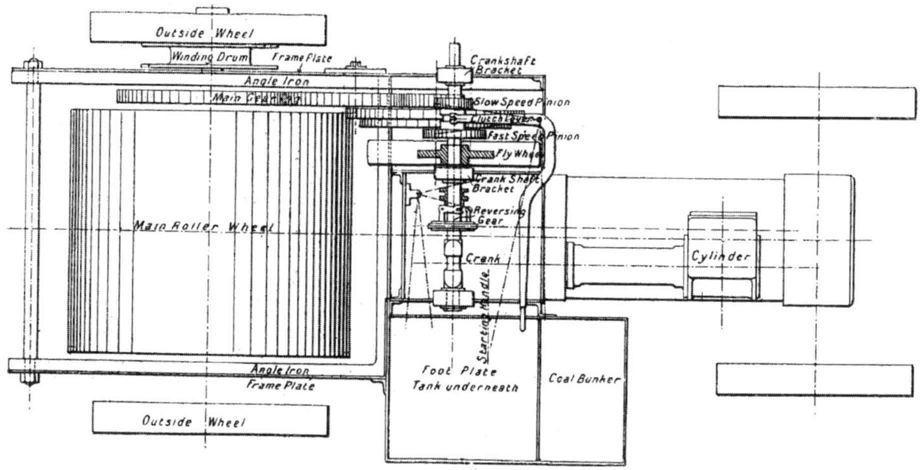

Figure 44: Plan Drawing of the Parmiter Steam Cart
The drawing helps to understand the construction of the Parmiter Steam Cart built in 1897 by Mann and Charlesworth. In this view the load cart is absent. *(The Engineer)*

Parmiter was not entirely happy with the report in *The Engineer,* [32] for he wrote to the journal shortly afterwards:

Parmiter's Steam Wagon

Sir, I must thank you for the notice of my patent steam wagon in your issue of March 25th last, particulars of which were supplied by Messrs. Mann and Charlesworth, who built the engine to my specifications, but I should have been a little more satisfied if you had headed the engraving and notice "Parmiter's Patent Steam Wagon", for whatever credit or discredit there may be to the design, I am anxious to claim it after the many years of work and waiting it has cost me. Before most engineers who are now large in business had completed their apprenticeship or had entered the profession, this engine was designed as perfectly as it is to-day; but agricultural depression and the failures of steam farming had been so complete that I found it impossible from agriculturists to get the slightest co-operation in my scheme, and traction engine builders were dead against it. In 1886, at the Royal Agricultural Society meeting at Norwich, I showed the model to the late Mr. David Greg, *(sic, Greig. of John Fowler & Co.)* who, with characteristic promptness, declared that "no roller wheel was worth a damn", and such has been the prevailing opinion of all to whom I have submitted my design. From the work the engine has now done I have the satisfaction of knowing that I have been correct, and I am convinced that it will prove the "other half of the loaf" in farm cartage, to which the late Mr. John Fowler once referred as wanting to complete the success of steam as applied to land tillage and general farm work. This little engine is as handy as a horse and cart, it will pull 10 tons on a road up 1 in 9, and carry 6 tons on any fallow or pasture that will carry a cart. It has before it the widest possible application, and no improvement can be made for agricultural work by differential gear, or otherwise in the present design.

PHILIP J, PARMITER.
Station Works, Tisbury, Wilts,
March 31st (1898)

Figure 45: Parmiter Wagon
This view of the Parmiter wagon is shown with its tipping cart removed and hauling a plough. The large rear roller and the smaller outrigger wheels are self-evident. *(John Middlemiss collection)*

Subsequently, Parmiter had cause to regret his involvement with Mann and Charlesworth, for in June 1898 they exhibited a remarkably similar steam cart at the R.A.S.E. show held at Four Oaks Park, Birmingham. According to the magazine *Engineering* the steam cart was not complete when shown at Birmingham: "Messrs. Mann and Charlesworth, of Dewsbury Road, Leeds, show a steam tipping wagon, which was entered for the motor van trials, but was not ready in consequence of the engineers' strike; indeed it is not yet complete." [33] An article in "*The Engineer*" was rather more pointed, particularly about the similarities with the Parmiter machine, remarking: "Messrs. Mann and Charlesworth, Leeds, show a steam wagon, which is not very unlike that illustrated in *THE ENGINEER* of March 25th, except that it has not got the broad centre wheel at the back, ..." [34] In a letter published in *The Engineer* dated June 28, 1899, Parmiter expanded on his grievance: "...they are attempting, without the slightest acknowledgement to me, to appropriate the developments of my design, led up to at my cost in building the experimental engine with them.

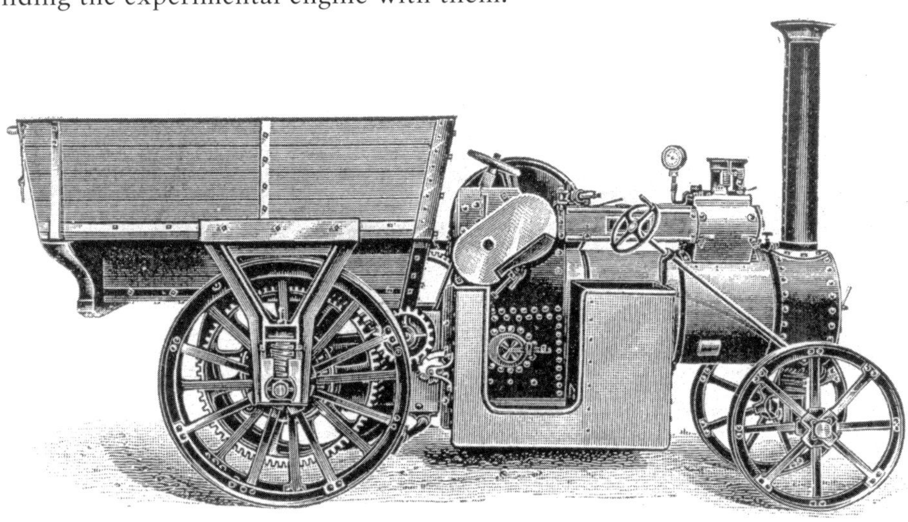

MESSRS. MANN AND CHARLESWORTH'S STEAM CART

Figure 46: Mann and Charlesworth Steam Cart
This engraving illustrates the vehicle exhibited at the Royal Show, Birmingham. The tipping cart now pivots about the rear axle, and is fitted with coil springs in the axle boxes. *(The Engineer)*

They excuse themselves by saying there is no infringement of patent – this will be a matter of legal enquiry. But besides the patent laws – which are extremely unjust in only giving a fourteen years' protection to an invention which, as in this case, required twelve years' advocacy and the spending of over £1000 to get its principle accepted – there is another law understood between business men.

When the order was in hand, I, in many interviews, freely discussed with them my entire scheme, and if, when they decided to build another engine on the same lines, they had made any proposition to me, I would have entertained it; but I now protest against their exhibiting this engine and taking the credit due to this design, and trading in my recommendations without the slightest acknowledgement." [35]

The catalogue for the Birmingham Show includes the light 7-horse-power traction engine, as exhibited at previous shows, but also describes the new wagon: "Steam Tipping Wagon £340. Compound steam tipping wagon, and farmer's general purpose engine, suitable for thrashing and hauling; fitted with exhibitor's patent single eccentric reversing gear. Extra wide road wheels, mounted on springs, and made to comply with the *Motor Car Acts of 1896.*" [36] (See appendix 4 for more details of British Road Traffic Legislation.) This same show also featured a competition of road vehicles with the title, 'Trials of Self Moving Vehicles'. A circular course of around 13 miles, in the vicinity of Tamworth, Coleshill and Sutton Coldfield provided the test route. Two classes of vehicle were tested, one for light loads and the other for heavy loads:

Vehicles for Light Loads, up to 1-ton

- The Daimler Motor Co., Shaftesbury Avenue, London – 4 n.h.p. petrol van, £350
- Messrs. Roots & Venables, Westminster – 6 b.h.p. oil motor, £370
- The Lancashire Steam Motor Co., Leyland, Lancs. – Van to carry 1 ton, £285
- H. P. Saunderson, Kempston Road, Bedford – Petrol vehicle, £250

In this class only the Daimler vehicle successfully completed the course and consequently was awarded the £100 first prize.

Vehicles for Heavy Loads, up to 3-ton

- T. Coulthard & Co., Preston, Lancs. – Steam Motor Lorry, £350
- Jesse Ellis & Co., Invicta Works, Maidstone, Kent – Steam Wagon, £550
- The Lancashire Steam Motor Co., Leyland, Lancs. – Steam Lorry, £375
- Mann & Charlesworth, Canning Works, Leeds – Steam Tipping Wagon, £330
- The Steam Carriage & Wagon Co., Homefield, Chiswick – Steam Lorry, £650

Only two of these machines completed the trials and the judges made the following awards; first prize to the Lancashire Steam Motor Co. and second prize to the Steam Carriage & Wagon Co. It is not recorded what happened to the Mann and Charlesworth entry, but given the comments in *Engineering* (see previous page), it seems that the vehicle never took part in the trial.

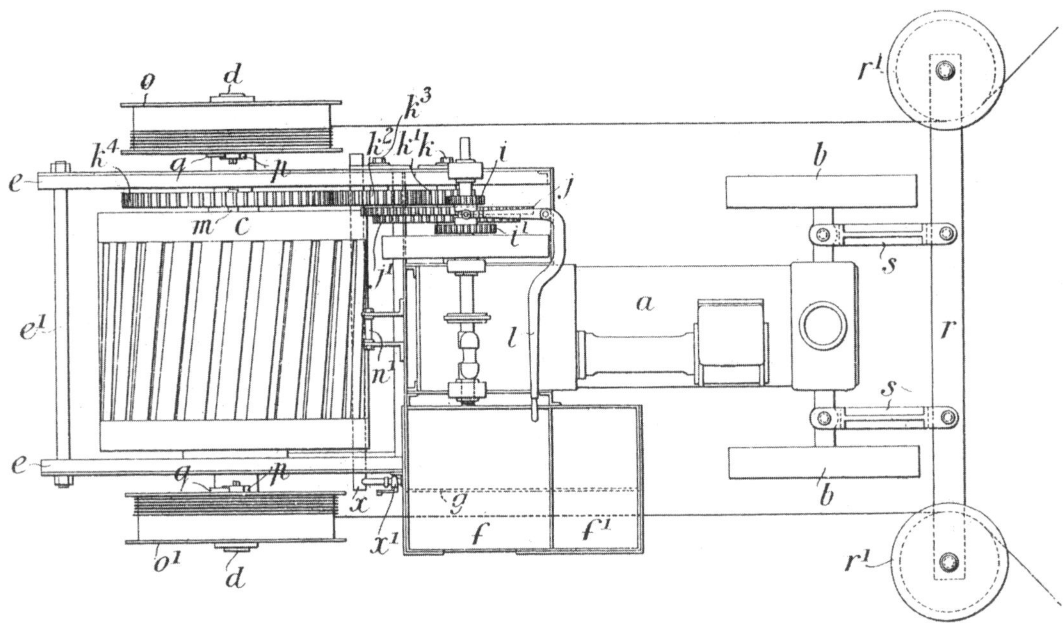

Figure 47: Patent Drawing, Parmiter Cart of 1898
Following the construction of the original cart by Mann and Charlesworth, Parmiter lodged a further patent on 4 July 1898 to protect his ideas. There is no evidence that this second-generation cart was ever manufactured. The wide load-spreading roller is still an important factor in this design, but it also includes cable drums for ploughing.

Philip Parmiter took out a second patent on his cart, number 14,739, lodged on 4 July 1898, entitled *Improvements in or connected with Road Locomotives for Agricultural and other Purposes.* There is no evidence that he pursued his ideas for a single roller drive, however he did go on to develop a very successful agricultural machinery business at Tisbury, Wiltshire. Following his death in 1922, the business moved away from the family, but today it is still a thriving independent agricultural machinery business. The works is still based at Tisbury, and exports over 60% of its production to regions such as North America, Europe, Australia and New Zealand.

The Mann and Charlesworth machine, exhibited at Birmingham, was built to comply with the new Locomotives on Highways Act (1896), with the total weight of wagon and engine being less than four tons. The intention of this act was to define a class of 'light locomotive' applicable to the developing private motor car. Mann and Charlesworth cleverly exploited these new rules to produce a commercial vehicle that fitted within the scope of the light locomotive specification. The 15 b.h.p. engine was placed on the top of the boiler with compound cylinders at the smoke-box end. A double-reversing gear of Mann and Charlesworth's patented design was used. The sides of the smoke-box were extended backwards, to carry the horn-plates for the engine wheels. The wagon was located partly between and partly overhanging the main wheels, but it also had a pair of wheels of its own, of the same size as those of the engine. These were placed wider apart, and carried by external bearings in such a manner that the wagon could be run over the tail of the engine, so that the pair of wheels on each side were concentric. Each pair was then bolted together at the periphery so that a pair of double-width wheels was formed.[37] This arrangement effectively

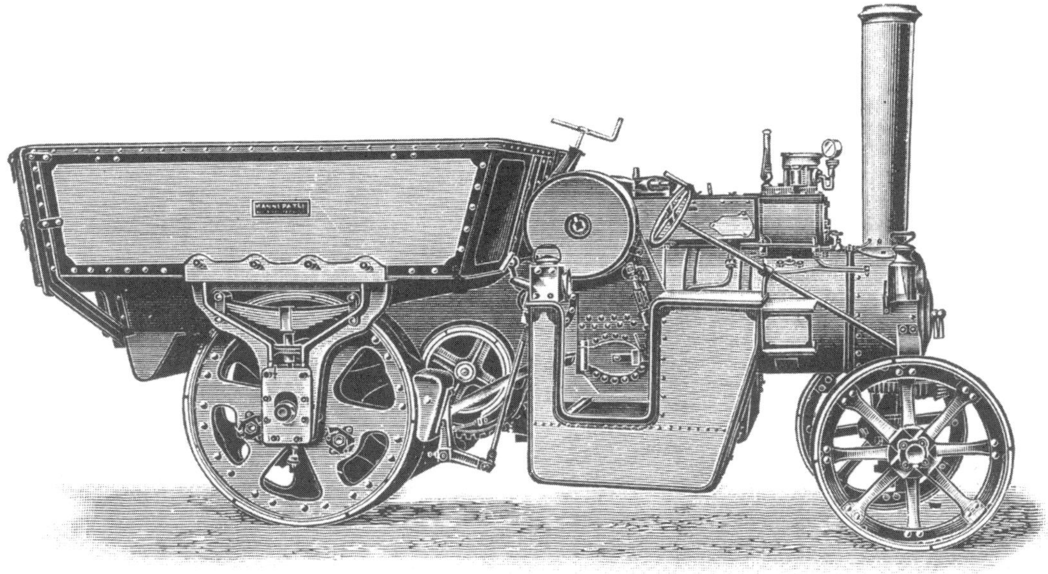

Figure 48: Engraving Mann and Charlesworth's Steam Cart
This view shows a later development of the steam cart with the tipping cart being supported on leaf springs. The pins that connected the two sets of wheels together can be seen on the rear wheel frame.

formed a single pair of wide wheels, which provided a low ground pressure and thereby enabled the wagon to traverse soft ground. The tipping wagon could pivot around the centres of its own wheels to discharge the contents. The driven wheels were directly geared from the engine, i.e. no chains were used, and an intermediate shaft and gears provided three road speeds. The driver's platform was on the offside of the engine, and was counterbalanced by a large water tank on the other side. The fire-door was in the side of the fire-box, with coke being used as fuel. The engine was steered by a worm and quadrant attached to the front axle.

The design was not entirely successful, as the following quotation from *The Engineer* illustrates: "To prevent any visible steam issuing from the funnel the exhaust is led into a small copper vessel on one side of the smoke-box, which acts in a measure as a condenser, part of the steam being thrown down in it, and the remainder is superheated as it passes through a tube in the smoke-box. This arrangement will probably be modified in future designs. It may accomplish its purpose but appears an unnecessary complication. The driving gear can be readily thrown out, when the engine is available to drive any farm machinery, or by removing the wagon body, which can be done in a few minutes, it forms a serviceable small traction engine."[38]

The act of plagiarism in adopting some of the features of Parmiter's cart was evidently the work of James Hutchinson Mann. This is demonstrated by the fact that patent 13,236, defining the Mann steam cart, lodged on 14 June 1898, is the first to omit Charlesworth's name. This was a turning point for the company, and it is suspected that Charlesworth was so offended and incensed by Mann's actions, that this was the reason for his eventual departure from the business. In defence of Mann, whilst there is little doubt that Parmiter's vehicle was the inspiration for Mann's cart, the primary feature of Parmiter's patent was the driven rear roller. The original Mann steam cart introduced a number of features that became synonymous with their vehicles and these continued in use until the company closed. In particular:

- The side mounted footplate and associated side entry firedoor
- Re-heating of the exhaust steam in the smoke box to reduce visible emissions
- The worm and quadrant steering direct onto the forecarriage
- The patent single eccentric reversing gear
- A horizontal connecting pipe from the safety valve exhaust into the chimney

This last feature was an ingenious but simple piece of engineering. The initial purpose of connecting the safety-valve exhaust to the chimney was to act as a silencer to minimise the upset of horses, as required by legislation. There is however a danger that introducing steam into the chimney might increase the draught and draw the fire stronger. To avoid this, the steam was not led up the chimney, but rather was fed in at right angles so that equal quantities went down as went up the chimney. This provided a neutral effect on the fire and so did not encourage even greater steam production. The undesirable effect of this was to dislodge the accumulated soot from the chimney interior and for it to fall on the driver and any others in close proximity.

Figure 49: Mann and Charlesworth worm and quadrant steering
The Mann and Charlesworth worm and quadrant steering was a feature that became one of the identifying features of their vehicles. In later years, the gears were enclosed in a casing and filled with oil to provide flooded lubrication.

Figure 50: Mann and Charlesworth safety valve exhaust
Road legislation required that vehicles were designed such that "no smoke or visible vapour is emitted therefrom". To achieve this, the exhaust from the safety valve was fed at right-angles to the chimney. This avoided increasing the blast, and prevented the fire from producing more steam.

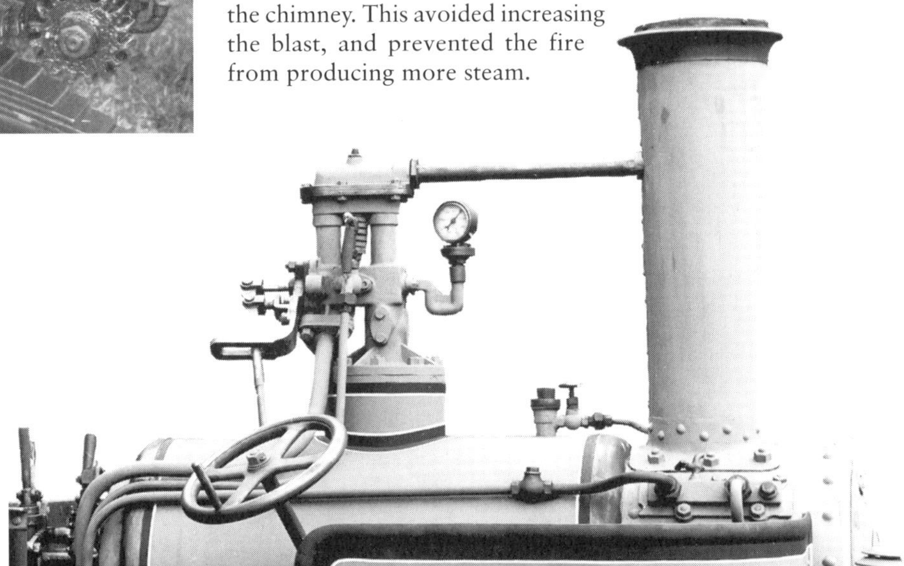

The first feature identified in the list above, the side mounted footplate, was to feature heavily in catalogues, with the company promoting this concept as a great advantage for many years:

> "Here we come to the many great, outstanding advantages of 'The Mann' side firing arrangement. This constitutes the greatest advance ever introduced into the designs of the overtype steam wagon.
>
> The Mann is absolutely the original and still the only genuine one man controlled steam wagon on the road; including the 'One Man' side firing, which allows the man to stoke, drive, steer and control the wagon with efficiency and perfect safety. This cannot be done by any other wagon, and no other wagon can truthfully claim the same efficiency.
>
> Our "One Man" arrangement of having the bunker placed directly in front of the driver, at a convenient height, enables him to fire up easily with his eyes always looking out ahead and without having to resort to the most dangerous practice of turning round to his fuel bunker, or as an alternative to carry a second man either as fireman or steersman." [39]

The concept of the side entry boiler firing was seen by some rival manufacturers as a valuable feature and was later used by them. William Allchin & Co. Ltd., of the Globe Works, Northampton, introduced their first wagon in 1906. This vehicle had a locomotive-type firebox with the fuel door in the side.[40] Other examples include Straker, of Bristol[41] and Tasker, of Andover.[42]

The Mann vehicle exhibited at the R.A.S.E. show at Birmingham was the subject of patent 13,236 lodged on 14 June 1898. This is "the" patent identified later in the company title, Mann's Patent Steam Cart and Wagon Company. The important words from this patent that define the vehicle that became associated with Mann are: "In a road engine constructed in accordance with my invention, the driver's platform and fuel bunker may be carried on one side of the firebox, and the tank on the other; the fire door being placed to one side to suit. The firebox shell sides are extended further back than usual, in order to carry at a suitable distance, the axle boxes or bearings for the hind axle of the engine. The outer ends of the axle carry two road driving wheels, connected by any suitable gearing to the crank shaft of the engine."

This last phrase was cleverly worded as it did not specify where the engine was located and, as we shall see later, Mann used this to advantage in adapting his machines for both overtype and undertype engines. These key features were not however the limit of this patent. Also defined in detail are:

- The means to tilt the cart about the axis of the rear wheels for discharging the cargo, and a method of raising the cart back to its travelling position with a windlass.

- A method of detaching the cart by the use of a second pair of rear wheels whose axle centres were coincident with the driving wheel axle centres, and normally locked to them when in transit.

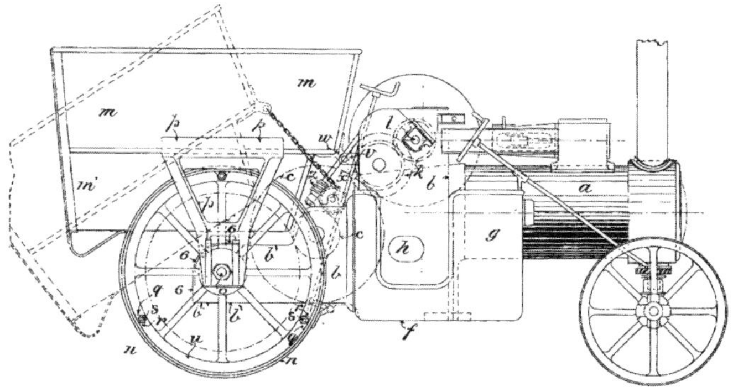

Figure 51: Patent Drawing, Mann's Steam Cart 1898.
Patent 13,236 lodged on 14 June 1898 is 'the' patent identified later in the company title, Mann's Patent Steam Cart and Wagon Company. It also signalled the end of the partnership between James Hutchinson Mann and Sidney Charlesworth.

Introduction of the Steam Lurry

In the following year, 1899, the company exhibited two vehicles at the Maidstone Royal Show. The first is described as the *Patent Steam Lurry* and was priced at £400.[43] The inclusion of the word "patent" in this phrase is somewhat erroneous, as the lurry (lorry) patent was not applied for until the following year. This lorry was said to come under the Motor Car Act, capable of hauling a load of 5 tons up an incline of 1 in 10, mounted on springs, and provided with a flywheel for driving barn machinery etc. The second vehicle is listed as the *'Patent Steam Tipping Cart'*, and was also priced at £400. This was the same machine as shown at Birmingham the previous year, however some enhancements had been made. The show cart was reported as being combined with a road roller, fitted with the patent single eccentric reversing gear, and suitable for general farm and road haulage. The road roller was not provided as standard, but was charged as an extra, however the price is not stated.

Some further technical detail of the steam lorry was reported in *The Engineer*.[44] The boiler was of the locomotive type, and was fitted with long side plates riveted to the firebox. These extended backwards and were formed into a box by top, bottom and end plates. This box was used as the water tank but also formed the bed for the engine that was fitted beneath the load platform. This was Mann's first use of the undertype engine arrangement.

The engine had compound cylinders and the salient dimensions of the vehicle were as follows:

- high pressure cylinder — 4in. diameter
- low pressure cylinder — 6 3/8in. diameter
- piston stroke — 8in.
- crank-shaft — 2 1/4in. diameter
- intermediate shaft — 2 1/2in. diameter
- main axle — 3 1/2in. diameter
- front wheels — 35in. diameter by 5 1/2in. wide
- rear wheels — 46in. diameter by 12in. wide
- heating surface — 36 square feet
- water tank capacity — 230 gallons
- fuel bunker capacity — 200 pounds of coke
- platform dimensions — 11ft. long by 6ft. wide
- vehicle dimensions — 17ft. long by 6ft. wide

Steam Lurry, Mann's System (General View).

General View of Trailer.

Figure 52: Maidstone Show, 1899, Steam Lurry
The steam lorry was not a direct development of the steam cart, although it did share some features. The main difference was that it was an undertype vehicle with the engine mounted beneath the load platform on top of the water tank. *(The Automotor Journal)*

The trailer platform was constructed of oak, using four longitudinal beams, and these were braced and tied together by means of plates and bolts. Steel side brackets supported the wheels, which were suspended on coil springs.[45] For the lorry, all the gearing was cast-steel, with the first motion gearing of $1^1/_8$in. pitch, and the main and differential gear of $1^3/_4$in. pitch.[46] The intermediate shaft passed through the water tank in a cast-steel pipe bearing. The other shafts were fitted through cast-steel brackets having turned projections on them that fitted through accurately bored holes in the horn plates. This was done to relieve the fixing bolts from the strain of the engine. A rectangular coke bunker was fitted on top of the boiler, with the driver's position being on the right-hand side of the firebox. The engine wheels and the cart wheels were of identical diameter and when running on the road were connected together by two bolts or pins on each hub, such that each pair acted as a wide single wheel. The exhaust from the engine passed through a swan neck pipe in the smoke-box to provide a measure of re-heating. Of this arrangement the article reported, "As it is close to the end of the fire tubes it is found that on ordinary occasions no visible vapour escapes." The lorry was said to weigh 3 tons 17 cwt. and the height from the driving platform to the top of the furnace was approximately 6ft. According to *The Automotor Journal* the boiler was constructed with 24 tubes each $1^3/_4$in. diameter. The firebox had 16 feet of heating surface, and $2^1/_2$ square feet of grate area, the total heating surface being 53 square feet. The boiler operated at 150 p.s.i. and was fitted with two feed pumps. When running at 250 r.p.m. the engine developed 14 b.h.p.[47]

References

1 *Kelly's Leeds Directory*, 1898
2 Duke, Alan, *Mann Engine List*, Road Locomotive Society, 1988
3 *Mann and Charlesworth Catalogue*, c1896, p4
4 Whitehead R. A. & J. E., *Garrett Portable and Fixed Engines*, Tonbridge, 2004, p3-2
5 *British Patent* 13,958, 1894
6 Yorkshire Agricultural Society, *Show Catalogue*, 1894
7 *The Engineer*, 8 May 1895, p209
8 *Mann and Charlesworth Catalogue*, c1896, p4
9 Clark, R. H., *The Development of the English Traction Engine*, Goose & Son, 1960, p201
10 *The Engineer*, 3 April 1896, p342
11 Whitehead R. A., *Garrett Traction & Ploughing Engines*, Tonbridge, 1997, p27
12 Clark, R. H., *The Development of the English Steam Wagon*, Goose & Son, 1963, p128
13 Clark, R. H., *The Development of the English Steam Wagon*, Goose & Son, 1963, p188
14 *British Patent 2571*, 1895
15 Royal Agricultural Society of England, *Catalogue*, Darlington Show 1895
16 *Engineering*, 28 June 1895, p827
17 *Mann and Charlesworth Catalogue*, c1897, p4
18 *Mann and Charlesworth Catalogue*, c1897, p2
19 Clark, R. H., *The Development of the English Traction Engine*, Goose & Son, 1960, p98
20 *The Engineer*, 3 April 1896, p342
21 Royal Agricultural Society of England, *Catalogue*, Leicester Show 1896
22 Royal Agricultural Society of England, *Catalogue*, Manchester Show 1897
23 *Mann and Charlesworth Catalogue*, c1896, p6
24 *Mann and Charlesworth Catalogue*, c1897, p11
25 Walker, John, meeting with author, Weeton, 10 October 2003
26 Rayner, D., *Steaming*, Volume 44, No1, National Traction Engine Trust, p25.
27 Clark, R. H., *The Development of the English Traction Engine*, Goose & Son, 1960, p183
28 *Mann and Charlesworth Catalogue*, c1897, p11
29 *The Engineer*, 25 March 1898, p278
30 Clark, R. H., *The Development of the English Steam Wagon*, Goose & Son, 1963, p4
31 *The Engineer*, 25 March 1898, p278
32 *The Engineer*, 8 April 1898, p340
33 *Engineering*, 24 June 1898, p786
34 *The Engineer*, 24 June 1898, p340
35 *The Engineer*, 7 July 1899, p19
36 Royal Agricultural Society of England, *Catalogue*, Birmingham Show 1898
37 *The Automotor and Horseless Vehicle Journal*, December 1898, p129
38 *The Engineer*, 24 June 1898, p598
39 Mann's Patent Steam Cart and Wagon Company, *Catalogue C.*, p47
40 Clark, R. H., *The Development of the English Steam Wagon*, Goose & Son, 1963, p65
41 Kelly, M. A., *The Overtype Steam Wagon*, Goose and Son, 1971, p120
42 Kelly, M. A., *The Overtype Steam Wagon*, Goose and Son, 1971, p124
43 Royal Agricultural Society of England, *Catalogue*, Maidstone Show 1899
44 *The Engineer*, 23 June 1899, p618
45 *The Automotor Journal*, March 1900, p283
46 *Engineering*, 23 June 1899, p820
47 *The Automotor Journal*, March 1900, p284

Chapter 4

Mann's Patent Steam Cart and Wagon Products, 1899–1914

As mentioned earlier, the new company, Mann's Patent Steam Cart and Wagon Company Limited was registered on 29 September 1899. This company , under the leadership of James Hutchinson Mann, became very successful in producing a whole range of steam powered road vehicles all evolving from the steam cart patent, lodged in June 1898. The next few years were a time of development that would see the emergence of products that would shape the company for many years to come.

The Development of the Mann Steam Cart and Wagon

York was the location of the Royal Show in 1900, and this was the first show for the products of the new company, Mann's Patent Steam Cart and Wagon Company Limited. Two vehicles were exhibited, these being very similar to the machines shown the previous year at Maidstone. The steam lorry had risen in price by £100 to £500, and is described as being fitted with a platform 12ft. long by 6ft. 4in. wide. Similarly the steam cart was £75 more expensive, being listed at £475. Whether this was due to increased manufacturing costs, or the company's perception of the market value of the product is not clear. These price increases are substantial and presumably the directors judged that their customers were prepared to pay a premium for their products. A short passage in *Engineering* reported, "Quite a considerable number of these carts are in use drawing bricks or coals; they will hold 5 tons of the former and 4 tons of the latter." [1] The low-pressure cylinder diameter was reported to be $6^1/_2$in., slightly larger that the previous year's machine at $6^3/_8$in., whereas the stroke and high pressure cylinder dimensions are quoted the same at 8in. and 4in. respectively.

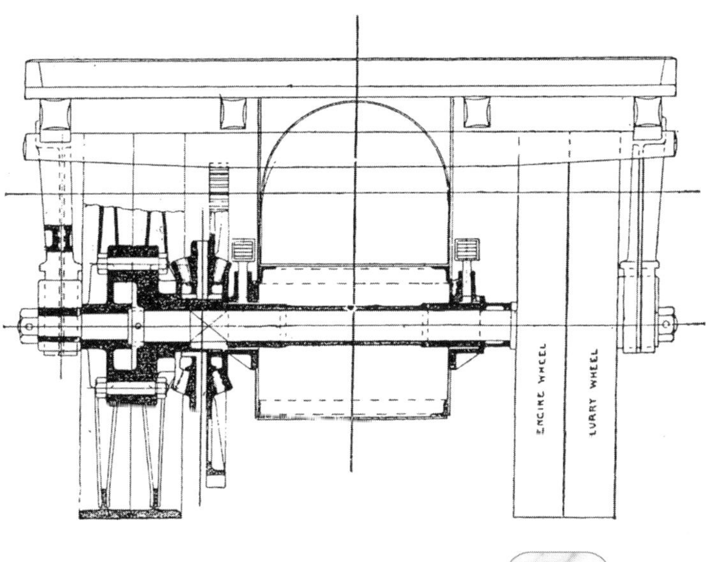

Figure 53: Steam Cart, Wheel Arrangement
This line drawing admirably illustrates the concept of the twin wheel-sets on the Steam Cart. One of the connecting pins "E1" can be seen below the hub of the right hand wheel. *(The Automotor Journal)*

The introduction of the Mann Steam Cart was not purely a British affair; in the New York journal *Scientific American*, an article was printed in 1900 extolling the virtues of the vehicle. When comparing the haulage of goods on trailers versus the use of the cart, they say, "The advantage of this is obvious. It dispenses with any connecting pins; it is not so unwieldy; it occupies less space; and it is far easier to handle." [2]

The Yorkshire Motor Car Show was held in Bradford on Saturday, 13 January 1900, and the Mann Cart was one of the entrants. The exhibition, at the Belle Vue Drill Hall, was organised by the Bradford and District Cycle and Motor Car Trades Association and, as a precursor, road trials were held on Tuesday 9 January. Professor Goodman of the Yorkshire College, Leeds, witnessed the trials, with assistance from Mr Cyril Lupton of Bradford.[3] Seven makers entered vehicles, however, in the event, only the Mann Steam Cart and a steam wagon by Messrs. T Coulthard & Co. of Preston completed the course, although the latter had problems with a steam pipe. In the trials, the Mann wagon was loaded with bales of wool weighing 4 tons, together with four passengers and the driver. The cart left Bradford at 10:25 a.m. and arrived back at 8:27 p.m., having travelled approximately 29 miles. The route covered a varied course along the valley of the River Aire via Keighley to Kildwick, and included some steep gradients and three very sharp turns. There were a number of stops en route to top up water and fuel, etc., accounting for 3 hr. 47 min. At the end of the journey, the average speed was calculated to be 4.6 m.p.h. and 330 pounds of coke had been consumed, together with 600 gallons of water. This equated to a fuel consumption of 10.4 pounds per mile. The committee considered the vehicle to be the most satisfactory solution to the problem of freight transportation on public roads and awarded Mann's Patent Steam Cart and Wagon Company the Gold Medal. At the presentation, the local newspaper reported, "The first award had been won by Mann's Patent Steam Cart and Wagon Company Limited, of Leeds, whose heavy motor, taken to Kildwick and back, proved in every respect thoroughly satisfactory. It climbed the hills magnificently, was prompt in stopping and starting, and could be very easily manipulated." [4]

James Mann had further thoughts about the detachable cart design, defined in his original patent, 13,236, for on 5 November 1900 he filed a further patent, number 19,786, dealing solely with this subject. The main topic is a means of easily securing the driven wheels to the cart wheels. Both these sets of wheels were located on the same axle centres, as in the previous patent. The connection between the two wheels was achieved by fitting a set of pivoting bolts on one set of wheels that, when required, were swung over and fitted into a radially slotted disc secured to the other wheel. To allow for the slight misalignment in the two wheels when mating up, the slotted disc could be rotated a small angular distance by being located on further semi-circular slots. The document makes it clear that the proposal applies whether the driven wheels were the inner pair or the outer pair. The drawing overleaf helps to understand this proposal.

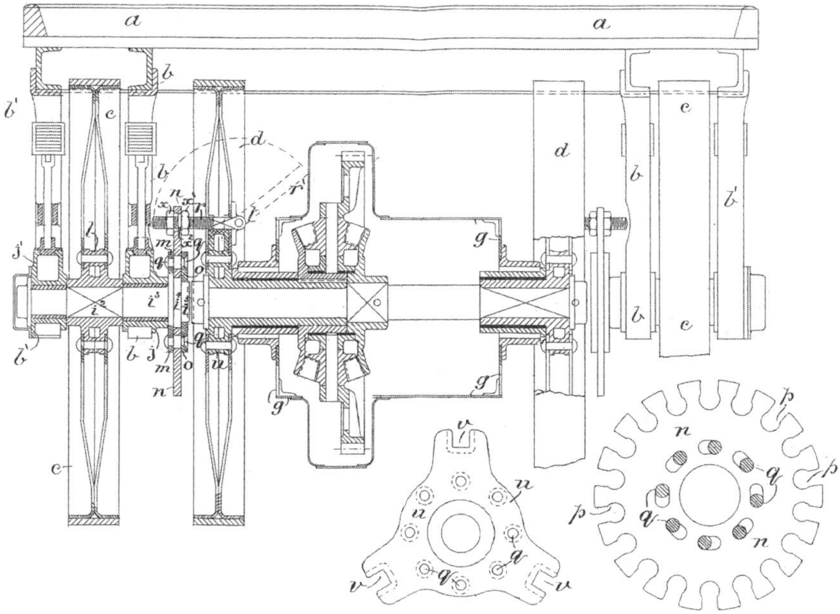

Figure 54: Patent Drawing, Detachable Cart Refinements.
On 5 November 1900, a patent, number 19,786, was registered covering refinements to the detachable cart arrangement. The main topic is a means of easily securing the driven wheels to the cart wheels. This was achieved by a combination of radial and semi-circular slots in the connecting disc.

Lorry Patent

Following very closely after the previous patent, on 22 November 1900 a further patent was applied for defining the Mann lorry, or lurry as it was spelt at the time. Patent 21,085 describes a steam vehicle for carrying goods on common roads - public roads as we know them today. This vehicle was not a variation of the steam cart, but a specialised vehicle with a flat load platform for carrying goods. The first statement of the patent states:

> "The object of our improvements is the construction of steam wagons or vehicles for travelling on common roads, so that they are adapted for conveying and for convenient loading and unloading of different kinds of goods, and for economising and fully utilising the space occupied by the combination of boiler, engine and vehicle body, whilst proving facility for inspection, cleaning and repairs of the engine; for obtaining the advantage of the weight, or the greater part of the weight of the vehicle and its load on the road driving wheels, so as to increase their tractive power;..." [5]

Furthermore this patent is the first recognition of the opportunity for carrying passengers by steam lorry. In the claims at the end of the document the following phrase is included: "In a steam wagon or steam vehicle for the conveyance of goods or passengers on common roads, ..." In keeping with his earlier patents, the locomotive-type boiler was fired from the side, however the major change was that long side plates were fitted, extending backwards from the side of the firebox to form a chassis for the load-carrying vehicle body. The driving wheels supported the chassis with stiff springs to avoid the transmission gears coming out of mesh.

Additional lighter springs were fitted between the chassis and the vehicle body to protect delicate loads from poor road surfaces. Another feature covered by the patent was the possibility of fitting the wagon with a tipping body, as necessary for the type of goods being delivered. The patent drawings illustrate some detail differences to the lorry exhibited at the Maidstone Show (described previously). The most obvious is the moving of the fuel bunker from the centre of the boiler to above the firebox. This also results in the steam collection header and safety valves moving in the converse direction so that they reside, conventionally, in the centre of the boiler on the latter machine. Another change is in the rear suspension. Here the original coil springs are replaced by leaf springs operated through push rods.

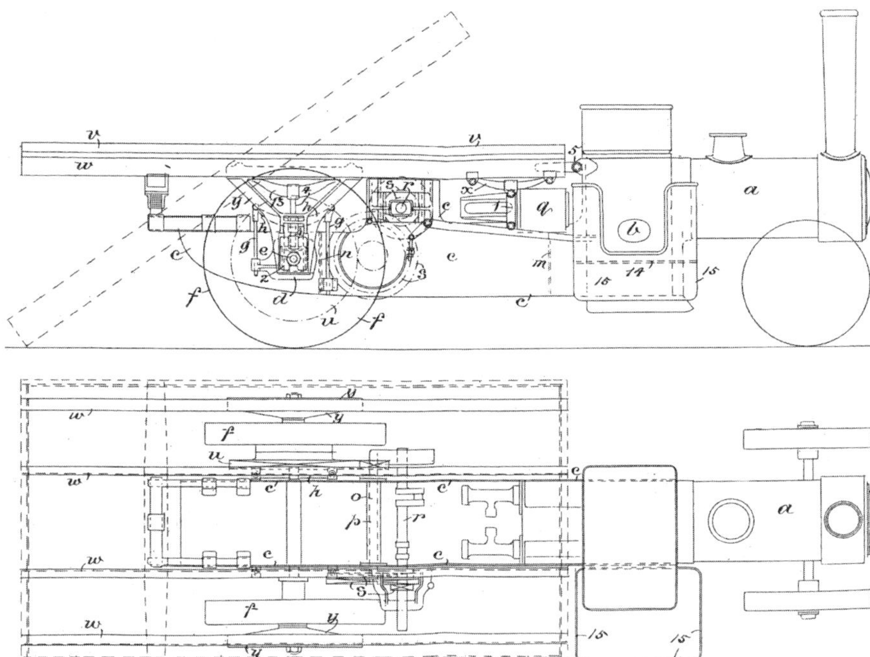

Figure 55: Patent Drawing, Mann Lorry.
Patent 21,085 describes a steam vehicle for carrying goods, and defines what was to become the standard Mann 5-ton lorry, or lurry as it was spelt at the time. The application was made on 22 November 1900. The undertype engine arrangement can clearly be seen.

Liverpool Trials, 1901

Over the period 3 June to 7 June 1901, the third in a series of road vehicle trials was organised by the Liverpool Self-propelled Traffic Association. The entrants could use motive power supplied by steam, electricity or oil (internal-combustion), and four categories were defined, Class A, B, C and D. Mann's Patent Steam Cart and Wagon Company entered two vehicles in Class D, a steam cart (D3) and a steam lorry (D4). Also entered in class D were four other manufacturers: The Thornycroft Steam Wagon Co. Ltd; T. Coulthard & Co. Ltd., Preston; Simpson & Bibby, Manchester and The Mechanical Transport Co., London, although the Simpson & Bibby machine did not complete the trial, and The Mechanical Transport Co. machine was not ready in time to compete. Class D was defined as: minimum load 4 tons; no tare limit; level platform area not specified; minimum width of driving tyres 4in.; speed 5 miles per hour.

The appointed judges were:

- Everard R. Calthrop (noted for his promotion of narrow gauge railways)
- S. B. Cottrell, Engineer, Liverpool Overhead Railway
- Professor H. S. Hele-Shaw, Liverpool University
- Boverton Redwood (noted for his definition of oil viscosity)
- Henry H. West

The trials were carried out over a variety of terrain to fully assess the capability of the machines:

June 3 - Hill climbing and manoeuvrability (Everton Brow, 1 in 9)
June 4 - Liverpool to Manchester via Widnes and Warrington (40.1 miles)
June 5 - Manchester to Liverpool via Bolton and St. Helens (42.9 miles)
June 6 - Liverpool to Blackburn via Wigan and Chorley (41.0 miles)
June 7 - Blackburn to Liverpool via Preston (44.5 miles)

The two Mann machines used boilers and engines with similar specification, that is, the boiler had an operating pressure of 160 p.s.i. with a grate area of 2.5 square feet and a heating surface of 51 square feet. This provided steam for the engine, which had compound cylinders of 4in and 6.4in diameter with a stroke of 8in. This combination provided 25 b.h.p. at a crankshaft speed of 360 r.p.m. Mann's patent reversing gear was employed. Both vehicles were direct gear driven, with no roller-chains employed. On the steam cart, the engine was carried on top of the boiler, i.e. an overtype, whereas with the steam lorry, the engine was fitted on a rearward extension of the fire-box sideplates, beneath the load-carrying platform, i.e. an undertype.[6] One of the refinements introduced on the steam lorry used in the Liverpool trials was the use of enclosed oil baths for the main transmission components.[7] On previous machines the engine bearings had used oil wick lubrication, which relies on the diligence of the operator to maintain adequate supplies of oil. When running non-stop for long distances, the use of an oil bath with its in-built reservoir was one of the reasons for the machines reliability.

The steam cart (D3) was 13ft. 6in. long by 6ft. 6in. wide. The load carrying area was 6ft. 5in. long, providing a surface area of 34.5 square feet. The front wheels were 33in. diameter, whilst the rear wheels were 48in. diameter by 5½in. wide, set on a wheelbase of 8ft. 3in. Fuel capacity was 3.4 cubic feet and water capacity was 144 gallons. The purchase price was £465.[8]

The steam lorry (D4) was longer at 18ft. 11in. but with a similar width to its partner at 6ft. 5in. The load carrying area was 12ft. long, providing a platform area of 69.8 square feet. The front wheels were 33in. diameter, and located just over 11ft. away were the rear wheels of 42in. diameter by 5½in. wide. The larger lorry was able to accommodate greater storage for consumables, with 5.8 cubic feet of fuel and 158 gallons of water, carried in two separate tanks of 86 gallons and 72 gallons. The purchase price was £500.

Figure 56: Liverpool Trials 1901, Steam Lorry, photograph
This photograph varies from the engraving in Figure 52 in that the safety valve has moved from the top of the firebox to the centre of the boiler. As a consequence the coke bunker has been moved nearer to the driver. *(Michael Walters collection)*

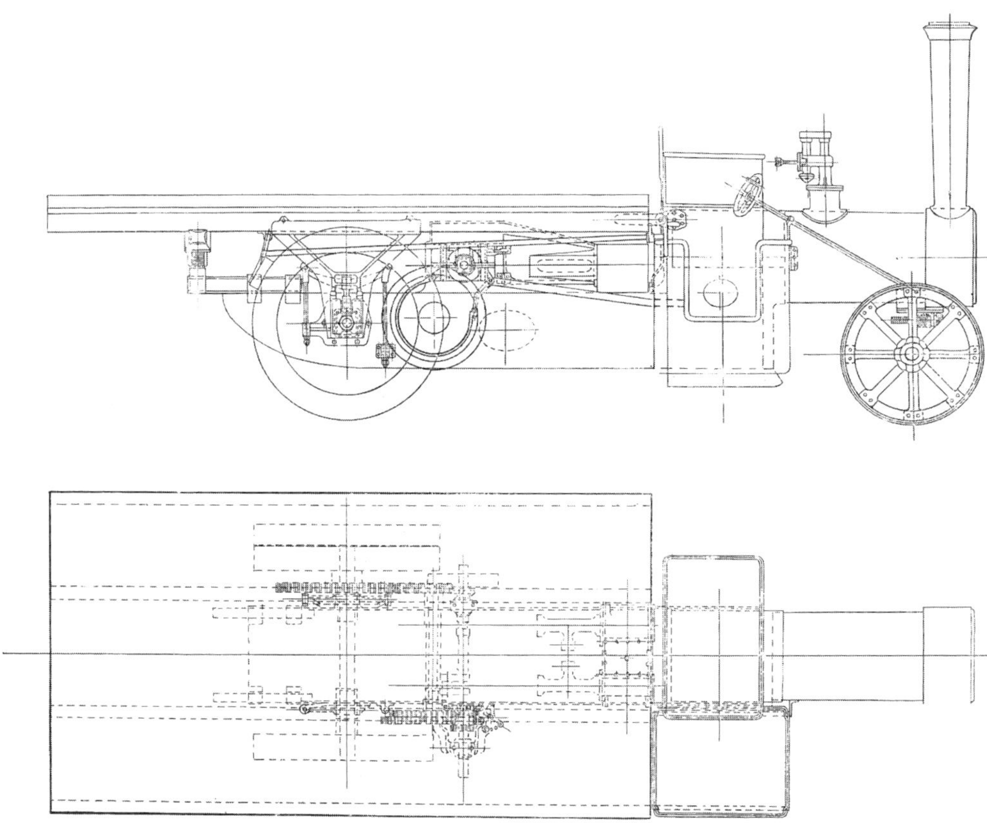

Figure 57: Liverpool Trials 1901, Steam Lorry, diagram
The horizontal undertype compound engine and gear transmission are well illustrated in this line drawing of the Steam Lorry. *(Judges Report, Liverpool Trials)*

In both cases the body was balanced to allow it to tilt to gain access to the engine and gearing. In the case of the cart, this was also used for tipping the contents. Also in both cases, the body was carried on separate wheels, which were the same diameter as, and ran concentric with, the main driving wheels. Braking was provided by two means: the first by a band-brake acting upon a pulley on the intermediate shaft, the second acting on the rim of the vehicle wheel. It was also possible to use the engine reversing gear to act as a brake.

Of the Mann engines, the journal *The Engineer* reported; "We understand that there are now about sixty of them at work in this country. The makers have modified considerably the construction of the road wheels. These were formerly made like traction engine wheels, this is, with T-iron rims, wrought-iron spokes, and cast iron bosses. It is found that a much stronger and lighter wheel can be constructed from dished and flanged steel plates, with cast-steel bosses riveted into them." [9]

Liverpool Trials, 1901 – Consumption Summary

Vehicle	Fuel Consumption - lbs. per ton-mile of load	Water Consumption - gallons per ton-mile of load
D1 - Thornycroft	3.31	1.90
D2 - Coulthard	3.78	2.29
D3 - Mann Cart	4.12	2.52
D4 - Mann Lorry	3.81	2.22

At the conclusion of the trials the Mann machines were jointly awarded the Silver Medal, whilst the judges considered the Thornycroft and Coulthard machines of equal merit and consequently were both awarded with Gold Medals. The Judges Report also observes, "Vehicles Nos. D3 and D4 were fitted with driving wheels having tyres which were not smooth. These vehicles, in addition, are not 'so constructed that no smoke or visible vapour is emitted therefrom except from any temporary or accidental cause.' They are, however, eminently suited for some kinds of heavy haulage work where visible vapour and smoke are unimportant."

The Royal Show for 1901 was held at Cardiff and Mann's Patent Steam Cart and Wagon Company were there to publicise their products. Interestingly, the Leeds firms of J. & H. McLaren and John Fowler & Co. occupied the adjacent stands, although these companies were showing traction engines, not steam wagons. The show catalogue contains details of the steam lorry and the steam cart, both priced as the previous year at £500 and £475 respectively. [10]

Military Vehicles

The subject of military vehicles was the next area for James Mann to investigate. Whether this was of his own volition or in response to a Government initiative is not known; nevertheless the resulting machine is very workmanlike. Patent number 8654 was filed on 27 April 1901 and titled, *Improvements in or in connection with the Mounting and Transport of Field Artillery*. This patent submission marks the transition from Dewsbury Road to Pepper

Road, in that the provisional patent, of April 1901, is addressed with the former location, whilst the final submission, of January 1902, is addressed with the latter location. The vehicle is essentially the Steam Cart but with a field gun mounted on recoil cylinders at the rear. The gun is fitted with the usual adjustments for direction and angle, whilst the vehicle has a drop arm and anchor plate to absorb the recoil of the gun. One of the features emphasised in the patent is the ability of the vehicle to approach the enemy position with the gun pointing forward, i.e. the vehicle moving backwards. The normal method of pulling the gun behind and turning round in a semicircle to fire is considered very dangerous, "during which the whole combination of the team, limber and gun are presented broadside, offering a very wide and vulnerable target to the artillery and long range rifle fire of the enemy; so that the gunners' team or gun may be considerably crippled,...., before the gun is even brought into position to fire a single shot." Mann's solution is defined as, "Now the object of the present invention is to obviate these disadvantages, and to bring the gun up to its firing position with the muzzle pointing in the firing direction, so that it can be directed or kept trained and fired at any moment during its advance, or even retirement, whilst keeping the gunners all the time more or less protected." The major drawback with all steam driven vehicles in military situations is the visibility of the exhaust from the steam and smoke, so whether this machine was ever put to use is doubtful.

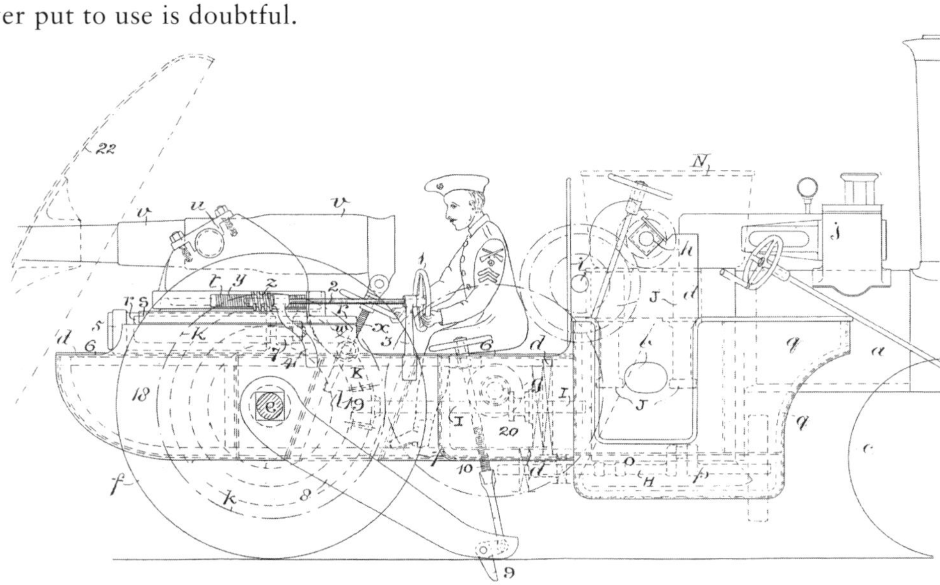

Figure 58: Patent Drawing, Mann Military Vehicle
Patent number 8654 was filed on 27 April 1901, entitled, *Improvements in or in connection with the Mounting and Transport of Field Artillery*. There is no evidence that this machine was put into production.

An advance on the original design of steam cart as defined in patent 13,236 was the subject of Mann's next patent, number 25,998, dated 20 December 1901. The principal change was that the driving wheels were placed outside the chassis, i.e. spaced wider apart, which allowed a deeper and broader cargo space. The important extract from the patent is:

> "The main road driving wheels are placed outside the extended fire box shell plates, an arrangement which allows of the floor of the cart being dropped between the wheels, thus increasing considerably the carrying capacity for loose materials and reducing the height from the ground.
>
> The arrangement of the engine cylinders and crankshaft on top of the boiler, also allows of the floor of the cart being placed lower, and keeps the engine away from the dust of the cart and facilitates inspection, repairs, and attendance of the engine."

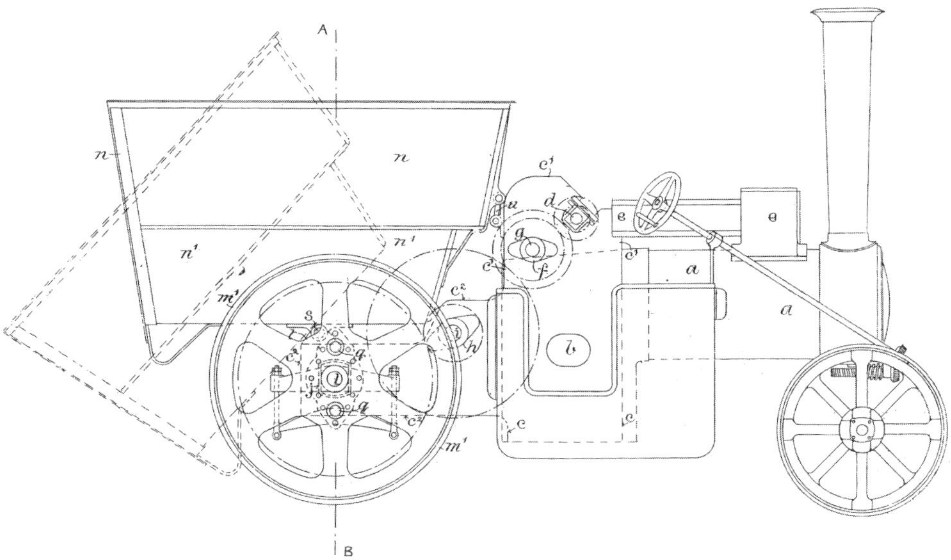

Figure 59: Patent Drawing Improvements to the cargo capacity
Mann's patent of 20 December 1901, number 25,998, shows a development of the steam cart where the driving wheels are placed outside the chassis to improve the load capacity.

The modern concept and advantages of interchangeable bodies, as used today by the ubiquitous articulated lorry, was the attention of James Mann as early as 1902. In his patent of 27 September 1902, number 21,044, he suggests, "This invention refers to improvements in or in connection with road locomotives and trucks, and wagons or carts forming part of the same or adapted to be used therewith; and has for its object to enable such locomotives to be used with interchangeable bodies or platforms for carrying goods, so that the proportion of time spent by the locomotive in hauling to that spent whilst waiting for loading and unloading and coupling up and uncoupling can be reduced enormously."

The load-carrying vehicle was effectively an independent unit with its own set of wheels and could be fitted with a draw bar, or indeed, horse shafts, so that it could be manoeuvred independently of the traction vehicle. When the two components required coupling together for onward transport, the traction unit with its low under-frame slid underneath the load-carrying vehicle. To ensure correct alignment between the two vehicles when the traction unit backed in, dovetail guides were fitted. A lifting mechanism of the screw or hydraulic type was then operated to lift the load-carrying vehicle wheels clear of the road.

This vehicle was exhibited at Park Royal, London on the occasion of the 1903 Royal Show. On this wagon the lifting mechanism, previously described, was operated by bevel wheels connected together by shafts, so that all four worked in unison. Furthermore, the jack mechanism could be operated from the engine crankshaft through worm gearing to provide powered raising and lowering of the platform. The three platform wheels were 24 in. diameter steel castings.[11]

Figure 60: Patent Drawing, Interchangeable Body Vehicle
In patent number 21,044 of 27 September 1902, the load-carrying vehicle was effectively an independent unit with its own set of wheels and could be fitted with a draw bar for manoeuvring whilst the traction unit was elsewhere.

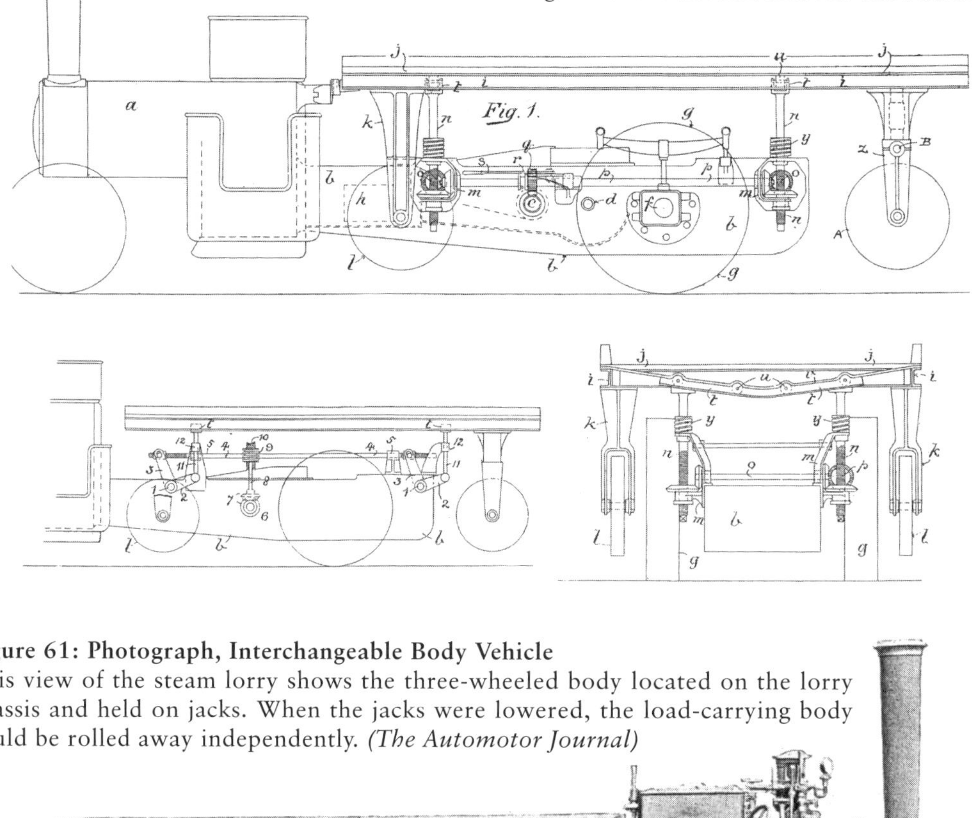

Figure 61: Photograph, Interchangeable Body Vehicle
This view of the steam lorry shows the three-wheeled body located on the lorry chassis and held on jacks. When the jacks were lowered, the load-carrying body could be rolled away independently. *(The Automotor Journal)*

By 1903 the production of the steam cart and the steam wagon was well established with standardised products being readily available. An article in *The Engineer* of that year states, "There have already been built upwards of 200 wagons." [12] The same article gives some very detailed information about Mann products at that time.

The driving wheels were built up of two pressed-steel flanged plates with a T-section steel rim stiffened with a rolled steel tyre. The spokes were stamped out in a press, whilst a steel casting of a modified triangular shape was used for the hub, with a bush made of phosphor-bronze. The cast iron cylinders were made in one casting, and were both bored on one machine, one cut and a finishing reamer completing the operation. The holes for bolts and studs were tapped by machine. All the gear wheels in the vehicles were of cast steel, except the crankshaft pinions, which were forged and cut from the solid and afterward case-hardened. The cast steel gear wheels only required finishing off by an emery wheel, and a purpose-built machine made by Wilkinsons of Keighley carried this out.

The boiler shell and side plates were all marked out to templates, and the plates were cut out by band-saw. The flanging was all done in a hydraulic press in one heat. The riveting was done hydraulically, and the caulking by hand.

Figure 62: Steam Carts at Clifford, Hay-on-Wye
These early steam carts, lying out of use, were photographed in 1935 at E. S. Chambers, Clifford, Hay-on-Wye, Herefordshire. RLS records show that E. S. Chambers owned engine numbers 96 and 99. *(John Middlemiss collection)*

As previously described, the lorry version was of the undertype arrangement, with the engine placed between the extended side frames, in an oil-tight chamber behind the boiler. In the case of the steam cart, the engine was placed traction-engine fashion on top of the boiler. The boiler was of traditional construction with a barrel of 1ft. $6^5/_{16}$in. internal diameter, and built from one sheet of steel $^9/_{32}$in. thick. The firebox and back end plate were of steel $^5/_{16}$in. thick, the front end plate being $^3/_8$in. thick. The rivets were $^5/_8$in. diameter, single joints being $1^{11}/_{16}$in. pitch, and double joints $2^1/_4$in. pitch, the rows being $1^3/_8$in. apart and arranged in zigzag fashion. Double rows of rivets were applied to the longitudinal seam of the barrel, the joint between the crown plate and horn plate, and the joint between the back plate and horn plate. There were 24 steel fire tubes, 3ft. long and $1^{3}/_{4}$in. diameter, swelled to $1^{7}/_{8}$in. diameter. The heating surface provided was 48 square feet, and the grate area 2.5 square feet. Two angle irons were placed back to back inside the back end plate for stiffening purposes. The two side plates, $^{5}/_{16}$in. thick, forming the extension for the frame, were riveted on to the fire-box, 1 ft. $10^{3}/_{4}$in. apart, and top and bottom plates were provided, forming a girder bed for the engines and water tanks. These side plates were made shorter for the cart than for the lorry. The compound cylinders were 4 in. and $6^{1}/_{2}$in. diameter with a stroke of 8 in. The crankshaft speed was about 350 revolutions per minute. For exhibition purposes, vehicles were painted "Midland" red, and lined with yellow and scarlet. These colours were regarded as the Mann house colours.[13]

Colonial Steam Wagon

A completely new design of engine was exhibited at the 1903 Royal Show, held at Park Royal, London. This wagon was designed to carry 7 tons on its own platform and was described as a Colonial Steam Wagon. The wagon could additionally haul a trailer loaded to 3 tons. This machine was destined for export, and because of the less prohibitive legislation, this enabled the vehicle to be larger than its British equivalent.

Its overall dimensions were 20ft. 6in. long by 6 ft. 6in. wide, with a platform length of 14ft. The platform was mounted on independent springs to isolate the load from the road surface. As with the conventional 5-ton lorry, the engine on the Colonial Wagon was mounted horizontally between the frames under the load platform, i.e. an undertype. The engine and gearing were mounted in a dust proof casing, which formed a box girder, and the whole unit ran on oil, allowing the moving parts to be self-lubricating. The engine's dimensions were high pressure cylinder $4^{1}/_{2}$in. diameter, low pressure cylinder $7^{1}/_{2}$in. diameter, both with a stroke of 8in. Power was transmitted from the crankshaft to the back axle through cast steel gearing, there being four shafts in all; the first shaft, driven from the engine, carried the two-speed change-gear, which provided speeds of 5 and $2^{1}/_{2}$ miles per hour.[14] The driving wheels were 3ft. 9in. diameter, with a tyre width of 14in. set on a wheelbase of 11ft. $10^{3}/_{4}$in. To provide the rear suspension, the main axle moved in horn-plates, and was supported on semi-elliptical springs. The front axle was fitted with transverse springs and mounted on a turntable for steering. The large boiler operated at 150 p.s.i. and provided a heating surface of 70.5 square feet. A 200 gallon water tank was fitted at the back of the chassis. Fire doors were provided on both sides of the firebox to enable a second man to assist the driver and to stoke the boiler. For shipping, the boiler could easily be detached from the chassis.[15]

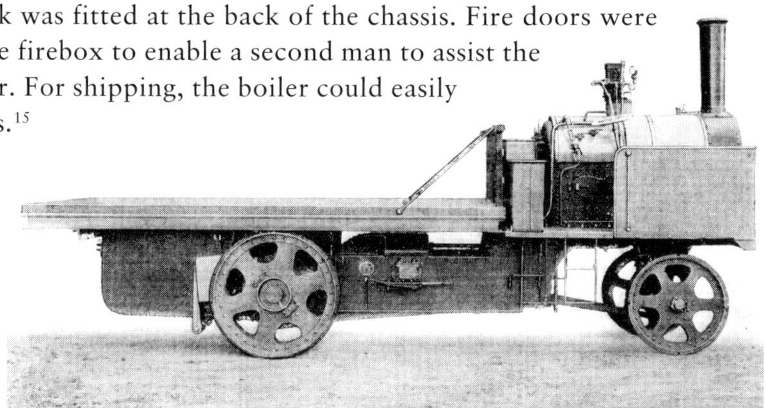

Figure 63: The 7-ton Colonial Wagon
This vehicle was designed for the export market and was larger and more powerful than the normal British 5-ton wagon. The main features are clearly a development of the 5-ton lorry. *(The Engineer)*

Spring Loaded Lubricator

On the 9 January 1904 a patent was registered in the names of Joseph Capel Cornock of 90 Tempest Road, Beeston Hill, Leeds and Mann's Patent Steam Cart and Wagon Company.[16] The document, patent number 584, is entitled "An Improvement or Improvements in or relating to Lubricators." In the patent, Cornock is identified as a Mechanical Engineer, and it appears that he was at this time a design engineer with the company. However, he must have been well respected for in 1906 he was elevated to the position of Company Secretary, which seems a curious transition. The patent describes a spring loaded grease lubricator, and in particular an easy method of fitting the lid when the lubricator was installed in a awkward and hard to see location, as might be found on the underside of a wagon. The cap avoided the use of a threaded fixing, as was normal; instead, a quarter-turn movement was all that was required, not dissimilar to a bayonet type fixing. The lubricator spring, which fitted to the cap, was pre-loaded before being fitted to the lubricator body. When the lid was closed, the retaining clip released the spring-loaded piston to allow it to act on the grease and force it into the bearing surface.

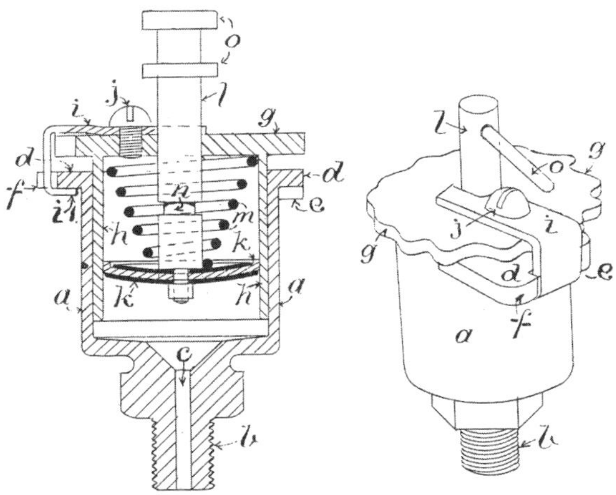

Figure 64: Patent Drawing, Cornock Lubricator
This lubricating device was registered at the Patent Office on 9 January 1904 in the joint names of Joseph Capel Cornock and Mann's Patent Steam Cart and Wagon Company.

Figure 65: Photograph, Cornock Lubricator
This photograph of the front wheel on a 2-ton wagon shows a Cornock lubricator between the spokes on the left hand side of the wheel. In this instance the unit was used for grease lubrication of the plain bearings of the wheel. *(Henry Roskilly collection)*

Wooden Tyred Wheels

The subject of patent 2109, filed on 28 January 1904, was wooden wheels. The opening statement reads, "This invention relates to the construction of the wheels of traction engines, road locomotives and the like, in which the tyre and tread of the wheels is formed of a series of wood blocks or segments." The use of wooden wheels appears today to be a backward step when steel wheels were in regular use and rubber tyres were available. The introduction of vulcanised rubber tyres for road vehicles (initially for cycles) was around 1850, with pneumatic tyres first appearing in 1888. This was principally through the efforts of John Boyd Dunlop, although another Scotsman, R. W. Thompson was the first to patent the idea. At this period, a set of rubber tyres cost around £100, a considerable sum at that time, representing around one fifth of the cost of a new steam wagon, and Mann's were keen to consider all the options available. In the company literature the following paragraph explains, "For country roads we strongly recommend the built-up steel wheels shown in most of the illustrations, which are the result of years of experience; but where the work is principally on granite setts, and rubber tyres are not used, it is sometimes advisable to have wooden wheels as they are somewhat quieter running than steel. If however, customers will give us particulars of the nature of their work we shall be pleased to advise them whether steel, wood or rubber tyred wheels are most suitable." [17]

In Catalogue A, the wooden wheel is described as Mann's Patent Winter Wheel. The wheel consisted of a cast steel inner wheel with a polygonal rim. Hardwood segments were bolted to the rim with the grain end-on. To prevent splitting, plate segments were bolted to both the wheel and the wooden blocks, to clamp them in position. The plate segments were slotted to allow them to be adjusted, so that as the wooden surface wore down, the plates would not come into contact with the road surface. The catalogue states, "These wheels enable wagons to travel in snowy and frosty weather, when the roads are impassable to ordinary steel-tyred machines, and when used in combination with a sanding box will climb steep hills." One user is quoted as saying, "We are pleased to say the wooden wheels have done remarkably well, and are undoubtedly a wonderful improvement." [18] A pair of wheels was priced at £33.[19]

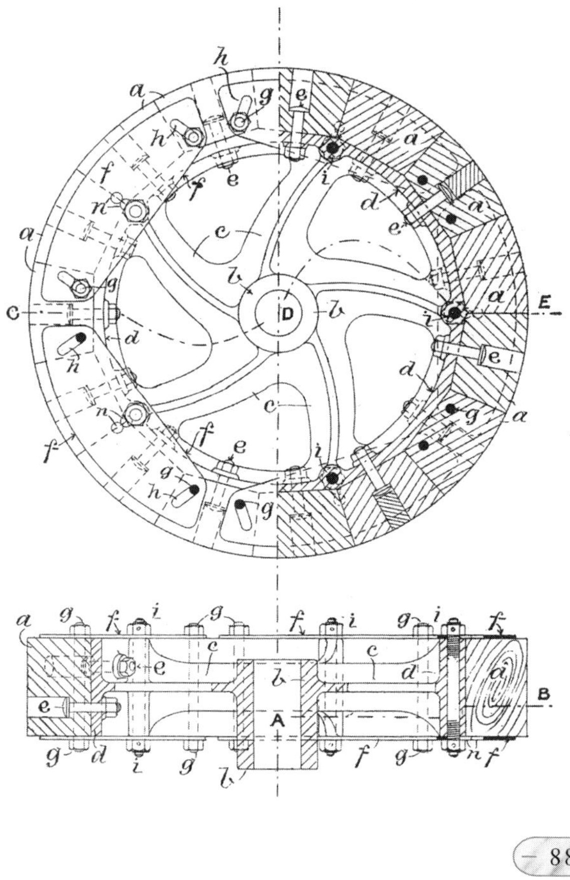

Figure 66; Patent Drawing, Wooden Tyred Wheel.
Wooden wheels were quieter than steel versions, and according to company catalogues were better in snowy and frosty weather. The Patent for this tyre was filed on 28 January 1904.

Mann's next patent was not directly connected with steam carts, but a method of filling them. The proposal was to pre-fill a hopper with gravel or grain for example, and then to discharge this into the cart when necessary. The patent states, "Our new method of filling steam carts consists of first filling a hopper, which is resting on or supported near the ground, with the material to be filled into the steam cart: the hopper having a capacity equal to that of the steam cart to be filled, or thereabouts. When filled the hopper is raised to a sufficient height, by means of an apparatus mounted on travelling wheels, capable of receiving the steam cart within it beneath the raised hopper. The steam cart is then moved into the position just indicated, and the content of the hopper discharged into the steam cart by opening a door in the bottom of the hopper." [20]

In support of his proposal, Mann relates the following benefits, "The object of this invention is chiefly the saving in the time, during which the steam cart is kept stationary whilst being filled; and as such carts have a capacity four to five times as great as that of horse carts, the saving in time compared to that now required to fill such steam carts by shovelling in the material is very considerable. Our new method and means thus enable a greater number of journeys to be undertaken in a given time, or in other words, more time in a day becomes available for making the journeys."

The hopper, which had approximately the same capacity as the body of the vehicle to be loaded, was lowered to a convenient height, filled by a labourer during the time the steam cart was away delivering its load, and hoisted into position ready for the cart to return. The hopper was fitted with wheels to enable it to be moved about in the yard and four shackles were fitted to connect it to a vehicle. Cross-stays were located in sockets so that they could readily be removed when the cart needed to back under the hopper. It was suggested that "Contractors and builders will find this system one offering great possibilities of economy." [21] The device was said to be suitable for road metal, coal lime, sand and bricks and would enable twice the number of journeys to be made, or in other words, double the number of tons carried in a day.

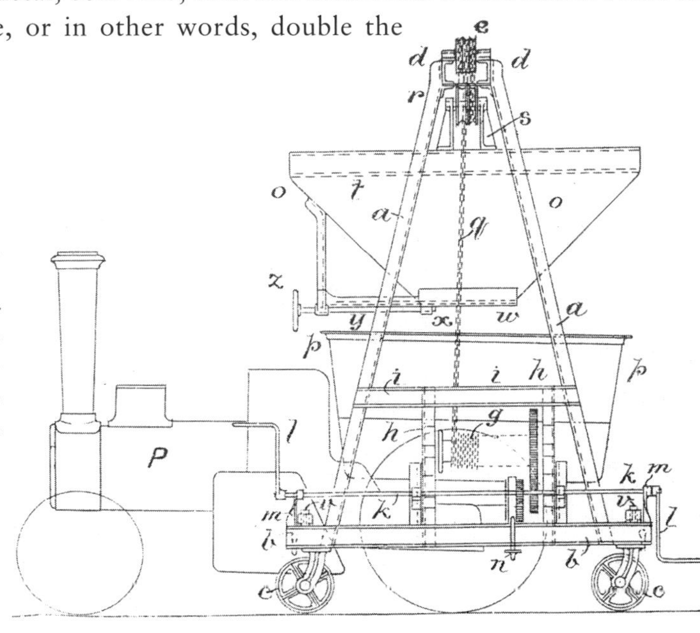

Figure 67: Patent Drawing, Loading Hopper.
Patent 1347 was submitted on 24 January 1905, and is entitled, *Improved Method and Means for Filling Steam Carts, Wagons and the like*. This product was offered for sale, however, no records have survived to indicate how many were sold.

Hand Pumps for Washing out Boilers

In common with most traction engine related manufacturers, Mann's offered a hand washout pump in their catalogues. This was priced at £3 10s.[22] The company made the following observation: "The principal reason why fire-boxes require frequent renewal is because they are not washed out as often as necessary to prevent the mud and sediment in the water spaces from depositing and caking on to the fire-box plates. This prevents the water coming in contact, and consequently allows them to burn and crack. Washing out without a Force Pump is a tedious and unpleasant job, inasmuch as the silt and deposit is most difficult to dislodge, especially from amongst the stays, and therefore it is only done as seldom as possible, and then in an unsatisfactory manner. We strongly recommend all users of Steam Carts, Lurries, Traction and Portable Engines to have these Pumps as a means of making "washing out" a more popular, and consequently, a more frequent and efficient job, thereby effecting a considerable saving in repairs to their boilers." [23]

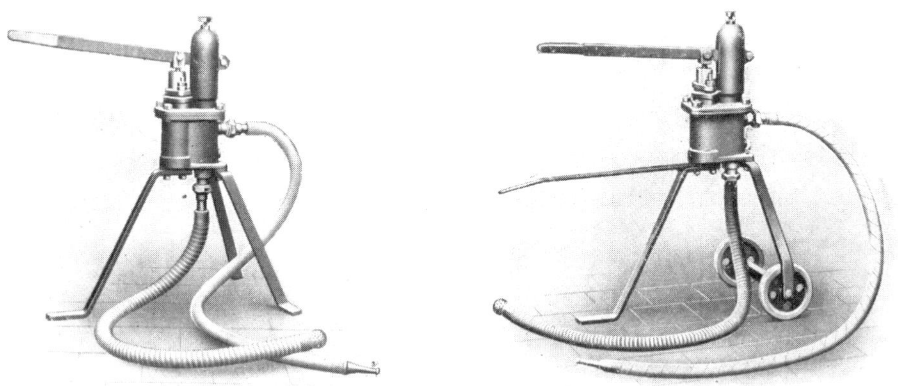

Figure 68: Hand Force Pump
These washout pumps were intended for cleaning out the wagon's boiler. The same design of pumps featured in catalogues throughout the company's existence. *(Mann Catalogue)*

Independent Suspension

The use of independent suspension, i.e. the two driven wheels being fitted to stub axles, each separately sprung, is considered to be a relatively modern innovation. It is therefore surprising to discover that James Mann patented this idea in 1905. In patent 2207, submitted on 4 February 1905, the text reads:

> "This invention relates to the construction of self-propelled road vehicles, heavy motor cars and the like, hereinafter for the sake of brevity referred to as vehicles; and consists in dispensing with the usual long rear or main axle having a road wheel at each end, and in providing instead two short axles, one on each side of the vehicle, quite independent of each other, and driven by separate trains of gearing from an intermediate or the crank or driving shaft of the motor."

In the patent, Mann gives the benefits of this proposal as:

> "This invention has the advantage of obtaining great flexibility in the connection between the body or frame of the vehicle and the main driving road wheels, and enables the road wheels to adjust themselves better to the ordinary roadway, so that much less damage is done to the roadway."

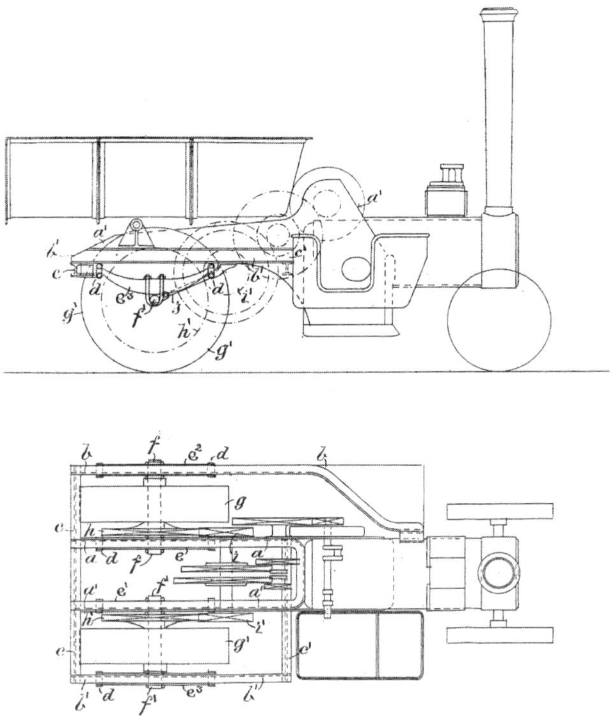

Figure 69: Patent Drawing, Independent Suspension
Independent suspension is considered to be a relatively modern innovation, however James Mann patented his ideas on the subject in 1905. Each driven wheel was fitted to a stub axle and powered by independent gearing.

Two-Ton Wagon

In response to the Heavy Motor Car Order 1904, a lightweight, fully sprung, 2-ton wagon was introduced in 1905.This was exhibited in 1905 at Cordingley's tenth annual Automobile Exhibition, held at the Agricultural Hall, Islington. The design of this machine was a departure from their previous vehicles and incorporated a number of changes. The wagon was an inexpensive, lightweight machine and therefore targeted at a new range of customers. Rolled steel channel was used for the chassis, to which was bolted the boiler. This was a major departure from previous practice, where the chassis was formed from steel plates riveted to the firebox sides, producing a composite boiler-chassis structure. The 40in. diameter rear wheels were able to operate up to 8 miles per hour under legislation that came into effect on 1 March 1905. A single cylinder engine of 4in. diameter and 7in. stroke provided the motive power. The horizontal undertype engine was connected to the transmission through a metal-to-metal friction clutch, allowing speed changes whilst on the move. In addition, the engine could continue running when the vehicle was stopped, thereby allowing the water pump to feed the boiler. The engine and quick running gear operated in the same oil bath. To slow the vehicle, a foot brake operated on a drum on the intermediate shaft, whilst a screw brake acting on the rim of the driving wheels provided a parking brake.[24] Writing in 1906, Norris [25] describes this vehicle somewhat differently. In particular he describes the engine cylinder as being 4.75in. diameter by 6in. stroke, developing 20 h.p, and these dimensions are confirmed by an article printed in March 1905 in the journal *Commercial Motor*. This may have been an engine development of the 1905 machine described by the *Engineer*.

Another new vehicle brought out in 1905 was a redesign of the 5-ton wagon, originally introduced in 1900. The primary differences were:

- the boiler was shorter, but larger in diameter than previous
- the engine was sunk lower between the main frame side plates
- a single pair of driving wheels was fitted, rather than the twin pair of concentric wheels previously used

The engine was of the horizontal compound arrangement with a low-pressure cylinder of $4^1/_4$in. diameter, a high-pressure cylinder of $6^3/_4$in. diameter, both with a stroke of 7in. The engine shaft and gearing were enclosed to keep out dirt thrown up from the road surface. This machine was not Mann's first undertype, as some commentators have suggested. The 5-ton undertype was introduced in 1899 at the Maidstone Royal Show, this design being patented in 1900, and subsequently entered in the Liverpool trials. A more detailed description of the 1905 wagon was given in *Commercial Motor*, although the size quoted for the low-pressure cylinder is different:

Boiler

As previously mentioned, the boiler was shorter in the barrel but larger in diameter than previous wagons and this provided several advantages: "It causes a less space to be taken up by the (steam) generator, whilst the provision of a firing door at the top of the fire-box allows the platform to be raised materially, thus giving the driver an excellent view all round." [26] The grate area was 3 square feet, and the total heating surface was about 80 square feet. The boiler was fitted with 50 tubes each $1^1/_2$in. diameter. A particular feature of the fire-box was the large radius of the vertical corners of the outer fire-box shell. The boiler was also designed for easy cleaning, and for this purpose it was fitted with the following items: a blow-off cock at a low level for easy access, a plug at the bottom of the front tube plate, wash-out doors at the corners of the fire-box, a large hand hole at the top of the fire-box, and the top of the tubes could be reached by removing the dome cover. The boiler operated at 180 p.s.i. and was fed with water by both a pump and a Penberthy injector.

Engine

The compound engine was rated 35 h.p. with cylinders of $4^1/_2$in. and $7^1/_2$in. diameter, with a stroke of 7in. A valve on the footplate allowed steam to pass direct from the regulator to the low-pressure cylinder when extra power was needed. The $2^3/_4$in. diameter crankshaft had gear wheels on both ends. The running speed of the crankshaft was 300 r.p.m. When the appropriate gear meshed with the countershaft the two road speeds of either three miles per hour or six miles per hour were obtained. The first motion shaft, which previously ran in a separate casing, was placed in the engine oil bath. This was located lower than before, thereby allowing access to the engine without tilting the platform. Cornock sprung-loaded units provided grease lubrication for the wheel bearings. These consisted of a grease cup that contained a spring-loaded piston. This forced the grease out slowly onto the bearing.

Figure 70: Mann 5-ton wagon with tipping platform
This immaculate new wagon is pictured at the back of the works with the chimneys of the Leeds Steel Works in the background. The vehicle is thought to be Mann number 431 supplied to Earl Fitzwilliam's Collieries, in 1908. The driver is Billy Wintringham. *(David Riley – www.photoarchives.co.uk)*

Running gear

The new 5-ton machine dispensed with the twin sets of concentric rear wheels that had been used on earlier wagons to get around the restrictive legislation. With the introduction of the Heavy Motor Car Order 1904, this complicated wheel arrangement was no longer necessary and therefore a single pair of driving wheels was fitted. These were 3ft. 6in. diameter and 10in. wide, and were supported by large bushes, 4in. diameter and 7in. long. The front wheels were 2ft. 9in. diameter and 5in. wide.

The rear leaf springs were 3ft. 6in. long and these were assisted by check springs that came into play when hauling a heavy load over rough ground. The front spring was 2ft. 6in. long. The steering operated by the usual Mann worm and quadrant arrangement. The hand brake operated block brakes on the rear wheels, whilst the foot operated brake acted on a band round the countershaft. In difficult circumstances, the differential could be locked to provide extra traction.

Overall dimensions

The length of the wagon was 17ft. 6in. with a wheelbase of 11ft. The flat body of the wagon was 12ft. long by 6ft. wide, and this overhung the rear axle by 6ft. 6in. The water bunker held 180 gallons, whilst the coke bunker carried 5 cwt of fuel.

Enclosed boiler front

A later revision of the 5-ton wagon, illustrated in the journal *Commercial Motor* of October 1906, was the hiding of the smoke-box door.[27] A machine supplied to Hancock's Brewery, Cardiff, was built with the sheet steel forming the bunkers continuing around the front of the boiler, thus hiding the smoke-box door. A large door was formed in the enclosure to gain access to the smoke-box door for cleaning and maintenance. Despite the very neat appearance of this machine, the variation did not persist, as later photographs do not include this feature. This may have been due to the hindrance incurred by limiting access through the steel door.

Timber Haulage

An interesting variation on the 5-ton wagon was featured by an article in *Commercial Motor*. The article describes a wagon that was sent to Austria in 1906 for hauling timber at the Dobrisch Castle Estate of Prince Colloredo Mannsfeld.[28] The complete vehicle consisted of wagon and a separate trailing truck. The trailer was used to support the long timbers after tree felling on the estate. The trailer was fitted with its own steering gear to make it more manoeuvrable, particularly when reversing. In addition, rollers could be fitted to the trailer for road making purposes. According to the article: "It has proved itself a thoroughly satisfactory machine for all-round estate work, including the haulage of coal, road metal or general produce, quite apart from its primary use in timber haulage and road construction around the Prince's seat, Dobrisch Castle."

Figure 71: Timber Haulage in Austria
This specialised wagon was delivered to Dobrisch Castle Estate of Prince Colloredo Mannsfeld, Austria in 1906. The basis of this machine was the standard 5-ton wagon. *(Mann Catalogue)*

Ten years later a similar application was reported in the press.[29] This report describes timber haulage at the estate of Lord Aldenham at Elstree, Hertfordshire. The timber was hauled into position on a four-wheeled pole-wagon by means of a wire rope from the winding drum of the tractor. This refers to the standard steam road tractor built to comply with the Motor Car Act. The article continues: "It is intended for other estate work besides timber haulage, since, when fitted with a governor, it may be used for driving a thrashing machine, saw bench, stone-breaker, &c., from the flywheel."

Figure 72: Timber Haulage, Elstree
This tractor and pole wagon was in use at the estate of Lord Aldenham at Elstree, Hertfordshire. This was engine number 1017, completed in May of 1916. *(Mann Catalogue)*

Steam Tractor

An adaptation of the steam cart, a new steam tractor, was the subject of an article in the journal "*The Engineer*" in 1905.[30] The machine's appearance was essentially a small traditional overtype traction engine, but with a goods platform above the rear wheels, capable of carrying about two tons. As with most of Mann's products, the fire-hole and associated footplate was placed on the side of the firebox, so as to provide maximum space behind the boiler for goods. The side location of the footplate, it was claimed, gave the driver a favourable position for seeing either backward or forward. Additional load, up to three tons, could be carried on a trailer, giving a total load of five tons.

The weight of the tractor was 4 tons 15 cwt., the length 12ft., the width 6ft., and the platform measured 5ft. 6in. by 6ft. The platform was supplied with detachable hinged side and loose removable ends. The engine was of the compound horizontal type, with cylinders 4in.

and $6\frac{1}{2}$in. diameter by 7in. stroke. The power was transmitted to the road wheels by spur gearing, giving two travelling speeds of 5 miles per hour and $2\frac{1}{2}$ miles per hour. Compensating gear was provided for turning corners, and no pitch chains were used. The steering gear consisted of a worm acting directly into a quadrant on the fore-carriage bracket, and the motion of the engine could be reversed by means of a single eccentric reversing gear, which could be notched up so that the engine itself acted as a brake. The boiler was of the locomotive pattern, with a firebox suitable for burning coke or smokeless coal. At the top of the firebox was placed a fusible plug to protect the boiler if the water was allowed to get low. Also fitted to the boiler was a man-hole for examination purposes and a mud door for cleaning out the residues that collected in the boiler bottom. The boiler shell was of Siemens-Martin steel plates, the edges of which were planed. It was constructed for a pressure of 150 p.s.i., and the firebox sides were extended to carry all engine shafts and axle brackets. The water tank had a capacity of 120 gallons. The main road wheels were 4ft. diameter and 10in. wide, the front wheels were 2ft. 9in. diameter. These were of mild steel, and had steel tyres provided with holes for cross bars. The crankshaft, intermediate shaft, and axles were steel forgings, and ran in long, hard, phosphor-bronze bearings carried in cast steel brackets, which were provided with turned projections accurately fitting into holes in the horn-plates. A winding drum and steel rope were provided to assist in difficult situations. Two forms of brakes were fitted: the first for use in traffic was of the band type, operated by a foot pedal within easy reach of the driver's foot; the second brake was a shoe brake, brought into action by turning a hand-wheel. The works price of the complete tractor was £425. [31]

Figure 73: Steam Tractor
This road tractor was based on the steam cart, and as the picture illustrates, was able to haul 2 tons on the platform and an additional load on a trailer. *(Henry Roskilly collection)*

Vehicle Load Weighing

A means of weighing portions of a vehicle's cargo was a subject that James Mann spent some time investigating during 1905, presumably in response to an enquiry by one of his clients. On 11 January 1906, he filed a patent, number 742 titled, *Improvements in or relating to Means for Weighing, whilst Filling and on Delivery, Definite Separate Portions of the Load of Motor Propelled Vehicles*. This patent[32] describes a vehicle with a number of independent, movable and self-emptying storage boxes, typically four or six. In the centre of the boxes and fixed to the lorry was a pillar crane, fitted with a suspension-weighing machine. The patent also included the use of a travelling beam crane with the two support tracks fitted across the front and rear of the load area. The crane was not used for unloading the boxes, merely for weighing. Individual tipping mechanisms were fitted to the underside of each box to discharge the cargo out of a door provided for the purpose.

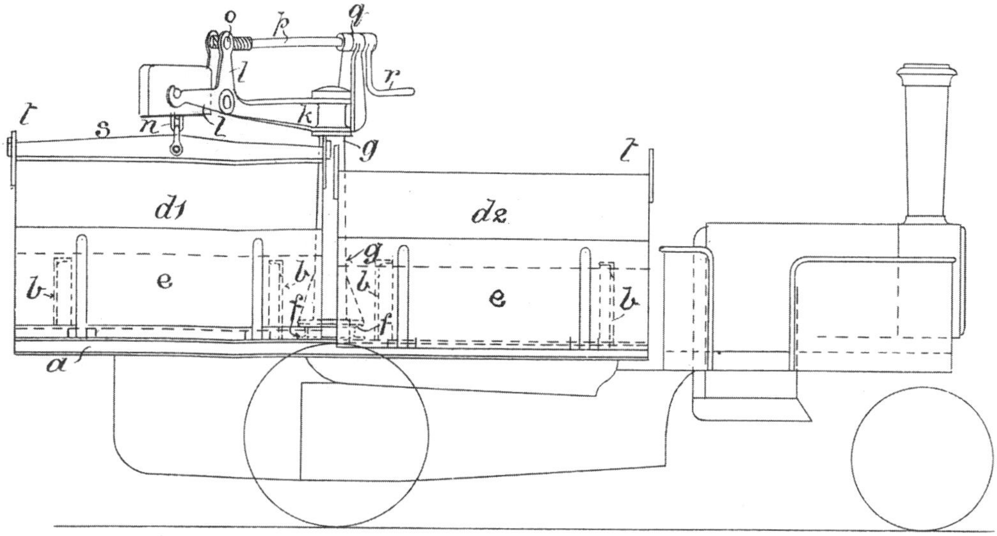

Figure 74: Patent Drawing, Vehicle Load Weighing.
James Hutchinson Mann filed this patent on 11 January 1906. The document, numbered 742 is titled, "Improvements in or relating to Means for Weighing, whilst Filling and on Delivery, Definite Separate Portions of the Load of Motor Propelled Vehicles".

Pipe Joints

Presumably as a result of his own bad experience, James Mann lodged a patent on the subject of Pipe Joints, on 20 January 1906. In his opening statement Mann states, "Screwed pipes which have to withstand vibration, frequently break off close to the flanges or bosses or other attachment into which they are screwed; caused by the point of greatest strain coming upon a portion of the pipe, which has been reduced in strength due to cutting of the screw." The proposal defines a screwed fitting that was longer than normal. This long extension accommodated the unthreaded portion of the pipe, and was split along its length and fitted with lugs. When the pipe was screwed into the fitting, a nut and bolt, passing through the lugs, was tightened to clamp the pipe. The drawing below illustrates this arrangement.

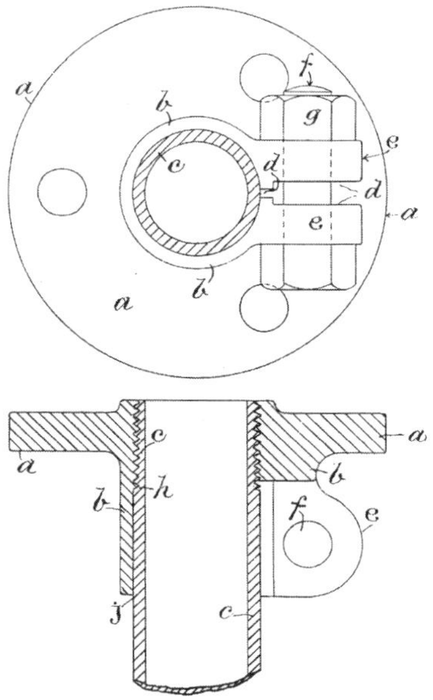

Figure 75: Patent Drawing, Improved Pipe Fitting
Patent 1539, was submitted on 20 January 1906, and is titled, *An Improvement in or relating to Pipe Joints*. This subject was presumably addressed from bitter experience of pipe joint failures.

Revised Two-Ton Wagon

At the Royal Show of 1906, held in Derby, a revised 2-ton wagon was shown. This was similar to the 2-ton undertype wagon introduced the previous year, but included a more powerful compound engine, rated 20 h.p. According to the journal *The Engineer*, this had a low-pressure cylinder of 6$^3/_8$in. diameter, and a high-pressure cylinder of 3$^3/_4$in. diameter, with a stroke of 6 in.[33] Curiously the rival publication, *Engineering*, records a different set of dimensions, these being a low-pressure cylinder of 5 in. diameter, and a high-pressure cylinder of 3$^1/_2$in. diameter, with a stroke of 6 in., operating at 350 r.p.m.[34] Later evidence agrees with figures quoted by *The Engineer*, which suggests that the data provided by *Engineering* was incorrect.[35] The Mann patent single eccentric reversing gear operated the valves. The boiler was of the shortened style, of similar proportions to the 5-ton engine, and had a working pressure of 170 p.s.i. Because of the shortened boiler, the distance from the back of the driver's seat to the front of the smokebox was only 4ft. 9in. The safety valve discharged directly into the funnel, and an exhaust steam superheater was fitted in the smokebox to render the discharge invisible. The motion ran in hard phosphor-bronze bearings and power was transmitted from the crankshaft to the axle through spur gears running in an enclosed oil bath. This gave two road speeds of 8 m.p.h. for normal running, and 3$^1/_2$ m.p.h. for hill climbing. Rolled steel channel was used for the chassis, to which was bolted the boiler. The main axle was supported by radius rods, to ensure good alignment of the transmission gears. The driving wheels were 3ft. 2in. diameter by 6in. width and these fitted on square axle shafts. A 100-gallon water tank was fitted and this fed water to the boiler via an engine driven pump or alternatively through an injector when the engine was stationary. A water lifter and 20ft. of suction hose was provided for replenishing the tank from streams. Steering was by the standard Mann arrangement of worm and quadrant on the fore-carriage. The lorry platform was 5ft. 6in. wide and 10ft. long. The vehicle weighed approximately 3 tons and the length was 15ft. 6in.[36] An example of the 2-ton wagon was shown at an exhibition in March 1907, having been built for Tangyes Limited, the Birmingham based, pump and engine makers. Of the 2-ton machine, a further article written in June 1907, relates some items of convenience for the driver, "The bunker is fitted with a lid, and has a firing-tray in front of it, on which the coke is raked out prior to firing. The tray is perforated, so that any fine dust formed passes through on to the road, in place of being blown about on to the attendant or into the machinery. The firing-tray is practically on the same level as the fire-door. A roomy seat is provided for the driver, who has all the steam-regulating and brake handles grouped within convenient reach." [37] The 1909 Royal Show catalogue gives the price of the 2-ton wagon as £400.[38]

Figure 76: 2-Ton Wagon
This photograph demonstrates one of the important features of the 2-ton wagon, i.e. that the boiler was bolted to a channel frame chassis, rather than being formed as an integral unit, as had earlier designs. *(Henry Roskilly collection)*

Revised Five-Ton Steam Cart

In the following year, 1907, a revised 5-ton steam cart was on display at the Lincoln Royal Show. The cart was fitted with an overtype compound engine mounted at a slight angle to the horizontal plane. This was probably done to ensure good lubrication of the various crankshaft bearings, which were contained in an oil-bath at the lowest point. The engine had a low-pressure cylinder of 6¾in. diameter, a high-pressure cylinder of 4in. diameter, and a stroke of 8in.[39] The boiler was designed for a working pressure of 200 p.s.i. and water tanks with a capacity of 120 gallons were fitted. With the introduction of the Heavy Motor Car Order, allowing higher tare weights, the vehicle was made with a larger body and corresponding increases in the boiler, tanks and engine size. Perhaps more significantly, this cart was fitted with a single pair of rear road wheels. It may be recalled that to comply with the legislation in force at the time, the original 1898 Mann steam cart was built in two parts, the engine, and the carrying platform, each with its own set of rear wheels, six wheels in all.

This complicated layout persisted until 1907. The new cart simplified this arrangement, and was built as a conventional integral unit with four wheels. The transmission from the engine to the crankshaft continued to be by spur wheels, however, the gear alignment was achieved by suspending the driving axle on radius rods to accommodate the movement of the leaf springs. Two road speeds were provided of 5 m.p.h. and $2^1/_2$ m.p.h. The main road wheels were 3ft. 10in. diameter and 10in. wide. The platform was 8ft. long by 6ft. 6in. wide. The overall dimensions of the vehicle were length 15ft. 6in., width 6ft. 6in. The load platform was arranged to take a swivelling bearer, so that it could be used for hauling timber. This was done by having the front of the logs resting on the swivelling bearer, whilst the rear of the logs rested on a trailer. The flexibility provided by this arrangement allowed the combination to take corners without hindrance.[40] When not in use for haulage, the cart could be used to drive adjacent machinery by the use of a flat leather belt from the crankshaft flywheel.[41]

Figure 77: 5-Ton Steam Cart
A revised 5-ton steam cart was exhibited in 1907 at the Lincoln Royal Show. The cart was extensively redesigned and importantly, the twin sets of rear wheels were removed and conventional wheels substituted. The pin-rack used to lift the body, was of open construction to prevent clogging with dirt, and thus proved very reliable. *(Henry Roskilly collection)*

7-Ton Undertype Wagon

In response to a request from the brewers, William Hancock of Cardiff, Mann's produced in 1907 a 7-ton delivery lorry. This machine, because of its weight, was outside the Motor Car Acts and therefore had to operate under a traction engine licence. The 7-tonner was a development of their standard 5-ton machine, but larger and more powerful. The cylinder dimensions are shown overleaf, compared with the 5-ton sizes.

Cylinder sizes	High pressure	Low pressure
7-ton wagon	5in.	8in.
5-ton wagon	4¹/₄in.	6³/₄in.

The 7-ton Colonial wagon had originally been introduced in 1903, however the Hancock machine, as described in the journal *Commercial Motor*, has some detail differences. These differences may have resulted from experience on the earlier machines, however it may simply have been the client's specification. The extra size of the 7-ton wagon provided a large platform 17ft. long by 7ft. 3in. wide, making the overall dimensions of the wagon 24ft. by 7ft. 3in. Similarly, the wheels were larger than normal, the main driving wheels being 4ft. diameter by 14in. wide. A water tank of 200 gallons capacity was provided.[42] The engine contained two oil baths. The first was used for lubricating the engine, crankshaft, first-motion gearwheel and pinion. The second oil bath contained the change speed gears, the differential and main axle. Reversing gear was by Mann's patent arrangement. The steering gear was duplicated so that a second man sitting on the opposite side of the boiler to the driver could operate the steering wheel if required. These large wagons were often referred to as Colonial types because their primary market was abroad. As mentioned earlier, because of their weight they did not comply with the Motor Car Acts and therefore had to operate under a traction engine licence. In the colonies, where the restrictive English road legislation did not apply, heavier wagons could operate freely and without financial penalty.

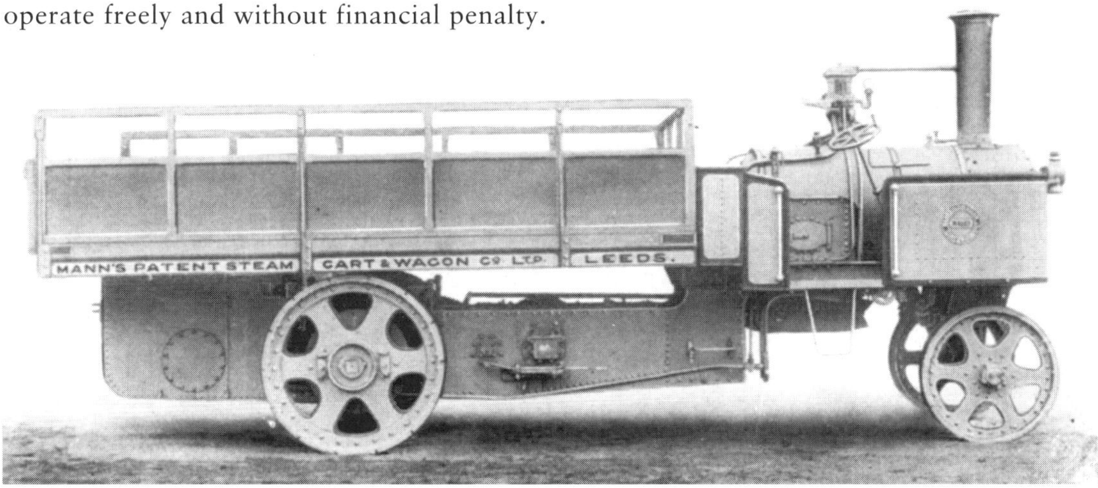

Figure 78: 7-ton Steam Wagon
A few British users operated the 7-ton steam wagon, however, because of its weight it could not operate within the Motor Car Act, as a result they were mainly sold abroad. *(Mann Catalogue)*

Fuel Hopper Wagon, 2-Ton

A development of the locomotive-type water-tube boiler was designed in 1907. The principal changes were the addition of an extended dome on top of the boiler, and the inclusion of a fuel hopper directly above the top of the firebox. These two ideas were the subject of two related patents, both filed on 24 June 1907, numbers 14,469 and 14,469A. The physical arrangement of these changes is best understood from observing the associated drawing, Figure 79.

The primary change to the boiler barrel was that it was formed in a D-shaped profile, with the flat surface on the top. In the centre of the flat boiler top was formed a circular flange, to which the enlarged dome was fitted. The enlargement of the dome was done both in height and in diameter such that it normally operated partially full of water. This is in contrast to a conventional locomotive-type boiler where the dome is used purely as a steam collector and water entry into this space is avoided to prevent priming, i.e. water passing through to the cylinders. The inclusion of water in the dome had the effect that the top of the firebox and the top of the boiler were always fully covered with water. The fixing of the large dome on top of the flat surface of the boiler added to the rigidity of the arrangement and helped to minimise the need for extra stays, as would normally be expected with a D-shaped boiler.

The patent claimed that the larger dome had the following advantages:

- Increased accessibility for examination and repairs
- A higher working water level, with more space above for dry steam
- Solid water over the firebox and front end of the tubes when descending or ascending hills

The second addition was the fitting of a fuel hopper directly above the firebox. This was fitted with two hand-operated slide valves. With the bottom valve closed, the top valve was opened first and then closed, thus allowing a fixed volume of fuel to collect in the space between the valves. Secondly the bottom valve was opened to discharge the fuel and then closed again. This sequence provided a measured volume of fuel to be held in the space, in so doing, preventing the entire contents of the hopper from discharging into the firebox. This space between the two valves also performed two other functions. The first was that the space was made from bars, rather than solid plate, so that the heat of the firebox was attenuated before passing to the fuel hopper. This reduced the risk of igniting the fuel in the hopper. Secondly, a door was fitted in the space between the valves so that the operator could examine the fire if the bottom valve was open.

According to the patent, the fuel hopper made it easier to fire the engine, as the only action required of the operator was the periodic movement of the two fuel valve levers. No manual lifting of fuel was required, until the hopper required replenishing.

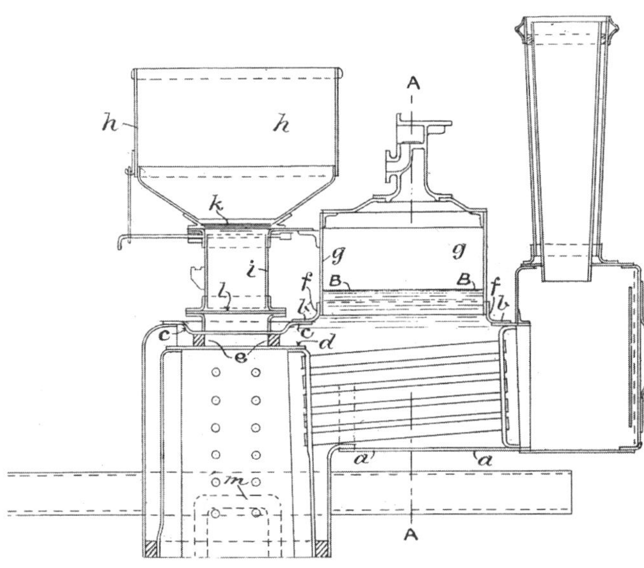

Figure 79: Patent Drawing, boiler with fuel hopper and extended dome

Two related patents were submitted on 24 June 1907. These cover a "D" shaped boiler with an enlarged steam dome, and hopper-fed fuel arrangement. Whilst the principle is admirable, this product was soon dropped from company catalogues. It is suspected that practical issues with firing and re-fuelling were the cause of its demise.

Figure 80: Fuel Hopper Wagon
This photograph of the hopper fed wagon illustrates the basis of this vehicle, i.e. the 2-ton undertype wagon, with the secondary springs under the load platform, however, the unique features are self evident, e.g. the fuel hopper and the large central steam dome. *(Mann Catalogue)*

The realisation of this hopper-fed engine was shown at Newcastle on the occasion of the 1908 Royal Show. The wagon was constructed to carry a load of 2 tons and to travel at eight miles per hour on metal tyres. With rubber tyres fitted, 12 miles per hour was possible.[43] The 1910 catalogue made the following observation, "Stoking with a shovel at these speeds is apt to occupy too much of the driver's attention, so to obviate this we dispense with hand firing altogether whilst the machine is travelling." [44] One of the practical advantages of the large steam dome was that it allowed easy man access for examination and de-scaling. This was possible because the upper portion of the dome was attached to the lower portion by screwed studs. The boiler was rated at 200 p.s.i. and the water tank provided 112 gallons of water. In keeping with their other engines of the period, the engine and transmission ran in an enclosed oil bath, no drive chains being employed. The engine was an undertype with a stroke of 6in., the low-pressure cylinder was $6^{3}/_{8}$in. diameter, and the high-pressure cylinder $3^{3}/_{4}$in. diameter.[45] A gunmetal water pump was installed, fitted with phosphor-bronze valves, additionally an injector was fitted for use when the engine was standing. Two road speeds were provided of 8 m.p.h. and $3^{1}/_{2}$ m.p.h. To reduce the vibration on the load platform, springs were fitted between the chassis and the platform, this was in addition to the main leaf springs on the axle, which were 4ft. long. The tare weight of the vehicle was 3 tons, and its overall dimensions were 15ft. 6in. long by 5ft. 6in. wide.

Despite the apparent benefits of the hopper-fed machine, it did not continue in production for a long time, which indicates that it was not popular with customers and therefore sold in small numbers. This may have been due to the cost premium of producing the extra-complicated boiler and hopper arrangement. There may also have been technical problems with the fuelling system, for example, the bottom fuel valve would have been subject to the intense heat of the firebox and would require frequent replacement to avoid leakage and reduced efficiency. Similarly, the upper fuel valve would be prone to jamming unless the fuel grade was carefully selected. Unfortunately this can only be conjecture, as there are no surviving examples of these wagons to allow an examination of these practical issues.

The journal *Commercial Motor* of 1907 describes a fascinating fire extinguishing machine that was produced for use in the port of Alexandria in Egypt. The machine was built for the Clayton Fire Extinguishing and Ventilating Co. Ltd. A standard Mann 2-ton wagon was used as the chassis and engine, whilst the extinguishing and disinfecting equipment was mounted at the rear of the vehicle. The machine generated sulphur dioxide, produced by burning sulphur in a chamber, and a steam driven blower circulated the gas through hoses. For extinguishing fires on ships, the gas was injected into the ship's hold and then returned back to the generator via a cooler. This continued for a period until the fire was starved of oxygen and thereby extinguished. Similarly, sulphur dioxide is widely used as a disinfectant, and therefore the same equipment was able to disinfect warehouses and ships' holds to exterminate rats and other vermin.[46] The fire extinguishing equipment was manufactured by Thwaites Brothers Ltd., of Bradford.[47]

Figure 81: Fire Extinguishing Wagon for Egypt
This machine, supplied in 1907, was based on a standard 2-ton chassis, and used for disinfecting and fire extinguishing at the port of Alexandria in Egypt. Note the rare use of Ackermann steering. *(David Riley – www.photoarchives.co.uk)*

The most popular of all the Mann vehicles was the 5-ton wagon, and in 1908 this was extensively remodelled. The major change was the use of a pair of rolled steel chassis members, a concept that was first introduced on the 2-ton wagon in 1905. Previous 5-ton wagons had used an integral boiler-chassis arrangement. On these older wagons the chassis was constructed as a box-section out of stout steel plates and these were riveted to the sides of the firebox to form a rigid construction. In the 1908 model the major components, i.e. engine, boiler, wheels and load platform were bolted to the chassis. This modular type of construction was easier to manage during manufacture, and also much simpler for the user in case of repair, as he could deal with smaller components. Another feature of the new wagon was the very short locomotive-type boiler. The construction of the boiler was in every sense conventional, however, the length from the back-plate to front tube plate was only 3ft. 4in. Consequently the furnace was larger in proportion than a conventional boiler. The primary objective of this was to avoid uncovering the tubes when ascending or descending an incline. With a long boiler this was more likely. The engine crankshaft and change-speed gears were enclosed in a steel casing and this was filled with lubricating oil. Of the engine arrangement the company reported that, "The compound-horizontal engine is placed rather low down, and it is quite possible to remove the top cover of the casing, in order to examine any of the parts, or to adjust the piston-rod, or valve-rod glands, without moving the load on the platform." [48] This wagon, as well as many other Mann vehicles, employed a very simple form of differential locking gear. A brake drum was keyed on to the extreme end of the driving axle, and encircling this was a brake band, anchored to the nearside driving wheel. To lock the differential gear, the brake band was drawn tight by means of a nut and bolt provided for the purpose. The new 5-ton wagon was first shown to the public at the Olympia Exhibition Hall, London, in March 1908.

Figure 82: New 5-ton Steam Wagon
The revised 5 ton wagon of 1908 was constructed with a rolled steel chassis, to which was bolted the major components, i.e. boiler, engine, wheels, and platform. This particular machine was delivered to Mr. T. D. Thomas, miller, of Castletownroche, near Cork, Ireland. *(David Riley – www.photoarchives.co.uk)*

Mann's new conventional 5-ton steam road tractor, a small, lightweight, traction engine, was exhibited on stand 53 at the 1908 Newcastle Royal Show. The tractor was particularly designed for road haulage and constructed to come within the Motor Car Acts. It was available with a single or compound engine and was geared from the crankshaft to the main axle by spur wheels on intermediate shafts. The single cylinder version was rated 10-12 h.p. and had a stroke of 9in. with a diameter of 5½in.[49] Mann's patent single eccentric valve motion was fitted. The boiler had a heating surface of 74 square feet and a grate area of 3.08 square feet. Cornock patent, spring-loaded grease lubricators were fitted to the bearings. The transmission was described as a four-shaft type, and the built-in flexibility allowed the road wheels to displace with ease when travelling over rough roads, (see description overleaf). The overall length of the tractor was 13ft. 3in. and the width 6ft. 3in. The main road wheels were 4ft. 9in. diameter by 9in. wide, whilst the front wheels were 3ft. diameter by 5in. wide.[50]

Figure 83: Mann 5-ton Road Tractor
This superb photograph is taken at the 1920 Royal Show, held in Darlington. The tractor is Mann number 1376, sold to Lunesdale Rural District Council, Lancashire. The vehicle in the background is a patching roller, believed to be Mann number 1431, sold to North Yorkshire County Council. *(David Riley – www.photoarchives.co.uk)*

The Mann 5-ton road tractor was exhibited again, at the Gloucester Royal Show of 1909. This lightweight conventional traction engine had a compound engine with a low-pressure cylinder of 6¾in. diameter, and a high-pressure cylinder of 4in. diameter, the stroke being 8in.[51] The compound tractor, however, was a major departure from previous Mann machines, in that the engine was fitted with link valve motion. A lever was provided close to the driver's platform for locking the differential gear, if the road was slippery. The transmission was described as a four-shaft type. The axle springs allowed a vertical movement of 1¼in. and to keep the main axle and intermediate shaft equidistant, the bearings of these two shafts were tied together on the offside, by a rigid link. The nearside intermediate shaft bearing was pivoted to allow for the angular movement. This allowed the main axle to rise and fall when travelling over bumps in the road but still maintained the gears in constant mesh.[52] The journal *Commercial Motor* was very enthusiastic, as the follow extract illustrates: "Although the first of its type, it has the appearance of being particularly well thought out, and its arrangement is as clean and compact as it well could be.....The clean design of this machine is sure to commend it to a large number of users; there are no steam fittings placed in awkward positions or where they are likely to be damaged by the driver while firing up, or when handling the machine in difficult places. All the usual and necessary engine and boiler mountings are provided, but these are conveniently placed, and out of harm's way." [53] Another feature observed by the publication *Engineering* was a drain-box or steam-trap on the exhaust from the engine. This drained off much of the moisture in the exhaust steam, which consequently required less superheating to render it invisible on discharge from the chimney.[54] The price quoted for the Road Tractor in the Show Catalogue was £400.[55]

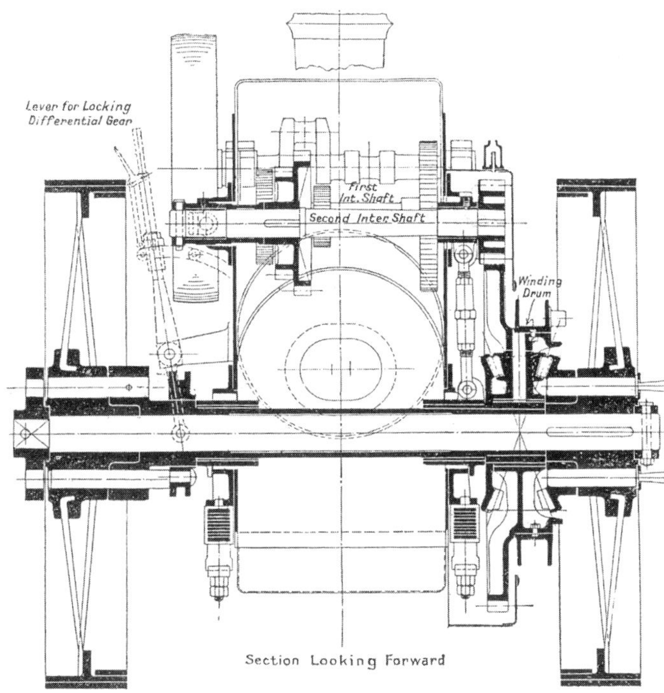

Figure 84: Line drawing of Mann 4-shaft Tractor
This superb drawing illustrates the way in which the driving gear was kept in mesh even when travelling over bumpy ground. The key element was the link between the two intermediate shafts. This can be seen on the right of this view. *(The Engineer)*

Using the steam cart as a basis, Mann's produced in 1908 a small road roller designed for road repair, as opposed to road construction. In consequence it was termed a patching roller. The first Mann patching roller was engine number 497, built to an order placed by Cheltenham Corporation in 1908, and this was illustrated in the journal *Commercial Motor* of that year.[56] According to W. P. Riley, these were sometimes referred to as "Pickering" rollers after Mr Pickering, the Cheltenham Borough Engineer, who had originally conceived the idea.[57] In the following year, this very practical roller made its first show appearance at the 1909 Royal Show. As previously mentioned, the machine was based on the standard Mann Steam Cart, however the wide rear roller did not allow the usual spur geared drive, and so it was fitted with roller chain drive from the intermediate shaft to the main axle. This was Mann's first use of roller chain drive in one of their road vehicles. A water ballast tank was fitted over the rear roller to serve two purposes. In the first place it allowed the weight of the roller to be adjusted for the road conditions, and secondly it provided a source of water for rolling hot macadam. The vehicle was sufficiently powerful to haul a trailer to carry road construction materials. The report also indicated that a smaller machine was available: "Some of our readers may be pleased to hear that the company also make a still smaller machine for rolling drives and paths, which should be particularly handy for park and estate purposes." [58]

It is interesting to note the similarities of the patching roller with the Parmiter Cart produced by Mann and Charlesworth in 1897. Whilst Parmiter's original vehicle was intended as an agricultural machine, his second patent of 1898 (number14,739) does refer to its use as a road roller, "When the locomotive is being used as a road roller, cylinder segments may be applied to the surface of the roller for making the same smooth or plain throughout. I advantageously arrange in connection with the water tank under the foot plate a water sprayer or distributor, which is adapted to deliver the water upon the road just in front of the main wheel."

At the 1911 Royal Show the light steam roller was again displayed and the press gave further details. The machine had a maximum rating of 8 tons when charged with ballast and a full tank.[59] The exhibition machine was built for use in Shanghai, China, but similar machines had been constructed for British customers. The vehicle was provided with an interchangeable body so that a variety of duties could be performed, e.g. patching or rolling tarmacadam roads,

Figure 85: Patching Roller
The Mann patching roller made its first show appearance at the 1909 Royal Show. This machine was based on the standard Steam Cart, however the wide rear roller did not allow the usual spur geared drive, and so it was fitted with a roller-chain drive. This view is of Mann number 623. *(John Middlemiss collection)*

street watering and haulage of road materials. The bulk of the weight was over the rear rollers, however as these were twice the width of the front rollers there was an equal distribution of weight over all four rollers. A tar tank, heated from the boiler, could also be fitted. When the vehicle was fitted with a trailer full of road metal, the unit was self-sufficient for patching damaged roads. The price quoted in the 1912 Show Catalogue for the Patching Roller was £475.[60]

Figure 86: Cheltenham Corporation Patching Roller
The first Mann patching roller was engine number 497, built in 1908 to the ideas of Mr Pickering, the Cheltenham Borough Engineer. Subsequently these machines were sometimes referred to as 'Pickering' rollers. *(Mann Catalogue)*

Undertype – Overtype Engine Arrangement

The use of the overtype or undertype engine arrangement was not a clear-cut choice for the user, as each had its advantages and disadvantages. The undertype engine was generally linked directly to the axle by means of spur gears. This was because the engine was located close to the back wheels and therefore it was relatively easy to connect the two in this way. Unfortunately, the closeness to the road allowed dust and dirt to accumulate on the wearing surfaces, which were coated with oil and grease. This combination provided an abrasive agent that was obviously detrimental to the moving surfaces of the engine and transmission. To avoid this problem, many designers opted for a fully enclosed and lubricated transmission system. This had the benefit of reducing wear, if the oil was topped up and replaced periodically. The disadvantage of this arrangement can be summed up by the phrase "out of sight, out of mind" i.e. because the engine was low down behind the driver, it was often neglected, unless a strict discipline of inspection was enforced. In addition, if something started to go wrong, perhaps indicated by a knocking sound, this could go unnoticed amongst all the other noises that are produced by a steel-wheeled wagon. Another disadvantage of the undertype engine was the losses caused by the remoteness from the boiler. These losses came from a variety of sources: firstly, the long length of pipe leading to the cylinder allowed heat to be lost from the steam so that its energy was reduced by the time it entered the cylinder; secondly, the passage of steam along a pipe creates friction within the pipe and results in reduced pressure at the cylinder, sometimes referred to as throttling loss. A further problem is the losses in the exhaust pipe taking the spent steam away from the cylinder. The losses in this pipe create back pressure in the cylinder, which reduces the force produced by the piston and thereby lowers the effective power of the engine.

With an overtype engine, mounted on top of the boiler, the power transmission to the wheels could be direct through spur gears to the wheels, if the wheelbase was not too long. Alternatively, a roller-chain was employed between the engine and axle, particularly for longer vehicles. The disadvantages of the chain drive were firstly that the chain was very heavy and added to the dead weight of the wagon, thereby reducing the effective load capacity. The second disadvantage of chain drive is that if the chain failed, the drive was completely lost, and hence engine braking was also lost. On many wagons, the engine was used as one of the primary brakes, and loss of this on a hill could be dangerous. Whichever type of transmission was employed, the overtype engine had the advantage of being very close to the driver's senses. This made him very aware of the sounds and vibrations that normally accompanied the engine. An unusual noise or vibration was an early warning that something was amiss and required attention before a more serious problem developed. The closeness of the engine to the driver allowed him to inspect, clean and lubricate the engine with ease. This was not always the case with undertype engines. Finally, the closeness of the cylinder to the boiler allowed minimal losses in transferring steam into the cylinder, always assuming that the port sizes were not restrictive. Thus the problems described previously with the undertype, i.e. losses caused by long pipe lengths, did not occur with the overtype. Conversely, in the overtype arrangement, the remoteness of the engine from the driving wheels gives rise to its own losses. To provide the transmission of power from the engine to the axle requires more components than is necessary with the close coupled undertype. These components consist of either a roller chain or additional intermediate gears. For each gear, its shaft will run in bearings and these will have friction that absorbs energy, thereby reducing the efficiency. Similarly, every interaction of gear tooth sliding on gear tooth, or chain link on chain wheel introduces yet more friction and hence losses. As stated at the outset, the use of the overtype or undertype engine arrangement was not a clear-cut choice for the user, and ultimately it was a matter of personal preference.

The original Mann vehicles used both undertype and overtype engine arrangements. The Steam Cart, introduced in 1898, was of the overtype layout with spur gear transmission. The Steam Lorry, introduced in 1899, used the undertype layout with spur gear drive to the axle. For the next decade, these two systems were used consistently, however, by 1908, James Mann was sufficiently confident with roller-chain drives to use them in the patching roller, followed in 1910 by the direct ploughing tractor. By 1911 overtype wagons were produced with roller-chain drives, and thus Mann's were able to offer both overtype and undertype wagons in their range of vehicles. Conversely, the short wheelbase Steam Cart, designed for rough usage, remained as an overtype with spur gear transmission, and was never produced with roller-chain drive.

Figure 87: Advertising Material, 1907
This advert illustrates the Tipping Steam Cart and includes a reference from the brewers Wm. Hancock, Cardiff. There must have been a good relationship with this company as they are often featured in promotional material. *(Commercial Motor)*

Reporting on the 1911 Royal Show, the journal *Commercial Motor* wrote, "It will be interesting to note that the steam wagons are of Mann's latest pattern, with overtype engines and chain drive to the live back axle – a striking departure from the practice to which this company has adhered for so many years." [61]

In the 1911 catalogue, Mann's made the following statement: "We have always made both patterns, although for some time we confined the 'Overtype' to our Tipping Cart, as its short wheel-base allowed the power to be transmitted by spur wheels without chains. The quality of driving chains has, however, been so much improved of late that for a considerable time we have felt justified in using a chain to bridge the distance between the Intermediate Shaft and Main Axle, and give the necessary length of wheel base to permit the long platform required for the Wagon. We thus build both the 'Overtype' wagon or the 'Undertype' according to the preference of the purchaser." [62]

This ambiguity about the different engine arrangements was not simply a problem in the early days of steam wagons, which resolved itself as the product matured. In a paper entitled *Steam Wagons of Today*, read before the Institution of Automobile Engineers in 1925, Joseph Capel Cornock (Mann's Works Manager and Company Secretary) made the following statement: "The real reason that the undertype v. overtype controversy is still unsettled is that each type is superior to the other for its appropriate class of work, while there is an indefinite border line where these two classes of work meet and mingle and for which an almost equal case may be made out for both. Speaking broadly, both makers and users admit the superiority of the geared overtype wagon for work about tips, quarries, building sites, and work of a similar hard and strenuous character, and of the enclosed undertype for long-distance work requiring speed and comfort and its performance reckoned more in miles than in tons." [63]

Wavertree near Liverpool was the location for the 1910 Royal Show, and at this event Mann's Patent Steam Cart and Wagon Company exhibited their Direct Ploughing Tractor. This machine had the outward appearance of a steam cart, with the usual side location for the driver, however the rear wheels were placed between the frames.[64] Also, a large water tank was fitted over the wheels in place of the cart. The fore-carriage was mounted on springs, with steering provided using the normal Mann arrangement of gear and toothed sector. One of the very obvious visual features of this machine was the external winding drum on the rear axle, with the differential lock inside the drum. This same engine was tested exhaustively at the August tractor trials at Baldock organised by the R.A.S.E.

Figure 88: Mann's 20 b.h.p. Direct Ploughing Tractor This machine had the outward appearance of a steam cart, but the large rear rollers and the associated external winding drum identify the direct ploughing tractor. The friction band for the differential lock is fitted inside the winding drum. *(The Implement and Machinery Review)*

Baldock Trials

The 1910 Royal Agricultural Society's tractor trials at Manor Farm, Bygrave, Baldock, Hertfordshire were covered extensively in the journal *The Engineer*. Six engines were tested; comprising three powered by steam and three using internal combustion engines. Mann's Patent Steam Cart and Wagon Company entered their new tractor for direct ploughing.

This machine was based on their steam cart but included a number of detail differences. Power was provided by a compound horizontal engine mounted on the top of the boiler, having cylinders 4in. and 7in. diameter by 7in. stroke. The reversing gear was Mann's patent single eccentric type. As previously mentioned, the chief innovation consisted of having the two back wheels inside the frame, instead of outside, and so bringing the track inside that of the two front wheels. The front wheels were 25in. diameter by 7in. wide, and were steered in usual Mann style with worm and quadrant. The back wheels, or perhaps more accurately back rollers, were each 4ft. diameter, 21in. wide, and between them carried about two-thirds of the total weight. The advantage claimed for this arrangement was that the weight of the engine was distributed over a greater area of ground and that the hind wheels did not travel over land that had already been run over by the front wheels. The staff at the journal were not wholly convinced and commentated, "It appears, however, to tend to reduce the stability of the machine on rough ground."[65] The boiler had a heating surface of approximately 60 square feet and a working pressure of 200 p.s.i. Sufficient coal and water could be carried for half a day's work, the water capacity being 200 gallons. Two road speeds were fitted of 5 m.p.h. and 2½ m.p.h., and like the patching roller, power was transmitted to the back wheels by means of a Hans Renold roller chain. An external winding drum was fitted to the main axle, and this was supported on leaf springs and located by radius rods. A flywheel for driving auxiliary machinery was fitted. The whole machine weighed 4¾ tons, and was sold for £400.[66]

The trials consisted of three tests, a road test, a brake test and a ploughing test. The road test was carried out over a 12-mile route with a mixture of gradients and road types. The fuel and water consumption were recorded as well as the time to complete the course. In the brake test, the engines were set up as though driving a threshing machine, although in fact the machine was a dynamometer. Finally, each engine was given the task of ploughing five acres of land. The time taken, along with the fuel and water consumption were recorded. Whilst the Mann engine performed well, it was no match for the McLaren engine, which was judged the overall winner and presented with the Show's Gold Medal.

Baldock Trials, Summary Table [67]

Name	Type	H.P.	Motive Power	Price £	Weight ton	cwt	qrs	Cost to plough one acre (shillings) *
J. & H. McLaren, Leeds	2 cylinder compound	40	Steam	530	4	19	3	3.11
Wallis and Steevens, Basingstoke	2 cylinder compound	32	Steam	410	4	19	0	3.66
Mann's Steam Cart & Wagon Co., Leeds	2 cylinder compound	20	Steam	400	4	15	0	4.03
Ivel Agricultural Motors Ltd., London	2 horizontal cylinders	18	Paraffin	275	1	13	0	4.47
Saunderson & Gifken, Bedford	2 vertical cylinders	25	Paraffin	360	3	5	0	7.02
Saunderson & Gifken, Bedford	2 vertical cylinders	45	Paraffin	450	4	15	0	7.45

* These figures include fuel, lubricating oil, motor drivers, ploughman's and boys' wages, and water, but do not include capital charges, maintenance or depreciation. They are arrived at by taking coal at 30s per ton, paraffin at 8 1/4d. per gallon, petrol for starting up at 1s. 3d. per gallon, water at 1s. per 100 gallons, and drivers' wages at 35s. per week

Overtype Steam Wagon

Overtype steam wagons (as opposed to the steam cart) were first produced by Mann's in 1911 and first shown at the Norwich Royal Show of that year, with the 5-ton model being sold to Lipton's, Ltd.[68] The 3-ton steam wagon with solid rubber tyres was described as a high-speed model and this was also shown at the Royal Show in June 1911.[69] The engine was an overtype horizontal compound type with cylinders of 3¾in. and 6⅜in. by 6in. stroke, operating at a working pressure of 200 p.s.i. The engine components used modern steel technology to provide increased strength and keep the weight down. The crankshaft and eccentrics were formed from one solid forging, and were made from 3 per cent heat-treated chrome nickel steel. The intermediate shafts and the quick running gears were also made from nickel steel. Other parts used conventional steels; the pistons, crosshead and piston-rods were steel forgings, whilst the main driving gear carrying the differential was a machine

Figure 89: Three-Ton Steam Wagon
This type of vehicle was the first Mann road wagon to use roller-chains for the final drive. This technique was used on the Patching Roller and the Direct Ploughing Tractor but not previously on a wagon. This particular machine was owned by Walthamstow District Council and was Mann number 614, built in 1912. (*John Middlemiss collection*)

cut crucible steel casting. The final drive was taken through a 2½in. roller pitch chain. Three road speeds were provided; for rubber tyred vehicles these were 12, 8, and 2.5 miles per hour, whilst for steel tyred wheels these were reduced to 8, 5, and 2.5 miles per hour. In the Royal Show catalogue this wagon was priced at £450, although in the following year, 1912, this had increased to £475.[70]

Agricultural Tractor

The Smithfield Show of both 1911 and 1912 featured the two types of agricultural tractors, and this provides a useful comparison between them.[71] One version had the rear wheels close together between the frames, whilst the other had the rear wheels outside the frames, but with closely spaced front wheels, as previously described. The advantages claimed for the former were that the weight of the engine was more evenly distributed over the ground and the last narrow strip between the 'lands' could be ploughed without the driving wheels travelling over the newly ploughed land. With outside wheels, the newly ploughed land was partly rolled by the driving wheels, which necessitated the last strip being ploughed by horses. The advantage of the outside wheel type was a slightly lighter engine for the same power, with more stability on very uneven ground. It was also a three-speed machine with an all-gear drive. The inside wheel engine was only a two-speed machine with a chain drive from the intermediate shaft to the main axle.

Figure 90: Mann Agricultural Tractor
The main visual feature of the Mann Agricultural Tractor was the large water tank above the rear wheels. This allowed the tractor to operate for extended periods but it could also be used to carry a load on top of the tank. When compared with figure 88, the wider spread of the wheels is evident. This tractor is Mann number 676 of 1912. *(The Engineer)*

The boiler and engine in both tractors were identical. The boiler was of the locomotive type operating at 200 p.s.i. The firebox was suitable for coal or coke, however a larger firebox could be provided for burning wood, if required. The engine was the compound type, developing 21 b.h.p., very similar to that fitted to the steam carts and wagons.[72] One of the identifying features of these agricultural tractors is the use of steering chains fixed to quadrants located on the outside of the front wheel axles. This contrasts with the conventional Mann direct steering using machine-cut worm and quadrant, mounted on the front axle perch bracket.

Prices quoted for Mann vehicles in 1914 [73]

Type	Load (ton)	I.H.P.	Drive	Price £
Wagon with rubber tyres	3	20	Chain	585
Wagon with steel tyres	5	30	Chain	555
Cart with steel tyres	5	30	Gear	550
Road tractor	5	30	Gear	475
Agricultural tractor	-	22	Gear	455

Despite the introduction of the wide range of vehicles, the short wheelbase steam cart continued to be sold in significant numbers. Catalogues published even in the 1920s continued to extol the merits of this useful machine. "The first motor vehicle which we made was a Steam Cart, and its special advantages for certain kinds of work still justify us in retaining it as a distinct design from our steam wagons, in spite of the fact that from a manufacturer's point of view it would reduce our cost of production to merge them into one"

The same catalogue goes on to explain why the steam cart retained some distinct advantages, particularly for rough applications. "The steam cart is the mechanical equivalent of a horse-drawn cart, and for hauling road metal, bricks, sand etc., and for rough contractor's work, possesses just the same advantages over a steam wagon as a horse-drawn cart does over a dray for these purposes. Its outstanding points are its larger and wider wheels for travelling over rough ground, its short wheelbase, which enables it to get into confined spaces, and its general compactness and strength." [74]

Figure 91: Steam Cart with Stone Breaker
In this view the steam cart is operating auxiliary machinery by a flat leather belt from the flywheel. The device is a Blake stone breaker, made by H. R. Marsden, Soho Foundry, Meadow Lane, Leeds. *(Henry Roskilly collection)*

Furthermore, the steam cart was a very versatile machine, which could haul a trailer to increase the payload, but could also be fitted with other attachments to further increase its usefulness. "When required, it can be fitted with governors, and from the flywheel will drive a threshing machine, saw bench, stone breaker, mortar mill etc. It can also be fitted with a winding drum and steel wire rope, and when thus equipped forms a unique machine for estate or contractor's work." Another adaptation of the steam cart was the attachment of a front road roller. This was not a permanent modification but a conversion that could be added to the standard machine when required. To achieve this, a heavy-section curved angle-iron was riveted to the top outer surface of the smokebox. When required, the normal front wheels were removed and the forecarriage-top, a heavy casting that carried the front fork and roller, was bolted to the curved angle-iron on the smokebox. The steering mechanism used chains that attached from the sides of the new roller fork to the original front axle, which remained in position. Thus when the steering wheel was rotated, the normal worm and quadrant turned the original front axle and this in turn pulled on the chain to turn the roller. Of this adaptation the company stated, "This Combined Cart and Roller will be found most useful and economical for carting stones on to the roadsides in summer, and rolling them in during winter. We strongly recommend it to District Councils, Estate Owners, Contractors, etc." [75]

Figure 92: Steam Cart Convertible Roller
One of the options available with the steam cart was a convertible roller. This was particularly targeted at small local councils where perhaps a dedicated roller would not be fully utilised. This is Mann number 805 built in 1913. *(John Middlemiss collection)*

Trailers

To accompany their range of steam vehicles, Mann's Patent Steam Cart and Wagon Company also produced in their own works a full range of trailers. From the outset, a separate joiner's shop was included at the Pepper Road Works. Here high quality wagon bodies were constructed as well as the separate trailers. The following extract from Catalogue C gives some indication of the construction of wagon bodies: "The fixed platform is carried direct on the main girders and constructed of heavy, thick, tongued and grooved floor boards reinforced at the sides by substantial oak rails with rolled steel coping irons. Solid board sides, and backgate are fitted, hinged at the bottom, and easily detachable." [76] The range of trailers included simple flat-topped trailers for products in bales or casks, as well as the more complicated end tipping and side tipping trailers for loose materials such as stone, coal, sand etc. The mechanism for the tipping trailers included steel rails on the main frame and grooved rollers on the body. The body was moved along the rails by a drum, worked by a hand-operated ratchet lever. When the body moved beyond its centre of gravity, its weight made it tip automatically, throwing the load well clear of the road wheels.[77] Trailers were built to accommodate 2, 3, and 5-ton loads. A three-ton trailer was exhibited at the 1916 Manchester Royal Show, and the show catalogue gives it a price of £65.[78]

Another variation of the trailer, manufactured by Mann's, was a 4-wheeled living van. The journal *Motor Traction* describes such a van built for the Aitken Tar Roads Syndicate of Glasgow in 1908.[79] The men employed by this firm were often working away from home constructing roads, and had difficulty finding suitable lodgings. The van was fitted with two bunks, lockers and a small cooking range, while at the other end, a bench and vice, together with other lockers, a table and chair were placed.

A Mann flat trailer was examined by John Middlemiss in January 1962, and comprehensive measurements were taken. The trailer was located at Brinkburn Priory Sawmill, Longframlington, Near Morpeth, Northumberland.[80] The following are the salient details:

Length	12ft. 1in.
Width	6ft. 0in.
Wheelbase	7ft. 2in.
Distance between inner wheel faces	4ft. 9in.
Front wheel diameter	36in.
Rear wheel diameter	40in.
Width of metal tyres	4.5in.
Front springs	10 off, 2.5in. wide
Rear springs	12 off, 2.5in. wide
Front axles	5.5in. wide and 5in. deep
Rear axles	5in. wide and 6in. deep

Figure 93: Mann's Flat Trailer
Mann's produced their own range of flat trailers from their well-equipped workshop in Pepper Road. These allowed a wagon to increase its payload at little extra cost. *(Mann Catalogue)*

Figure 94: Mann's Side Tipping Trailer
For products such as coal, stone, and sand etc. the tipping trailer was an ideal carrier as it allowed the goods to be quickly removed at the destination. *(Mann Catalogue)*

Figure 95: Mann Flat Trailer, Brinkburn Priory Sawmill
This is a rare photograph of a Mann trailer, long out of use, but nevertheless in good condition. The photograph was taken in January 1962. *(John Middlemiss)*

References

1 *Engineering*, 22 June 1900, p812
2 *Scientific American*, 8 September 1900, p148
3 *Bradford Daily Telegraph*, 10 January 1900, p3
4 *Bradford Daily Telegraph*, 15 January 1900, p4
5 *British Patent* 21,085, 1900
6 *Engineering*, 31 May 1901, p699
7 *Commercial Motor*, 10 June 1924, p519
8 Judges' Report on the Third Liverpool Trials, p165
9 *The Engineer*, 31 May 1901, p574
10 Royal Agricultural Society of England, *Catalogue*, Cardiff Show 1901
11 *The Automotor Journal*, 25 July 1903, p775
12 *The Engineer*, 29 May 1903, p539
13 *Commercial Motor*, 24 June 1909, p328A
14 *The Automotor Journal*, 25 July 1903, p774
15 *The Engineer*, 3 July 1903, p16
16 *British Patent 584*, 1904
17 Mann's Patent Steam Cart and Wagon Company, *Catalogue* B, p12
18 *Commercial Motor*, 22 June 1905, p299
19 Royal Agricultural Society of England, *Catalogue*, Park Royal Show 1905, p28
20 *British Patent 1347*, 1905
21 *Commercial Motor*, 28 September 1905, p41
22 Royal Agricultural Society of England, *Catalogue*, Derby Show 1906, p101
23 Mann's Patent Steam Cart and Wagon Company, *Catalogue A*, p56
24 *The Engineer*, 24 March 1905, p289
25 Norris, William, *Modern Steam Road Wagons*, Longmans, Green and Co., 1906, p96
26 *Commercial Motor*, 29 March 1906, p63
27 *Commercial Motor*, 25 October 1906, p156
28 *Commercial Motor*, 23 August 1906, p517
29 *The Implement and Machinery Review*, 1 September 1916, p538
30 *The Engineer*, 14 July 1905, p42
31 *Commercial Motor*, 28 September 1905, p40
32 *British Patent* 742, 1906
33 *The Engineer*, 6 July 1906, p17
34 *Engineering*, 6 July 1906, p7
35 *Engineering*, 28 June 1907, p860
36 *Commercial Motor*, 7 March 1907, p611
37 *Engineering*, 28 June 1907, p860
38 Royal Agricultural Society of England, *Catalogue*, Gloucester Show 1909, p151
39 *The Engineer*, 5 July 1907, p17
40 *Engineering*, 28 June 1907, p860
41 *Engineering*, 5 July 1907, p22
42 *Commercial Motor*, 21 November 1907, p267
43 *The Implement and Machinery Review*, 1 July 1908, p360
44 Mann's Patent Steam Cart and Wagon Company, *Catalogue*, 1910, p40
45 *The Engineer*, 5 June 1908, p592
46 *Commercial Motor*, 21 November 1907, p267
47 *Motor Traction*, 5 December 1908, p509
48 *Commercial Motor*, 26 March 1908, p74

49 *Commercial Motor*, 2 July 1908, p433
50 *The Implement and Machinery Review*, 1 August 1908, p508
51 *The Engineer,* 25 June 1909, p655
52 *The Engineer,* 11 February 1910, p153
53 *Commercial Motor*, 2 July 1908, p434
54 *Engineering*, 25 June 1909, p852
55 Royal Agricultural Society of England, *Catalogue*, Gloucester Show 1909, p151
56 *Commercial Motor*, 3 December 1908, p258
57 Riley, W. P., *Portfolio number 27*, Road Locomotive Society, 1955
58 *The Implement and Machinery Review*, 1 June 1909, p205
59 *The Engineer,* 7 July 1911, p26
60 Royal Agricultural Society of England, *Catalogue*, Doncaster Show 1912, p168
61 *Commercial Motor*, 22 June 1911, p326
62 Mann's Patent Steam Cart and Wagon Company, *Catalogue*, 1911, p10
63 *The World's Carriers*, 15 May 1925, p248
64 *The Engineer,* 24 June 1910, p636
65 *Engineering*, 12 August 1910, p234
66 *The Engineer,* 19 August 1910, p193
67 *The Engineer*, 30 December 1910, p704
68 *Commercial Motor*, 29 June 1911, p364
69 *The Engineer,* 9 June 1911, p604
70 Royal Agricultural Society of England, *Catalogue*, Liverpool Show 1910, p168
71 *The Engineer,* 8 December 1911, p594
72 *Engineering*, 8 December 1911, p772
73 *Commercial Motor*, January 1914, p8 (supplement)
74 Mann's Patent Steam Cart and Wagon Company, *Catalogue B*, p34
75 Mann's Patent Steam Cart and Wagon Company, *Catalogue*, 1911, p45
76 Mann's Patent Steam Cart and Wagon Company, *Catalogue C*, p55
77 *Motor Traction*, 19 December 1908, p546
78 Royal Agricultural Society of England, *Catalogue*, Manchester Show 1916
79 *Motor Traction*, 15 August 1908, p163
80 *Portfolio number 27,* Road Locomotive Society

Chapter 5

Mann's Patent Steam Cart and Wagon Products, 1914–1918

In the years leading up to the outbreak of the First World War, the British government offered subsidies to purchasers of petrol-engined motor lorries in anticipation of the forthcoming conflict. The understanding was that the vehicles would be made available to the Army in the event of war. The details were announced in August 1912, and covered two classes of vehicle, those capable of carrying a useful load of 1½ tons, and those capable of carrying a useful load of 3 tons. To qualify for the subsidy the lorry had to meet a specification set by the War Office, and in addition, the vehicle had to undertake a trial of not more that 80 miles in a satisfactory manner.[1]

From the date of acceptance, each lorry was subsidised for a period of three years. The subsidy consisted of a purchase premium of £50 paid half yearly over the three year period, and an annual grant of £20, paid in half yearly instalments, i.e. totalling £110 over the three years. In addition, a rather curious stipulation provided a further £10 if the vehicle had "a body of the approved type for the carriage of meat slung from the roof". This provided a grand total of £120 over the three years of the subsidy.

Initial qualification was not the only requirement for the subsidy. The owner was also obliged to comply with the following long term stipulations regarding the lorry:

- It must remain the property of the owner
- It must be kept in the United Kingdom
- It must be certified by an inspecting officer of the War Department to be in a thoroughly serviceable condition and satisfactory state of repair
- It must be inspected every 6 months and the inspecting officer may go out in it on a run of approximately 25 miles when the lorry is fully loaded
- It may be purchased outright by the War Office if so desired
- It must be kept in a suitable covered-in building where protection from frost will be properly ensured
- It must at all times be driven by a properly qualified driver

These incentives to purchasers of petrol-engined lorries would have long term consequences for the steam wagon industry, however in the short term it was a time of full orders at the Pepper Road Works.

The first ten or so years of evolution of the Mann wagon gave rise to two standard vehicles that would continue in production until the mid-1920s. These were the 3-ton and 5-ton wagons, and they provided the bulk of activity at the Pepper Road Works. The standard specification for these wagons was as follows:

Capacity	5-ton	3-ton
Horsepower	35	30
Cylinder bore	4in. & 6¾in.	3¾in. & 6⅜in.
Stroke	8in.	6in.
Wheelbase	12ft. 5in.	11ft. 8½in
Tyres front	850 x 160 mm	850 x 140 mm
Tyres rear	1070 x 160 mm	1030 x 140 mm

Both machines shared many common construction features. The frame was constructed of a rolled steel channel to which was attached the front axle made from a steel forging. The live rear axle was also a steel forging with suspension being achieved by semi-elliptical springs. The transmission consisted of a four-shaft arrangement using machined gears and these drove the main roller chain to the rear axle. The driver's position remained on the side of the vehicle, as was common to most of the Mann vehicles. Braking was provided by quick acting foot brake on the wheel brake drums, in addition, a screw brake was provided for parking. Reverse gear could also be used to retard the vehicle. Steering was again provided in typical Mann fashion, by direct worm and quadrant. Whilst these two vehicles were the standard products at Pepper Road, the body applied to this basic vehicle was extremely varied. Some of these variations were:

- Articulated 6-wheeler
- Brewer's wagon
- Bus bodied wagon
- Canvas covered wagon
- Cold storage box van
- Compartment wagon for collieries
- Flat back wagon
- Flour miller's wagon
- Gully cleaning wagon
- Market gardener's wagon
- Municipal dustcart
- Pantechnicon for removals
- Street watering wagon
- Tar spraying wagon
- Three-deck mineral water wagon
- Tipping wagon (side and rear tipping)

Figure 96: Mann Side-tipping Wagon
Quarries, mines and civil contractors used side-tipping wagons where rock or aggregate needed tipping alongside the vehicle, for example, in road widening. *(Mann Catalogue)*

Figure 97: Mann Cold Storage Box Van
The cold storage wagon was built in small numbers for transporting goods that required to be kept cool. Before the widespread availability of refrigeration, specialist companies could provide ice that was delivered in this type of vehicle. *(Mann Catalogue)*

Figure 98: Mann Flour-miller's Wagon
This shiny new 5-ton wagon was supplied in 1908 to Whitworth Brothers, flour millers of Victoria Mills, Wellingborough, and was reported to be their 6th Mann wagon. The enclosed undertype engine is plain to see. *(David Riley – www.photoarchives.co.uk)*

Low Cost Steam Tractor

A low cost steam tractor was introduced in 1915 to provide a machine that was available to a wider range of customers than their traditional product. It was claimed that this was achieved, not by reducing the quality, but by reducing the number of working parts to a minimum, for example, no winding drum or injector was fitted. Overall the weight of the tractor was reduced by approximately half a ton when compared with the compound machine. The low cost tractor had a single cylinder, 5in. diameter by 8in. stroke and fitted with link motion reversing gear.[2] The flywheel was fitted on the left-hand side of the tractor, and to allow the driver to swing the flywheel from the right-hand driving position, barring gear was provided. This was necessary with a single-cylinder engine as there are 'dead spots' at the extremes of the piston stroke. Barring was achieved by spinning a hand wheel adjacent to the driver. This turned a shaft to which was attached a spur-gear. This gear engaged with teeth cast on the inside rim of the flywheel, and hence the flywheel was turned. A spring was provided to throw the gear out of mesh when the engine commenced running. The boiler was of the locomotive type with a working pressure of 150 p.s.i., and provided with 57.5 square foot of heating surface. The crankshaft was 2¼in. diameter and this drove through a series of gears onto the differential and hence to the main axle. No roller pitch chains were used. The road wheels were 4ft. 3in. diameter by 1ft. 6in. wide. Two road speeds were provided of 5 miles per hour and 2.5 miles per hour. The front wheels were 3ft. diameter by 8in. wide and were steered by chain links. A 150-gallon water tank was attached above the driving wheels and on top of this was a platform with detachable side and end boards, to carry a load up to 2 tons. The engine was provided with brake, pump, water lifter and governor. The company undertook some trials of the tractor and it was able to plough two and one-fifth of an acre in two hours, using just over two hundredweight of ordinary Yorkshire coal. The plough was a four-furrow device, and the land was fairly strong stubble and not level. It was claimed that the engine would pull a four-furrow plough in strong land, or two self-binders, or loads of five to six tons on the road. Similarly, from the flywheel, sufficient power was available to drive a 4ft. 6in. threshing machine with chaff cutter or straw elevator.

Figure 99: Low Cost Agricultural Tractor
This single cylinder steam tractor was introduced in 1915. The machine was made very simple, to make it more affordable, thereby assisting to increase food production during the First World War. *(Henry Roskilly collection)*

The Smithfield Show of 1915 had on display the Mann's Patent Steam Cart and Wagon Company's compound-engined tractor. This was rated 25 b.h.p. and was said to be specially designed for farm and estate work.[3] It was capable of hauling a five-furrow plough in good land or a four-furrow plough on heavy land when ploughing 7in. deep. Coal consumption was reported to be around 1 cwt. per acre of ground ploughed. The cylinders were 4in. and 6 $^{3}/_{8}$in. diameter by 7in. stroke, and the associated valves were actuated by the Mann patent reversing gear. The steel boiler was rated at 200 p.s.i., and a 200-gallon water tank was fitted above the rear wheels to replenish the boiler. Volute springs supported the front wheels, these being 2ft. 11in. diameter by 8in. width. The driving wheels were 4ft. 3in. diameter by 1ft. 8in. width, and the front wheels were 2ft. 11in. diameter by 8in. wide. Three-speed gearing was provided with a top speed of 5 miles per hour.[4] In a later article by the journal *The Engineer*, it was reported that the speed range of the gears was 2 miles per hour to 6 miles per hour.[5] The three speeds were selected from a single lever, such that it was impossible for more than one set of wheels to be in gear at the same time. The slow speed was for ploughing and the high speed for road use. A lever was provided on the footplate to lock the differential compensating gear when travelling on soft ground, for example, when ploughing. The tractor was intended to be an 'all rounder' for driving, threshing, grinding, chopping, pulping, and other barn machinery, as well as saw benches, stone breakers; hauling ploughs, cultivators, self-binders and reapers, farm

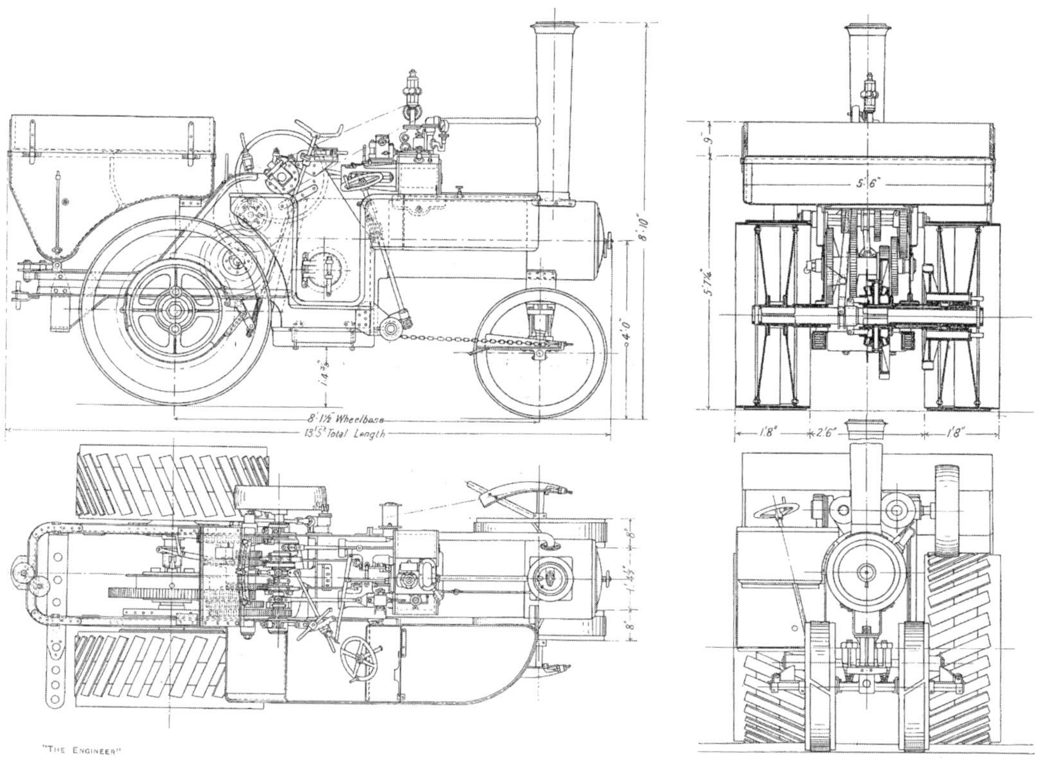

Figure 100: Line Drawing of Compound Tractor
The low-cost agricultural steam tractor was introduced in 1915. This drawing illustrates the compound version. The obvious differences include the narrow track of the front wheels and the chain steering. *(The Engineer)*

wagons, manure wagons, and road work such as delivering corn or produce to the market or railway station. The firebox was intended for burning coal or coke but a larger firebox could be fitted for burning wood. The fuel bunker had a capacity of 6¼ cubic feet. For driving threshing machines and the like, the governor was set to run the 2ft. 3in. diameter flywheel at 300 r.p.m. Steering was traction engine style, with chains connected to the extreme ends of the front axle and actuated by a worm and wheel. For braking, a hand-wheel operated band brake on the axle was provided. By removing the driving pins on the right hand side road wheel, a winding drum could be used for hauling logs, for example, or extricating the tractor from a difficult situation. The overall length of the tractor was 13ft. 5in. on a wheelbase of 8ft. 1½in. The width was a narrow 5ft. 10in. One observer commented about this tractor, "An obvious advantage with tractors of this type is that their working is extremely simple, and can be easily understood by any farm hand who has been used to driving traction engines or portable engines." [6]

The Highland and Agricultural Society Trials, 1915

The Highland and Agricultural Society held trials of motor tillage implements at King's Park Farm, Stirling, commencing Tuesday, 5 October 1915.[7] Prizes were not offered, but the society paid the carriage and carting expenses of the implements to and from the trial. The society also provided the necessary fuel and lubricating oils. The official observers appointed by the society were: Mr John Edmond of Gallamuir, Bannockburn; Mr James Kidd, Main of Errol; Mr James Walls, Muirton, Stirling; and Professor Stanfield, the Society's Consulting Engineer. Five machines were entered:

International Harvester Co., London	Mogul Oil Tractor	£265
Mann's Patent Steam Cart & Wagon Co., Leeds	25 h.p. Steam Tractor	£465
Mills & Sons Ltd., London	Sandusky 40-45 h.p. Petrol Tractor	£557 10s
Overtime Farm Tractor Co., London	Overtime 24 b.h.p. Paraffin Tractor	£231
Wyles Motor Ploughs, Manchester,	11 b.h.p. Motor Plough	£172 10s

The trial contained four stages, ploughing heavy land, ploughing light land, threshing using a 4ft. 6in. Burrell implement, and finally a road haulage test. The judge's conclusion about the Mann tractor was very positive:

> "This tractor is well designed, and of strong construction; the depreciation of a motor of this type should be very small. It is suitable for all kinds of stationary, field, and road work, and is very simple to manage; it is mounted on springs, to come under the Motor Car acts. On the light land the work done did not show to advantage. On the carse (sic) land, however, on the afternoon of the second day, the work done was very satisfactory. The plough used was a four-furrow one, and the work was accomplished very rapidly and without a hitch. This tractor drove the thrashing-mill, and took a load of 6 tons gross over the selected route without the slightest difficulty, and in a perfectly satisfactory manner. The observers are of the opinion that, in view of its comparatively light weight for a steam tractor, and its ease of handling and turning, this machine would be a desirable implement for a large farm. There can be no question as to its reliability."

On a similar note the journal *The Implement and Machinery Review* made the following observation of the Mann light agricultural tractor: "Both the engine and plough have been in evidence at many of the recent County Council demonstrations, and at one such event at York the outfit was, we are informed, awarded the premier position at the end of the day's work." [8]

Figure 101: Mann Agricultural Tractor, with reapers
This pleasant agricultural view shows a Mann Agricultural Tractor harvesting with reapers. The large water tank over the rear wheels dominates the tractor. *(Implement and Machinery Review)*

Implements

Agricultural implement manufacture is not usually associated with Mann's Patent Steam Cart and Wagon Company, however there are several references to this subject in agricultural journals. At the 1915 Royal Show the following description is included in a paragraph about their stand: "The light steam agricultural tractor shown by Mann's Patent Steam Cart and Wagon Company Ltd., Pepper Road Works, Hunslet, Leeds, had been sold to a farmer in Norfolk, who had also purchased a 4-furrow plough of their manufacture for use in conjunction with it." [9] Similarly at the 1916 show, the following statement expands on this: "The example shown had been sold to Messrs. Peck & Sons, of Boston, and is provided with three speeds and a winding drum...Large numbers of Mann wagons are at work in various parts of the country, and in many cases their owners also employ the Mann's four-furrow ploughs which are made specially for use with this tractor. Such a plough was present, a glance at which was sufficient to impress us with its strong and rigid appearance. It can be converted into a three-furrow implement very speedily if desired, and is provided with a double lifting lever, by which the depth may be regulated as it travels along. In addition, it has a system of wheel steerage, which greatly lightens the operator's labour and materially assists in the production of straight furrows." [10] The R.A.S.E. Show catalogue for 1916 indicates that the plough could be altered from three to five furrows and also included an arrangement for regulating the depth of ploughing. The list price was £50.[11] In 1917, an article about the light steam agricultural tractor gives a further snippet: "About five acres is considered a fair average day's ploughing for this tractor in medium land, the coal consumption being estimated at $1^1/_2$ cwts. per acre. For use in association with this tractor a powerful 4-furrow plough is also manufactured by Messrs Mann." [12]

Figure 102: Mann's Four-furrow Plough
Agricultural implements are not normally associated with Mann's Patent Steam Cart and Wagon Company, however, they were manufactured during the First World War. It is not clear when plough manufacturing stopped. *(Mann Catalogue)*

The Impact of the First World War

In general the impact of the First World War on Mann's Patent Steam Cart and Wagon Company was a buoyant order book and an increase in the female workforce, as many of the men were on active service. It has not been possible to find any documentary evidence as to the role of the Pepper Road Works in providing armaments, however a note by Wilf Cole indicates that shells were manufactured alongside the continued production of steam wagons.[13] The works became a Government Controlled Establishment, although what precisely this involved is not clear. One obvious effect is illustrated in the catalogue of the 1916 Royal Show, where the following entry is included:

> Stand No.182. – Mann's Patent Steam Cart and Wagon Company, Limited, Pepper Road Works, Hunslet, Leeds.
>
> 1974 – Steam Tractor, for direct ploughing, road haulage, driving thresher, &c., £490.
>
> 1975 – Pump, for washing out boilers of wagons, traction or portable engines, £3 10s
>
> 1976 – Trailing Wagon, to carry 3 tons, strongly constructed to withstand heavy vibration, £65
>
> 1977 – Plough, suitable for use with agricultural tractor; can be altered from three to five furrows. It has an arrangement for regulating the depth of ploughing, £50.
>
> (Owing to restrictions imposed by the Ministry of Munitions the following articles are not allowed to be exhibited.)
>
> 1978 - Steam wagon, to carry 5 tons, platform 12ft. 8in. by 6ft. 6in., speed five miles per hour, £610.
>
> 1979 - Steam cart with tipping gear, for general farm haulage and driving barn machinery, £590.
>
> 1980 - Steam wagon, to carry 3 tons, mounted on rubber tyres, to run at 12 miles per hour, platform 11ft. by 6ft., £635.

It is clear from these restrictions that the production of steam vehicles was a priority and that the effort involved and the delay to production that resulted from showing them at the Manchester Show was not considered justified by the authorities. However, because the agricultural business was being promoted to help the country become more self sufficient, these products were allowed to be shown. This had a major influence on the type of product manufactured at Pepper Road. The evidence indicates that, in the latter years of the First World War, the production of agricultural tractors exceeded the number of wagons, and this was the only period in the company's history that this occurred.[14]

GOVERNMENT-CONTROLLED ESTABLISHMENT.

TELEGRAMS:-"CANNING, LEEDS."
TELEPHONE Nº 972.
CODE USED:- A.B.C. 5TH EDITION.
CONTRACTORS TO
H. M. WAR OFFICE.
H. M. INDIA OFFICE.

MANN'S PATENT STEAM CART & WAGON CO. LD

PEPPER ROAD WORKS,
HUNSLET, LEEDS.

March 7th. 1917

London Office:
9, FENCHURCH AVENUE, E.C.
TELEGRAMS: "INTENSELY, LONDON."
TELEPHONE: 12283, CENTRAL.

JCC/JM.

CUSTOMERS' WAGONS ONLY DRIVEN BY OUR MEN AT THE CUSTOMER'S RISK.

Any time of delivery is named subject to the non-occurrence of Accidents to Machinery, Strikes of Workmen, or other unforeseen contingencies.

Figure 103: Letterhead, 1917
This letterhead from the First World War period had been overprinted at the top GOVERNMENT-CONTROLLED ESTABLISHMENT. Unfortunately no records have been uncovered to determine what this actually involved.

The University of Leeds Agricultural Trials, 1916

The serious shortage of male labour during the First World War not only affected industrial production but also agricultural output. In addition, the import of foodstuffs was severely restricted because of the requisition of much of the merchant shipping fleet by the government. One solution was to introduce more mechanised methods of farming. To enable farmers to judge for themselves the efficiency of labour saving appliances for the cultivation of land, the University of Leeds in conjunction with the Yorkshire Agricultural Society and the Yorkshire Council for Agricultural Education undertook a two day trial, held at the North Riding Asylum Farm at Rawcliffe near York, commencing on 4 November 1915.[15] Eight suppliers agreed to take part in the trials, although this was not a competitive situation, and no awards were given. The machines entered were:

Machine	b.h.p.	Price	cwt.	fuel	ground loading*
Fowler Motor Plough.	10	£158	16	Petrol	5.0
Saunderson & Mills Universal	20	£325	58	Paraffin	5.4
International Harvester Mogul Tractor	16	£272	50	Paraffin	4.7
International Harvester Mogul Tractor	25	£432	91	Paraffin	6.6
Overtime Tractor	24	£231	39	Paraffin	4.2
Sandusky Tractor	38	£577	81	Petrol	4.7
Daimler Tractor	40	£600	120	Petrol	6.0
Mann Steam Tractor	22	£465	95	Steam	4.6

*cwt. per sq. ft. of driving wheel

In the trial, the Mann tractor pulled a 4-furrow plough, and the figures obtained indicated that over a 10 hour day, 8.5 acres could be cultivated. Despite its weight, the large wheels of the Mann tractor provided a ground loading comparable with the lighter motorised tractors.

The Highland and Agricultural Society Trials, 1917

Following the success of their earlier tractor trials, The Highland and Agricultural Society undertook a further demonstration in 1917. This event was a much larger affair, attracting thirty-eight entries. As before, no prizes were awarded, but the society paid the carriage and fuel costs of the participants. The trials were undertaken at three separate locations, the first being held near Edinburgh on the Earl of Rosebery's East Craigie Home Farm, Cramond Bridge, on 17 and 18 October. The second was on the farm of Mr W. G. Imrie, Blackhill, Maryhill, Glasgow, on 22 and 23 October, whilst the final trial was held in Perth on 26 and 27 October. Only twenty-nine machines took part in the trials, eight of British construction and twenty-one of American origin. The British entrants were:

Company	Machine	Weight
Alldays & Onions, Birmingham	Alldays tractor 25-30 h.p	55 cwt.
W. Weeks & Son, Maidstone	Weeks-Dungev New Simplex 22.5 h.p.	35 cwt.
J Fowler & Co., Leeds	Fowler motor plough 12-14 h.p.	
Jas Hodgson, Carlisle	Hodgson's motor tractor 20 h.p.	
Mann's Patent Steam Cart & Wagon Co.	Steam Tractor 25 h.p.	4.5 tons
Martin's Cultivator Co., Stamford	Martin's motor plough	
Saunderson Tractor & Implement Co,	Universal tractor 20-25 b.h.p.	52.5 cwt.
Wyles Motor Ploughs Ltd., Manchester	Wyles motor plough 11 b.h.p.	21 cwt.

The Edinburgh event was well attended with about 1,000 spectators. The record of the Mann tractor was: "The only steam tractor on the ground was Mann's light agricultural tractor and Mann's tractor plough, which arrived about noon on the second day, having been borrowed for the demonstration from Mr. C. G. Ogilvie. The plough is capable of cutting four 10in. furrows, and this it did with remarkable ease to a depth of 9 in. and sometimes more." [16]

No specific observations are made of the Mann tackle at the Glasgow event, however, at Perth the text reads: "Mann's steam tractor encompassed a large area in a short time both lea and stubble, but the general opinion was that it was a bit too heavy, especially for stubble work, although all right on lea." [17]

A subsequent report on the Edinburgh trials in the journal "The Implement and Machinery Review" relates the following praise, "Testimony is before us that the Hon. A. H. Baring finds his Mann tractor runs admirably, and that with overtime, from 6 to 7 acres can be ploughed with it in a day." [18]

The Society of Motor Manufacturers and Traders (S.M.M.T.) ran a series of tractor trials from 22 to 27 September 1919 at South Carlton, which is approximately three miles north of Lincoln. Six judges were appointed: P. J. Bradshaw, G. A. Bellwood, E. G. H. Maddy, W. H. Passmore, E. W. H. Slade and E. J. Storm, all members of the Council of the National Farmers' Union. The event attracted fifty-six entrants, although on the day, five of the machines did not run. The Mann machine was entered in Group V, the steam category, and was the only runner in this group.[19] The compound steam tractor was rated 25-h.p. at 300 r.p.m., and on this occasion it was hauling a Robert's 4-furrow riding plough.[20] The specification was as follows: [21]

Figure 104: Mann Agricultural Tractor, Cross Ploughing
A pair of Mann Agricultural Tractors operating as direct ploughing machines. This photograph is believed to have been taken at the Edinburgh trials in 1919. *(Implement and Machinery Review)*

- Cylinders: 4in. and 6¾in. diameter by 8in. stroke
- Valve gear: Stephenson's link motion
- Flywheel: solid 2ft. 6in. diameter, 6in. face
- Governor setting: 300 r.p.m.
- Boiler: steel with 1¾in. diameter tubes, pressure 200 p.s.i.
- Boiler feed: plunger pump from second motion shaft, plus injector
- Superheater: coil in smokebox
- Water tank: mounted over driving wheels, 3 hours running capacity
- Front wheels: 36in. diameter, 8in. wide
- Rear wheels: 51in. diameter, 20in. wide
- Compensating gear fitted on second lay shaft, locking gear was provided
- Steering: by swivelling front axle controlled by chains
- Wheelbase: 9ft.
- Suspension: fully sprung to comply with the Motor Car Act
- Road speed: 5 m.p.h. and 2.5 m.p.h.
- Drawbar pull: 6,000 lb. at 2 m.p.h. in low gear
- Weight, full laden: 4¼ tons
- Price: £825

The trials consisted of an initial Drawbar Dynamometer Test using a machine provided by the National Physical Laboratory, followed by a Ploughing Resistance Dynamometer Test. In the latter case, the drawbar dynamometer was provided by Messrs. Hyatt Ltd. of London. Following on from this, practical trials were undertaken of ploughing on heavy clay land, ploughing on light to medium loam, a haulage test, and finally a threshing test.[22] Of the 56 vehicles entered, the Mann tractor performed superbly and provided the best performance in the following tests: [23]

- Dynamometer test: pull to skid of tractor wheel, 6,000 lb. (other contenders ranged from 2100 lb. to 5000 lb.)
- Dynamometer test: sustained pull at ploughing speed, 4,700 lb. (other contenders ranged from 1500 lb. to 4200 lb.)
- Drawbar horsepower: 22 h.p. (other contenders ranged from 6 1/4 h.p. to 19 h.p.)
- Field trial, light and medium land: Acres per hour – 1.08 (other contenders ranged from 0.40 to 0.93)
- Field trial, light and medium land: Fuel cost – 1.50 d (old pence) per 100 lb. of drawbar pull (other contenders ranged from 7.44 to 1.86)

On the heavy land the Mann tractor was not so successful. This was a difficult trial and only 34 machines took part. The aggregate score for the Mann tractor in the three tests in this category was 18th out of 34, i.e. around middle ranking.

Considering the superb performance of the Mann tractor, particularly its ploughing performance and its fuel cost on light land, the conclusion of the judges was somewhat reserved: "This is a well built compound tractor, weighing about 5 tons. It is well adapted for road haulage, threshing and other forms of belt work. Owing to its weight we consider it unsuitable for land work, except when the soil is dry. On the heavy land its work was not satisfactory, but on the light land, very good work was done." [24]

Figure 105: Mann Agricultural Tractor, South Carlton
This photograph taken from the S.M.M.T. official report shows the actual engine used at South Carlton. The tractor appears to be fitted with a feed-water heater along the boiler side. The machine is lettered, John Phillips, Rowston Farm, Stackpole, Pembroke, and is believed to be engine number 1400. *(S.M.M.T. Trial Report 1919)*

Figure 106: Mann Agricultural Tractor, Threshing
The Mann Agricultural Tractor was fitted with a solid flywheel, 2 ft. 6 in. diameter, and with a 6 in. face, specifically for driving farmyard machinery such as threshing machines. *(Mann Catalogue)*

References

1 *The Engineer*, 16 August 1912, p174
2 *The Engineer*, 12 February 1915, p165
3 *Engineering*, 15 October 1915, p394
4 *The Engineer*, 29 October 1915, p409
5 *The Engineer*, 4 January 1918, p5
6 *Engineering*, 15 October 1915, p395
7 *The Implement and Machinery Review*, 1 December 1915, p927
8 *The Implement and Machinery Review*, 1 January 1916, p1049
9 *The Implement and Machinery Review*, 1 August 1915, p482
10 *The Implement and Machinery Review*, 1 August 1916, p432
11 Royal Agricultural Society of England, *Catalogue*, Manchester Show 1916, p85
12 *The Implement and Machinery Review*, 1 April 1917, p1347
13 *Yorkshire Steam,* Yorkshire Evening Post, 22 May 1971, p9
14 Duke, Alan, *Mann Engine List*, Road Locomotive Society, 1988
15 *Report on Demonstration with Motor Tractors*, York, 1915, The University of Leeds, 1916
16 *The Implement and Machinery Review*, 1 November 1917, p718
17 *The Implement and Machinery Review*, 1 November 1917, p720
18 *The Implement and Machinery Review*, 1 December 1917, p837
19 *Engineering*, 3 October 1919, p445
20 *The Implement and Machinery Review*, 1 October 1919, p847
21 *Engineering*, 3 October 1919, p446
22 *Report of the Tractor Trials held at South Carlton, Nr. Lincoln*, S.M.M.T., 1919, p12-23
23 *Engineering*, 16 January 1920, p91
24 *The Implement and Machinery Review*, 1 February 1920, p1486

Chapter 6

Mann's Patent Steam Cart and Wagon Products, 1918–1929

One of the major factors affecting Mann's Patent Steam Cart and Wagon Company after the First World War was competition from petrol powered vehicles, particularly for road haulage, but increasingly for agricultural applications. To counter this, the company published in their catalogues a forthright defence of steam vehicles.

The first point raised was that the steam vehicle used coal that was a 'home product', whereas paraffin and petrol were imported products that required other exports to balance the payments. In addition, because petrol and paraffin were expensive fuels, it was more costly to carry out a task using an internal combustion powered vehicle rather than a steam vehicle.

Another argument made by the company was that steam powered vehicles were more robustly made than the lightweight petrol powered vehicles. This gave the machines a much longer life expectancy. The purchase price of a petrol vehicle was, if taken at face value, cheaper than its steam equivalent. However, given the longevity of the steam vehicle, the overall cost taken over the lifetime of the machine was comparable.

The final point identified in the catalogues was the time to raise steam: "Steam Tractors certainly take about three quarters of an hour to raise steam, but it is not lost, as not only do they work quicker, but this time enables the driver to thoroughly oil round, and make any necessary adjustments before starting work for the day, which are frequently neglected in the so-called instantaneous starting engines. Moreover, steam engines have the advantage that when steam is up they will start without any handle turning or grinding, which is such a trouble with internal combustion engines after standing in a field on a cold night." [1]

With such a determined view on the benefits of steam power, it is perhaps not surprising that James Mann continued the development of his machines along these lines, as the following patents illustrate.

Boiler Patents

A new style of boiler of the locomotive type was the subject of a patent, number 175,851, lodged on 20 December 1920. The object of this proposal was to simplify the construction of the boiler and thereby reduce the cost of manufacture. This patent defines a boiler shell made from only three plates, namely, one for the barrel, a second for the back half of the firebox, and the third for the front half of the firebox. The front tube-plate and internal firebox were constructed as normal. The two important features of this arrangement that simplified construction were the rounded top of the back half of the firebox, and the angled connection between the front half of the firebox and the boiler barrel. This is best understood by examining the associated drawing, shown overleaf. To construct such a boiler required the plates to be pre-formed to a much greater extent than was conventional practice. In a traditional boiler, the throat plate (the plate connecting the barrel to the firebox) was normally

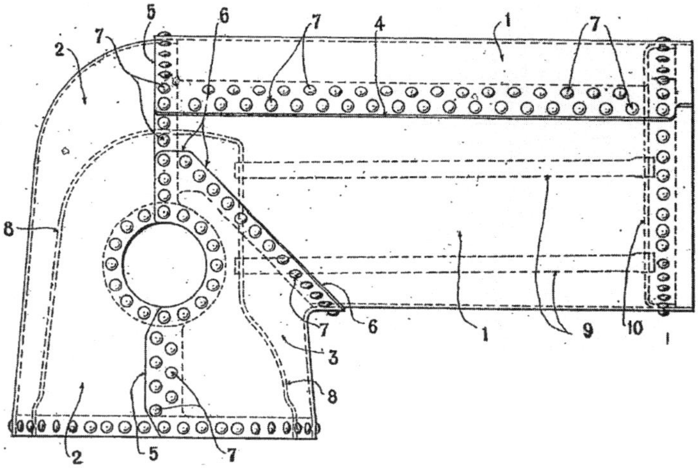

Figure 107: Patent Drawing, three-plate boiler arrangement. A new style of boiler of the locomotive-type was the subject of patent number 175,851, lodged on 20 December 1920. The object of this proposal was to simplify the construction of the boiler and thereby reduce the cost of manufacture, however it would have needed investment in ovens and large hydraulic presses to form the plates.

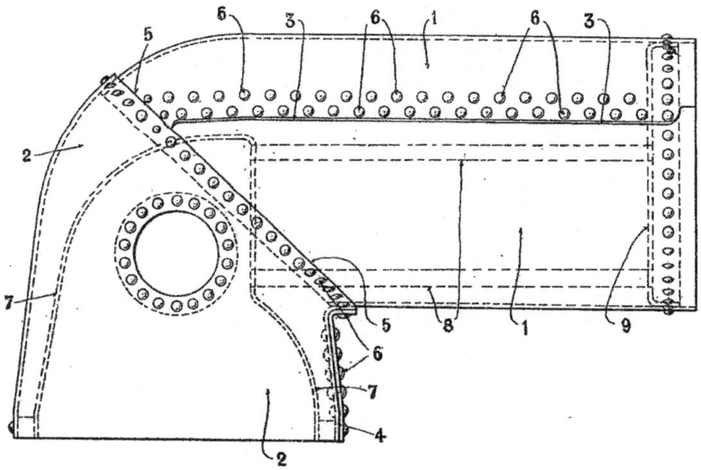

Figure 108: Patent Drawing, two-plate boiler arrangement. The boiler shown in the previous drawing was further refined in patent number 173,698, registered on 18 January 1921. In this proposal, the boiler shell was made from only two plates, one for the boiler barrel, and the second for the external firebox.

constructed by pre-heating the flat plate and hydraulic pressing using a former. This new boiler extended the use of pre-formed plates such that all the firebox shell was constructed in this manner. This type of boiler was often referred to as a 'pistol' type, owing to its profile in elevation view. In the 1920s, another steam wagon producer, Robey, of the Globe Works, Lincoln, adopted this style of boiler, although it was produced from eight plates.[2]

An associated second patent, number 173,698, was registered on 18 January 1921 with an enhancement of the simplified boiler. In this proposal, the boiler shell was made from only two plates, one for the boiler barrel, and the second for the external firebox. The boiler barrel was rolled circular as in conventional practice, however the firebox end was curved downwards. The external firebox was rolled tubular or slightly conical with the back face curved inwards, towards the top of the barrel. The throat between the boiler barrel and the external firebox was formed by riveting an overlapping joint on a diagonal line, nominally at forty-five degrees, although the patent also covered welded or butt joints. The foundation ring, front tube-plate and internal firebox were constructed in the conventional fashion. Despite the extra complexity of forming these plates, the patent claims that these were simpler to construct and consequently cheaper to produce.

Royal Agricultural Society Show, 1920

The 1920 Royal Show was held at Lincoln, and stand number 297 was occupied by Mann's Patent Steam Wagon Company. The after-effects of the First World War were still evident and in particular the price of goods reflected the effects of inflation and the shortage of raw materials e.g. steel. The following extract from the Show Catalogue illustrates this effect on prices: [3]

> Stand No.297. – Mann's Patent Steam Cart and Wagon Company, Limited, Pepper Road Works, Hunslet, Leeds.
>
> 3936 – Steam Agricultural Tractor, for direct ploughing, road haulage, driving threshing machines, &c., £1,030. [*pre-war price £450*]
>
> 3937 – Steam Wagon, to carry 5 tons, fitted with rubber tyres, and geared to run at 10 miles per hour; can be fitted with tipping gear, £1,360. [*pre-war price £540*]
>
> 3938 – Steam Wagon, to carry 3 tons, mounted on rubber tyres, speed 12 miles per hour; can be fitted with tipping gear, £1210. [*pre-war price £475*]
>
> 3939 – Steam Cart, to carry 5 tons, fitted with tipping gear, suitable for hauling stones, bricks, &c., and for general estate work, £1220. [*pre-war price £535*]
>
> 3940 – Steam Tractor, for general road haulage, driving saw bench, &c., £1,230. [*pre-war price £450*]
>
> 3941 – Steam Roller, for patching ordinary macadam and rolling tar macadam; can be converted into steam wagon when required, £1,285. [*pre-war price £475*]
>
> 3942 – Pump, for washing out boilers of steam wagons, traction engines, &c., £12 10s. [*pre-war price £3 10s*]

Unfortunately, the trade recession of the 1920s was "just around the corner" and by 1924 these prices had almost halved, as the company fought to retain its share of the dwindling market.

Tractor Trials, Lincoln, 1920

In 1920 the R.A.S.E. in conjunction with the Society of Motor Manufacturers and Traders ran a series of tractor trials at Aisthorpe near Lincoln. The event commenced on Tuesday, 28 September 1920 and was well supported, with around 40 vehicles entered. To provide a fair comparison, seven classes were defined to group together steam vehicles, petrol vehicles, direct ploughing and cable ploughing.

The Mann vehicle was entered in Class 4, which was defined as, "Direct traction steam engine plant, suitable for ploughing four furrows, 10in. wide by 8in. deep. Engines to comply with Light Road Locomotive Acts." [4] The machine used was very similar to that shown at the 1915 Smithfield Show, i.e. an overtype compound tractor with the front wheels placed close together.

The specification was as follows: [5]

- Engine: two cylinder compound
- Engine rating: 25 b.h.p. @ 450 r.p.m.
- Boiler, grate area: 3 square feet
- Boiler, total heating surface: 57.5 square feet
- Boiler feed: slow speed plunger pump, plus Penberthy injector
- Superheater: none
- Bunker capacity: 3 cwt. coal
- Water capacity: 200 gallons (sufficient for half a day's ploughing)
- Front wheels: 35in. diameter, 8in. wide
- Rear wheels: 51in. diameter, 20in. wide
- Wheelbase: 97in.
- Turning circle: 24ft.
- Brakes: drum on rear axle, 25in. diameter drum, 3in. wide.
- Ground clearance: 9in.
- Suspension: fully sprung to comply with the Motor Car Act
- Road speeds: 5 m.p.h., 3.5 m.p.h., and 2.25 m.p.h.
- Haulage drum: 19.5in. diameter
- Haulage drum speed: 29, 46 or 66 r.p.m. or 150, 235, or 340ft. per minute
- Weight, full laden: 5.4 tons
- Overall dimensions: 13ft. 5in. long by 5ft. 10in. wide

The journal *The Implement and Machinery Review* commented, "Mann's Patent Steam Cart and Wagon Co. Ltd., Leeds, had their five-ton 25-h.p. direct traction steam tractor at work in the category for this class of plant. It hauled a four-furrow riding plough, six inches deep, at a good four miles per hour, so that it did just over an acre per hour, with ample reserve of power. There were experienced ploughmen who found here some of the best ploughing of the meeting, for the full acreage was neatly turned over in even furrows. Some there were feared for the compression of the land, but, as the tractor has a 4½ft. wide bearing surface on the land at any time, this danger of packing was more apparent than real. The Mann outfit by the way, was the sole entrant in this class, and cut 5¼ acres in five hours, at a fuel expenditure of 1¼ cwt. to the acre." [6]

As a result of this superb performance, in the direct ploughing class, the Mann tractor was awarded the Gold Medal.[7]

The 1922 Royal Show contained a good cross-section of Mann products. A 5-ton tipping wagon was present, which had the tipping body and the water tank interchangeable, to allow water spraying and haulage. The basic 5-ton wagon with rubber tyres but without tipping body had a list price of £850. Similarly, the 3-ton machine was priced at £800. The shorter wheelbase 5-ton tipping cart was also shown, priced at £850. This machine was driven by spur gearing, whereas the wagon was driven by a roller chain from the third motion shaft to the main axle. Two steam tractors were also shown. The road tractor was built with the 4-shaft inside gear arrangement. The agricultural tractor for direct ploughing was of the type that took part in the Lincoln trials, and could be fired from coal or coke, or if fitted with a large firebox, fired with wood.[8] This was priced at £700.[9]

Four-Ton and Six-Ton Overtype Wagons

The year 1923 saw the replacement of the 3-ton wagon by the 4-ton wagon and its larger brother, the 5-ton wagon replaced by the 6-ton wagon. This was in response to the increase in unladen weight allowed in the 1920 Roads Act. The new 3-speed machines were largely an evolutionary development of the earlier machine with detail changes, such as larger bearing surfaces where necessary, and different diameter shafts, but in the main, the essential features were retained.[10] This approach whilst not "breaking new ground" did provide customers some comfort and reassurance that the new machine was very much like the machines they were used to and trusted to give good, long, reliable service.

The 6-ton overtype wagon adopted many of the Mann characteristic features, such as the locomotive boiler and the side firing with one-man control. Similarly, the transmission used the four-shaft system with all gears being located between the horn plates. The drive to the axle was by 2.5in. pitch roller chain. The steering used the familiar worm and bevel gear acting directly on the pivoting front axle. The most significant changes were in the increased dimensions of the boiler and engine. The boiler provided a heating surface of 71.3 square feet, of which the tubes contributed around 52.6 square feet, and the firebox 16.375 square feet. Each boiler was tested to 350 p.s.i. but its normal working pressure was 200 p.s.i. The engine was fitted with compound cylinders of 4in. and 7in. diameter with an 8in. stroke. This provided an increase in the low-pressure cylinder diameter, which had previously been 6³/₈in. Detail changes provided shorter and straighter steam ports to give greater efficiency of operation. The 'D' type slide valves were operated by Stephenson's link motion. To further improve the thermal efficiency, a feed-water heater was provided. This consisted of an exhaust steam jacket through which passed a large diameter copper tube carrying the boiler feed water. A low speed mechanical pump, running off the second motion shaft, provided lubrication of the cylinders. This was reinforced by a steam displacement lubricator. In addition, the differential gears were fully enclosed in an oil and dirt-proof casing. Three-speed gearing was provided with ratios of 5.4:1 (top), 9:1 (intermediate), and 17:1 (low), giving road speeds 12, 8 and 4 miles per hour at normal engine speed. The main axle was constructed using nickel-steel of 55-tons tensile strength. One visual alteration was the removal of the water tank from between the boiler and the body and replacing it by two tanks, each located either side of the chassis, in front of the rear wheels. This allowed the platform space to be extended by 18in. to 14ft., as compared with 12ft. 6in. in the old type. The platform width was 7ft. The brakes consisted of a band brake on the intermediate shaft operated by the foot pedal. For the hand wheel brake, Ferodo lined band brakes were provided on the rear-wheel drums. The Mann catalogue indicates that under average working conditions the 6-ton wagon would run 14 to 16 miles on 1 cwt. of fuel, and travel 25 to 30 miles on a tank of water.[11]

Similarly, the same catalogue suggests that the 4-ton wagon would run 16 to 18 miles on 1 cwt. of fuel and travel 25 to 30 miles on a tank of water. This lighter weight vehicle was also fitted with three-speed gearing, and this provided road speeds of 16, 10 and 4 miles per hour at normal engine revolutions. The platform was 12ft. 6in. long by 6ft. wide. Where sides were fitted, these were 1ft. 9in. high. The new 6-ton wagon was shown at the Yorkshire Agricultural Society's Sheffield Show of 1923. In the show catalogue the 6-ton wagon was priced at £875. The direct ploughing tractor, which was also exhibited, was priced at £600.[12] This was £100 less than the previous year and demonstrates the impact of the trade depression that was prevalent at the time.

The tipping gear for these wagons was the same type that had been used for earlier wagons. To operate the tipping mechanism, the road drive was taken out of gear and a friction clutch engaged. From this a roller chain drove a worm and wheel onto a rack pinion, which engaged with a pin rack to raise or lower the body as desired. The mechanical advantage provided by the reduction gearing provided a powerful means of moving the body without any chance of slippage at the clutch. This method was claimed to be more reliable than lifting screws as it was able to cope with dirt, grit and rough usage that could damage a screw mechanism. Similarly, the hydraulic jack approach was equally dismissed for its complication and additional pipes and joints, giving rise to inconvenience and expense due to leakage, freezing and bursting. The company were very sure of the capability of the tipping mechanism as this extract illustrates, "The Mann Tipping Gear is easily the most satisfactory yet invented, and as this has been employed as the standard type for so many years without any necessity for the least modification, it follows that its absolute reliability has been proved conclusively." [13]

Figure 109: Publicity for the 4-ton and 6-ton wagons
This advertisement from May 1925 is promoting the newly introduced 4-ton and 6-ton wagons. *(Motor Transport)*

Figure 110: The new 6-ton Steam Wagon during trials on Leathley Bank
In the spring of 1923 the new 6-ton steam wagon was introduced to the press, and as a demonstration of its capabilities the wagon was run along the Wharfe Valley in Yorkshire. This is Mann number 1606 and was sold to R. L. Dilworth of Lancaster. *(John Middlemiss collection)*

To demonstrate the capabilities of the new 6-ton wagon, the press were invited to a test run along the Wharfe Valley and up Leathley Bank and Pool Bank, which climb, at a maximum gradient of 1 in $4^1/_2$, approximately ten miles to the North of Leeds. The press were accompanied by James Mann's son, Arthur Mann, who was by this time a director of the company. The route commenced in Moortown, Leeds and ran through Harewood, Arthington, Pool, Leathley Bank, Pool Bank, Otley Road, and back via Headingley to Leeds. "Running quietly and easily, the wagon averaged 19 to 20 miles per hour. Of course the crucial point was Leathley Bank, whose gradient is as pronounced in one part as 1 in $4^1/_2$. Half way up the hill the steamer was stopped to be photographed, and was then restarted on a gradient of 1 in 5 without any difficulty, passing over the subsequent most acute rise in an untroubled effort. It was indeed, quite a fine performance. Following other severe hill tests, the run was completed after 22 miles had been covered. It was then found that 184 lbs. of coal and 130 gallons of water had been consumed, the return of coal per mile being 8.36 lbs., while the capacity of the water tank, allowing for the halt on the crest of the hill where full steam had to be maintained, was $27^1/_2$ miles." [14] Subsequent trials were made with and without a trailer. In the first trial, the wagon carried a 6-ton load a distance of 47 miles at a speed of $13^3/_4$ miles per hour. This produced a coal consumption of 7.1 lbs. per mile, whilst at the same time evaporating the tank capacity of 150 gallons of water in $32^3/_4$ miles. A further trial using the trailer and hauling 10 tons over the same route gave a fuel consumption of 9.53 lbs. per mile. The 150 gallons of water was used in $24^1/_2$ miles.

A variation to the 6-ton overtype was the six-wheeler wagon with a flexible connection between the front tractor unit and the load-carrying platform. The vehicle was designed for loads up to 12-tons and could be supplied with a platform up to 25 feet long with a variety of sides to suit the user's requirements. The six-wheeler had a maximum legal speed of 12 miles per hour, which together with its heavy capacity was ideal for long distance haulage.[15]

Figure 111: Mann Articulated Wagon
The articulated wagon is a common sight on today's motorways, but it must have been a rare occasion to see a machine like this in the 1920s. The vehicle was designed for loads up to 12 tons and could be supplied with a platform up to 25ft long. *(Mann Catalogue)*

In the years immediately after the First World War, the dominant position of the railways for the transport of goods started to be eroded by road haulage. This was the combined result of improved roads, together with advances in road vehicle reliability. The original Mann steam cart had been developed to the limit for its particular application, and on this subject the company wrote: "The Mann overtype has proved itself so unequalled for the strenuous work for which the type was originally evolved that it is almost impossible to produce another type to equal it, and we therefore were convinced that the correct procedure was to perfect this for the rough work of tips, building sites or quarries, with short distances only, ..." [16] However, for long distance transport a different machine was needed. Mann's Patent Steam Cart and Wagon Company set about designing such a machine with the following objectives:

- High load carrying capacity
- High speed both uphill as well as on the level
- Economy of fuel and maintenance
- Reliability and durability of the vehicle
- Pleasing appearance
- Quietness and comfort

One of the first pieces of tangible evidence of the development of the new wagon was the registering of a boiler patent. A new vertical boiler arrangement was the subject of a patent, number 193,316, lodged by Mann's Patent Steam Cart and Wagon Company on 12 April 1922. In this patent design, the internal shell of the boiler formed the tube plate, to which the water tubes were connected. The tube plate cross-section was made star-shaped, formed by two squares offset at forty-five degrees. This unusual cross-section was used to strengthen the internal boiler shell. Within each square section, water tubes passed across, inclined at a slight angle. The central portion of the boiler was left empty to accommodate the firing tube, which was suspended from the top of the boiler. According to the patent, "By employing tube plates of the star formation above described, vertical corrugations are obtained, which give a strong construction capable of withstanding external pressure

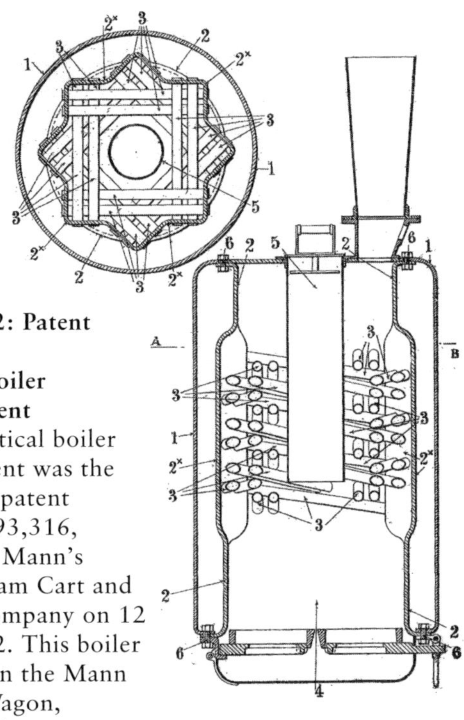

Figure 112: Patent Drawing, Vertical Boiler Arrangement
A new vertical boiler arrangement was the subject of patent number 193,316, lodged by Mann's Patent Steam Cart and Wagon Company on 12 April 1922. This boiler was used in the Mann Express Wagon, introduced in 1924. The strength provided by the corrugated shell avoided the need for stays.

without being dependent on the support of the water tubes. The arrangement further provides for a large area of tube surface to be exposed to the radiant heat of the fire and hot gasses, while a suitable inclination can be given to the water tubes to permit of free steaming by which the general efficiency and durability of the boiler is materially increased." [17]

After several years of development, the Mann Express Wagon, as it was named, was first shown to the press in the summer of 1924. The wagon was displayed at the Yorkshire Agricultural Society Show at York alongside its overtype equivalent. The show catalogue indicates that the Express Wagon was initially offered at £850, whilst the overtype of the same load capacity was sold for £820.[18] Unfortunately, the new Fowler steam wagon, with a similar specification and similar appearance, was introduced at the same time. This was regrettable, as the market for steam powered vehicles was contracting rapidly. The Express Wagon was a 6-ton undertype with a vertical boiler, as previously described, and an engine with two high-pressure cylinders, suspended under and across the frame. The two-speed gearbox was built as a unit with the engine. This was connected by a propeller shaft to the final drive bevel-and-spur double-reduction gearing. One of the most significant changes from normal Mann practice was the vertical orientation of the boiler. The main benefit of this is that it took up less space along the length of the wagon. According to publicity material, the cab was only 5ft. 6 in. long, which allowed 75 percent of the wagon area to be used for useful load. This could not have been achieved with a horizontal locomotive-type boiler.

Chassis

The main frame of the vehicle was constructed from steel channel sections with cross members, and this directly supported the load platform. To avoid weakening the chassis, all fixings were attached to the web rather than the flanges.

Boiler

As previously described, the boiler was a vertical type rather than the horizontal locomotive arrangement previously used. A domed top was fitted and this space was used to fit two coils for superheating. For inspection or repair, the whole of the inner member could be dropped from the bottom of the boiler without disturbing any mountings. To protect the boiler when the water level was low, a fusible plug was fitted opposite a small cover in the outer shell. The firebox provided a heating surface of 29 square feet, and the tubes provided 41½ square feet.[19] The operating pressure was 250 p.s.i.[20]

Figure 113: Express Wagon Boiler
The Mann Express boiler was a complete departure from Mann's previous practice, the primary difference being that it used a vertical boiler. The design was patented in 1922. The corrugated shell is readily seen. *(John Middlemiss collection)*

Engine

The engine was a two-cylinder undertype, fitted between the frames, with each cylinder being $5^3/_4$in. bore, with a stroke of 7in.[21] The running speed was 500 r.p.m. The innovative feature of the engine was the use of poppet valves for steam admission and exhaust. In a traditional steam engine with slide or piston valves, the admission, expansion, exhaust and compression of steam are interconnected. This is because the four ports that direct the steam are all controlled by valves fixed to a common shaft. The result of this is that the timing of the engine events is a compromise and does not allow the engine to run at best efficiency. With poppet valves the two inlet and the two outlet valves are all individually operated by cams and this allows the timing of the valves to be optimised to achieve best efficiency.

In the Mann Express Wagon the valves were provided with two cut-off points, to allow good tractive effort when starting, whilst allowing good economy when running at speed. These were set at quarter cut-off and three-quarter cut-off, respectively. In addition, the exhaust valves were located at the bottom of the cylinders. The benefit of this was that by putting the camshafts into the neutral position and opening the steam valve, any water lying in the bottom of the cylinders was blown out of the exhaust. Maintenance and durability of the engine was thought of at the earliest stage of design, with large access covers being fitted to the sides of the engine. As well as giving access to the engine it also revealed the main water pump. The crankshaft was a solid forging of high-tensile steel running in Hoffman roller bearings. Outside these bearings the shaft was splined to carry the gear pinions and was further supported by a third roller bearing. The whole of the engine motion and gears were contained in a steel oil-bath, to ensure good lubrication. The connecting rods were of girder section for lightness, and made of high-tensile steel stampings, to which was attached large die-cast alloy big-ends. These were fitted with oil-scoops to direct the oil to the crank pin, even when the oil level was low. Separate camshafts were used for the inlet and exhaust valves, these being driven from the crankshaft by spiral gears. To provide the different cut-offs and the reversing of the engine, the camshafts were moved laterally so that, in the different positions, a different set of cams acted on the valves. The crossheads and bored guides were lubricated direct from the oil-bath, while steam or water from the cylinders was excluded by double stuffing boxes.

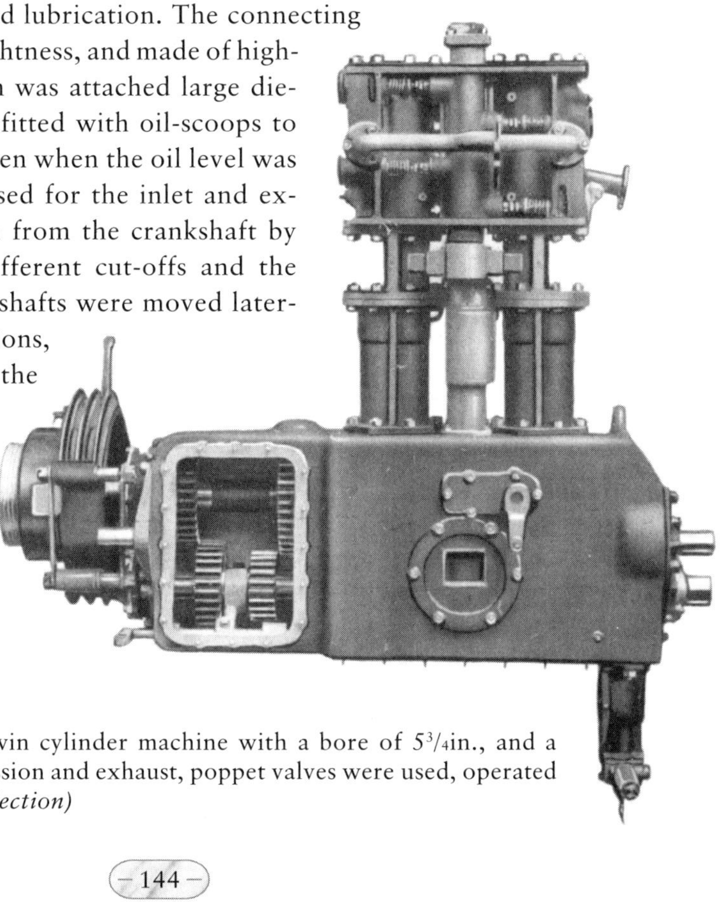

Figure 114: Express Wagon Engine
The Mann Express engine was a twin cylinder machine with a bore of $5^3/_4$in., and a stroke of 7in. To control steam admission and exhaust, poppet valves were used, operated by camshafts. (*John Middlemiss collection*)

Figure 115:Mann Express Tipper Wagon
This tipping variant of the Mann Express is thought to be Mann number 1695, supplied in 1925 to N. Furness of Eyam in Derbyshire. (*John Middlemiss collection*)

Transmission

The transmission provided two road speeds and was totally enclosed, running in oil. The gear ratios were 5.3 to 1 and 8.6 to 1. The propeller shaft, of high-tensile steel, was driven through a universal joint from the countershaft, which in turn carried nickel-chrome gear wheels driven by gear wheels on the crankshaft. At the other end of the propeller shaft, the bevel pinion drove the differential, and all the wheels and pinions were of tempered nickel-chrome steel. The differential gear was built as a self-contained unit, which could be removed from the axle casing without having to be taken apart. All the gear wheels were cut to a special involute curve to provide a strong, quiet and durable component. The main axle was of the fully floating type, so that all the weight of the load was carried by the main laminated leaf springs. Extensive use was made of roller bearings for the main shafts, conversely large floating bronze bushes, to resist the heavy road shocks, supported the main wheels. Cast steel wheels were employed all round, those at the front being dished and with T-section spokes. The front wheels were pivoted approximately 1 in. away from the centre thus ensuring stability at high speeds, as exact centring can cause wheel wobble. Channel section steel was used for the front axle and to this was attached cast steel fork ends which, as well as supporting the wheels, provided the seats for the springs.

Economy

The exhaust steam from the engine was taken through a feed-water heater of the copper-coil type, the intake and outlet for the water and steam respectively being so arranged that the water flowed in the direction of the incoming steam. The device also acted as a silencer, and by bringing the water almost to boiling point promoted economy and relieved the boiler from undue stress caused by unequal contraction and expansion.

Fuel and water

The water tank was carried longitudinally at the back of the frame, the supply to the boiler being by injector and pump, and it held sufficient for 30 miles to 35 miles operation. Baffles were fitted inside the water tank to prevent surging. The water from the tank was taken off by two independent pipes, one for the pump and the other for the injector. Each of these pipe-lines was provided with a strainer at the tank end, and a cock permitted each strainer to be cleaned without difficulty while the tank was full. A simple idea was used to prevent, so far as possible, the stranding of the wagon through lack of water; this was done by fitting the injector supply pipe to the bottom of the tank, and at a slightly higher point the pipe for the pump; thus, when the pump supply gave out there was still sufficient water in the tank to keep the injector working for another three or four miles. The fuel bunker, which was situated between the seats in the cab, held sufficient coal to travel 100 miles.

Driver controls

The Mann Express Wagon was designed for long distance haulage and the designers took into account the needs of the driver in this situation. In the first instance, the driver's cab was weather protected with a front windscreen. Cushioned seats were fitted, and all the main control levers were readily accessible for the driver. The steering was of the Ackermann variety and the large steering wheel actuated the wheels via a nut and worm. The hand brake was of the screw type, operating contracting shoes on the transmission drum. The main brake acted on the rear wheel drums and operated directly off the main boiler. This was achieved by means of two pistons moving in cylinders bolted to the frame. This was said to "give perfect safety even at the high speeds obtained". The main brake was operated by a foot pedal, as was steam admission to the engine. For slow running, a hand throttle was provided. Where tipping bodies were fitted, a hydraulic cylinder operated the tipping mechanism; this was operated by a separate pump. The fuel bunker was placed between the driver and mate's seat.

Dimensions

The leading dimensions of the Mann Express were: overall length, 21ft. 3ins; width, 7ft. 4ins; wheelbase, 11ft. 5ins; body, 15ft. 6ins. by 7ft; loading platform, 4ft. from ground. Rear tyre size: twin 160 mm. by 850 mm. Front tyre size: 180 mm. by 771 mm. Turning circle 35ft. The unladen weight was approximately 6 tons, and speeds up to 25 m.p.h. could be achieved.

Some owners of Mann Express Wagons are listed below: [22]

Owner	Engine Number
Frederick Sokell, Ferryhill, Co. Durham	1683
Alfred Thorne, Eaton Bray, Beds.	1692
H. R. D. Maconochie, Buxton	1695
B & W Transport, Mirfield, West Riding	1696
David Llewellyn, St Brides Major, Glamorgan	1703
Leggott & Son, Manchester***	
N. Furness, Eyam, Derbyshire***	
Morgan Pritchard, Carmarthen***	

*** ref: *The World's Carriers*, 15 July 1925, page 319

Figure 116: Mann Express Wagon
The Mann Express Wagon was of modern appearance and not dissimilar to its Leeds rival, the Fowler Steam Wagon. This machine, number 1692, was purchased by the flour millers Alfred Thorne of Bedfordshire, and is shown at the back of the Pepper Road Works. (*John Middlemiss collection)*

In the following winter, the journal *The World's Carriers* gave an account of a trial run, which they had witnessed. "The route selected was from the works at Hunslet, along the Tadcaster Road for some 10 miles, then turning right to Aberford, thence to Garforth, Oulton, and back to the works, a distance of some 28 miles. The wagon carried a full load of 6 tons." The route was of mixed gradients and mixed road quality, with the journey taking 1 hour 55 minutes, however, allowing for photographic stops the actual travelling time was 1.5 hours, giving an average speed of 17.7 miles per hour. The same article reported very favourably on the performance of the Express Wagon: "We rode on the wagon for some miles, and during the whole time the pressure gauge held steadily to about 10 lbs. above the working pressure mark. Evidently, the steaming qualities of the boiler are all the makers claim for it. The running of the vehicle was excellent, being both smooth and silent, vibration becoming apparent only at speeds of 20 miles per hour, and upwards. After the journey we found all accessible bearings cool, perfectly cool. At no point of the journey when hill climbing, was there any evidence of labouring or forcing." [23]

The salient details of the run were as follows:

- Average speed: 17.7 miles per hour
- Miles per tank of water: 33.4
- Miles per cwt. of coal: 16.5

Of the trial, the report in *World Carriers* concludes, "These results we regard as being very excellent even for a demonstration run, on which it is up to the manufacturer to have everything in perfect order. We congratulate the firm for having produced what in our opinion is a very excellent vehicle, and if its wearing qualities prove to be as good as the performance it puts up, it is a vehicle which will rapidly become popular, and we hope to make a journey on it at a later date, under actual working conditions for the purpose of comparison, and for the information of our readers."

Unfortunately, sales of the Mann Express never reached expectations and one of the reasons may have been early problems with poppet valves breaking.[24] As mentioned earlier, steam admission was controlled by poppet valves operated from a camshaft. These components are subject to high stresses because of the temperature differential along their length. This is compounded in a high-speed engine because they are required to operate approximately ten times per second. It is possible that the wrong grade of steel was used, however we shall never know, as this level of detail has not survived.

Figure 117: Advertisement, Mann Express Wagon
The attractive Mann Express Wagon was designed for long distance haulage, and the designers provided such refinements as weather protection with a front windscreen. *(The World's Carriers)*

In subsequent years the Mann Express continued to be exhibited at agricultural shows around the country. The Yorkshire Agricultural Society ran their annual show at a variety of locations in the North of England with Bradford being selected in 1925, Darlington in 1927, and Halifax in 1928. At all these shows the Mann Express was given a list price of £835 in the show catalogue. The 1925 Bradford Show also included the 4-ton overtype and this is listed at £760 including tipping gear.[25] This was likely to be the same machine exhibited at the Royal Show and this was sold to Thomas Maiden, builders' and contractors' merchants, Lime Kiln Lane, Ardwick.[26] The company did not exhibit at the 1926 Harrogate Show.

Tipping Gear Patent

The final patent submitted in the name of Mann's Patent Steam Cart and Wagon Company was number 252,947, dated 5 September 1925. This patent, titled *Improvements in or relating to Tipping Gear for Motor Road Vehicles*, details the use of a hydraulic cylinder to raise the body of a road vehicle in order to discharge the contents. The tipping body was able to tip to the right, left or rear of the vehicle by a single cylinder, which could only pivot in one plane. When tipping to the rear, the lifting cylinder, being supported at its top in trunnion pivots, could thereby provide the necessary movement to take up the changing angular position of the lifting body. The top of the piston rod, where it connected to the underside of the body was also connected via trunnions. When tipping to either side, instead of the cylinder tilting,

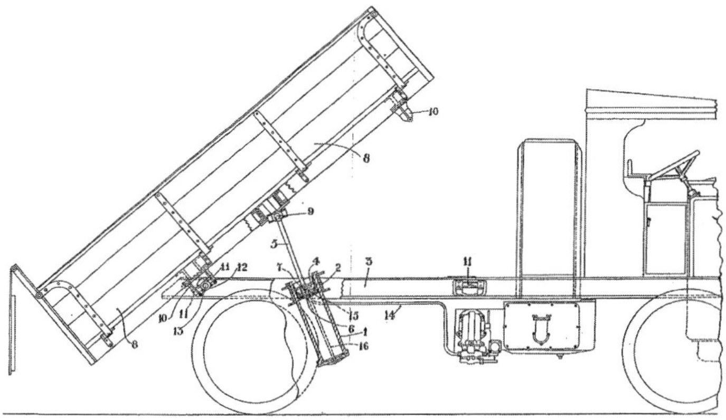

Figure 118: Patent Drawing, Rear Tipping Arrangement for Road Vehicles.
The final patent submitted in the name of Mann's Patent Steam Cart and Wagon Company was number 252,947, dated 5 September 1925. This patent is titled *"Improvements in or relating to Tipping Gear for Motor Road Vehicles"*.

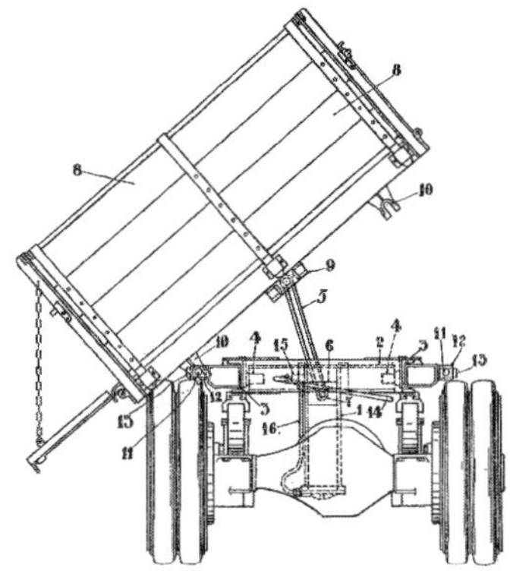

Figure 119: Patent Drawing, Side Tipping Arrangement for Road Vehicles.
Patent number 252,947 details the use of a hydraulic cylinder to raise the body of a road vehicle in order to discharge the contents. Because of the symmetry, the same mechanism could be used to tip either to the right or to the left.

the piston rod pivoted at its connection with the trunk piston, as is done at the gudgeon pin of a modern internal combustion engine. Again, the top of the piston rod, where it connected to the underside of the body, connected via trunnions to provide the necessary angular flexibility. However, the patent makes it clear that other types of connection e.g. ball joints, were not excluded from the definition of the design.

At the 1927 Royal Show, a 6-ton wagon was fitted with a three-way tipping body using this arrangement. A report in a journal relates, "In the latter case, oil is used instead of water, but as the oil is returned to the tank to be used over and over again, there is no waste." [27]

Proposed Mann Vehicles

In 1926 a new range of steam-powered vehicles was placed on the drawing board, all based around the Mann Express engine and vertical boiler. The first of these was the 6-wheeled haulage tractor. The four rear wheels were 4ft. diameter and 18in. wide and were all chain driven from a centrally located shaft. The wheel axles were pivoted by radius shafts located at the same centre as the chain drive, and suspension was provided by half elliptical springs. The engine was mounted horizontally with its cylinder pointing towards the rear. From the engine-gearbox unit, a pinion drove a large spur gear, which provided a big reduction for the differential countershaft, from which each wheel was separately driven through roller chains. The 250-gallon water tank was located above the driving wheels to improve adhesion. Ackermann steering was provided for the 3ft. diameter front wheels. The overall length was 14ft. 10in. The article in *Commercial Motor* suggests, "This tractor is chiefly intended for use in undeveloped countries, and for heavy agricultural haulage, ploughing, etc." [28]

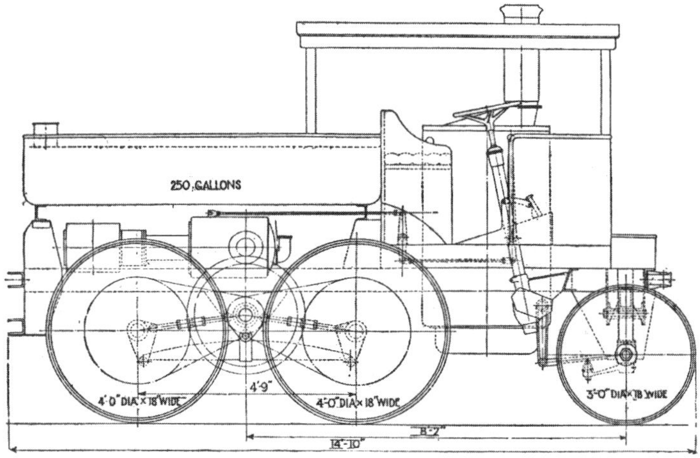

Figure 120: Line Drawing of proposed 6-wheeled tractor
This 1926 proposal for a heavy haulage tractor has a very powerful appearance. Unfortunately the steam vehicle was becoming less attractive for the road haulage business, and coupled with events within the company, this machine never became reality. *(Commercial Motor)*

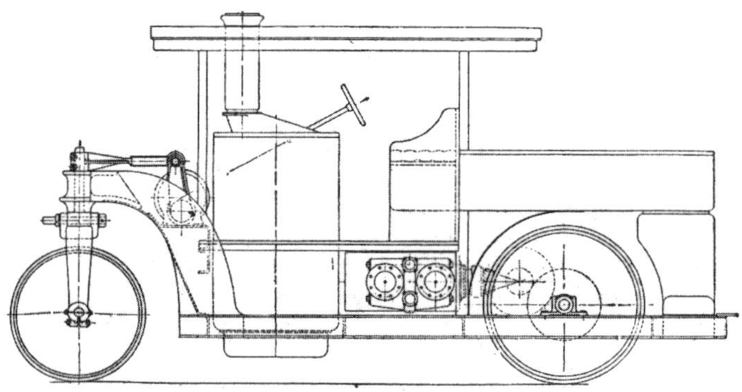

Figure 121: Line Drawing of tandem steam roller
This machine has a rather old-fashioned appearance and, by 1926, sales of internal combustion powered road rollers were starting to become significant. It is doubtful if this Mann proposal could ever have been a commercial proposition. *(Commercial Motor)*

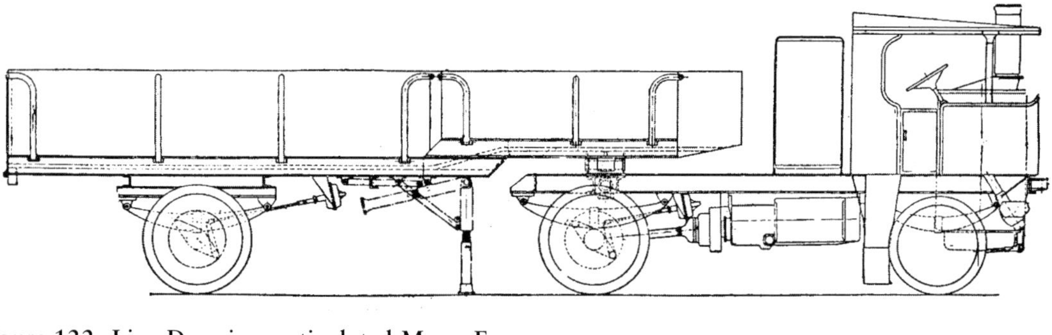

Figure 122: Line Drawing, articulated Mann Express
Given different financial circumstances within the company, this 1926 proposal could have been a success. Whilst steam wagon usage was declining, their application for heavy haulage was still viable. The Sentinel wagon, built in Shrewsbury, continued to be sold into the mid-1930s. *(Commercial Motor)*

A second proposal was for a tandem road roller. In this machine the engine was arranged across the chassis and drove first through a bevel reduction gear and then via a spur reduction gear to the rear roller. The front roller was steered using a conventional arrangement, however the power was provided by steam cylinders responding to the steering wheel position, rather like a ship's steering gear. The main chassis was constructed from straight channel steel, to which the forecarriage was fixed.

The third proposal was for an articulated lorry, consisting of a short wheelbase, 4-wheeled tractor unit and a 2-wheeled trailer attachment, connected to the tractor by a turntable. A combined front support and jack could be used to lift the front of the trailer out of the turntable, and then to carry the weight. Steam or Westinghouse (vacuum) brakes could be fitted. The tractor unit was essentially a shortened Express Wagon with poppet valve engine and vertical boiler.

By 1928 the range of vehicles manufactured in Leeds was slimmed down to three, presumably in an effort to reduce costs. The three vehicles were; the Express 6-ton shaft-driven wagon, the 6-ton chain driven overtype, and lastly the 4-ton chain driven overtype. This latter machine was the subject of a trial carried out by the journal *Motor Transport* in 1928. The engine is defined as having $3^7/_8$in. diameter high-pressure cylinder and $6\ ^5/_8$in. low-pressure cylinder, both with a stroke of 6in. Steam was controlled by double D-slide valves worked by Stephenson's link motion. Three speeds were provided and a single roller chain transmitted the drive to the back axle. This was a nickel-chrome steel forging and carried the three-bevel pinion differential gear. The axle was fitted with a large-diameter drum for the screw-down brake, whilst the pedal brake acted on drums bolted directly to the rear wheels. All four wheels were of the cast steel spoked pattern, fitted with twin 1,030 x 140 mm. solid tyres on the rear, whilst the front wheels had 850 x 140 mm. single tyres. The flange mounted road wheels could easily be detached by the removal of the retaining bolts.

The boiler had thirty-seven $1^1/_2$in. fire-tubes giving a heating surface of 42.36 sq. ft., which, with the firebox heating surface of 14.8 sq. ft. and the front plate of 1.78 sq. ft. gave a total heating surface of 58.94 sq. ft. The grate area was 3 sq. ft. A mechanical feed pump provided water for the boiler from the 150-gallon water tank that was slung from the chassis in front of the rear wheels. An auxiliary boiler feed injector was also fitted.

A powered tipping body was fitted to the trial wagon and this operated using a pin-rack and pinion. This was driven through a bevel gear by a shaft connecting to a cross-shaft from a worm gear. The cross-shaft was in turn driven by a chain from the transmission countershaft, the whole being controlled by a cone clutch. The steering used was the Mann worm and sector arrangement, however this was enclosed in an oil bath, and easy steering movement was ensured by mounting the forecarriage on ballbearings. The reporter also noted a number of improvements from previous models, of which some were: circular crossheads and guides to increase the wearing surface, improved safety valves fitted with double springs, the fitting of a feed-water heater, a larger diameter back axle with larger bearing surfaces, and to provide quicker gear changes, a trigger clutch lever was provided in connection with the three-speed gear. The comfort of the driver was also considered in these improvements and to this end the cab was fitted with windscreen, side plates and doors.

The road trial followed a route from Hunslet to York via Tadcaster and back to Leeds through Wetherby, a distance of 50.9 miles. The fire was lit at 8:57 using Ferndale Welsh coal, and by 9:35, 50 p.s.i. was showing on the gauge. At 9:45 the safety valve was blowing at 220 p.s.i. and the machine was ready for the off, having consumed sixty pound of coal in lighting up. The speed when running on the level was 25 m.p.h. so that Tadcaster was reached at 10:50 having covered 14 miles at an average speed of 14.5 m.p.h. The next 10 miles to York was done at an average speed of 24 m.p.h. arriving at 11:15. On the return journey a 9-minute water stop was necessary at Rufforth, and Wetherby was reached at 12:12, having covered 14 miles at an average speed of 14.7 m.p.h. The arrival time at Hunslet was 13:09 with an average speed on the last leg of 16.4 m.p.h. Fuel and water consumption figures are tabulated below and compared with figures obtained for similar earlier machines.[29]

Date	Type	Distance miles	Time mins.	Fuel lb.	Fuel/mile lb.	Water lb.	Water/mile lb.
1913	3-ton	23	140	244	10.6	1,450	63.0
1918	3-ton	27.5	150	223	8.12	1,440	52.3
1924	4-ton	27.5	123	216	7.85	1,490	54.2
1928	4-ton	50.9	180	255	5.0	2,290	44.9

The 1928 machine shows a significant improvement in fuel and water consumption, these being 38% and 17% respectively when compared with the 1924 machine, and even better when compared with earlier wagons.

The final Royal Show at which Mann's Patent Steam Cart and Wagon Company exhibited was the Nottingham Show in 1928. Stand 116 was occupied by a 6-ton steam wagon and a 4-ton steam wagon. These were described as follows: [30]

> 1109 – Steam Wagon, to carry loads up to 6 tons, fitted with three speeds, rubber tyres, and a three-way tipping body, £860.
>
> 1110 - Steam Wagon, to carry loads up to 4 tons, fitted with a tipping body, one-man controlled machine, for running at a fast speed, £770.

References

1 *Catalogue, Mann's Light Steam Agricultural Tractors*, c 1922, p5

2 Kelly, M. A., *The Overtype Steam Wagon*, Goose and Son, 1971, p107

3 Royal Agricultural Society of England, *Catalogue*, Lincoln Show 1920, p160 and p161

4 *The Implement and Machinery Review*, 1 October 1920, p898

5 R.A.S.E., *Trials of Agricultural Tractors*, 1920, p29

6 *The Implement and Machinery Review*, 1 October 1920, p894

7 *The Implement and Machinery Review*, 1 May 1921, p82

8 *The Implement and Machinery Review*, 1 July 1922, p346

9 Yorkshire Agricultural Society, *Hull Show Catalogue*, 1922, p10

10 *Commercial Motor*, 24 April 1923, p302

11 Mann's Patent Steam Cart and Wagon Company, *Catalogue C*, p17

12 Yorkshire Agricultural Society, *Sheffield Show Catalogue*, 1923, p3

13 Mann's Patent Steam Cart and Wagon Company, *Catalogue C*, p51

14 *The Implement and Machinery Review*, 1 June 1923, p216

15 *The Implement and Machinery Review*, 1 November 1923, p806

16 *Catalogue, Mann's Express Wagon*, c 1924, p2

17 *British Patent* 193,316, 1922

18 Yorkshire Agricultural Society, *York Show Catalogue*, 1924, p14

19 *Motor Transport*, 14 July 1924, p47

20 *The Engineer*, 18 July 1924, p81

21 *Commercial Motor*, 17 June 1924, p547

22 Duke, Alan, *Mann Engine List*, Road Locomotive Society, 1988

23 *The World's Carriers*, 16 February 1925

24 Cole, W., *Steaming*, Volume 19, National Traction Engine Trust, p 136

25 Yorkshire Agricultural Society, *Bradford Show Catalogue*, 1925, p37

26 *The World's Carriers*, 15 July 1925, p319

27 *The Implement and Machinery Review*, 1 July 1927, p301

28 *Commercial Motor*, 2 February 1926, p837

29 *Motor Transport*, 31 December 1928, p794

30 Royal Agricultural Society of England, *Catalogue*, Nottingham Show 1928

Chapter 7

Specialist Vehicles

The majority of vehicles emerging from the Pepper Road Works were of the standard 3-ton and 5-ton variety, latterly 4-ton and 6-ton, and these were fitted with a flat load platform, which could be fitted with fixed or hinged sides. There were, however, many customers who wanted special bodies constructing to suit their own needs.

Compartment Wagon

Compartment wagons were primarily aimed at colliery owners, coal agents and municipal authorities. Instead of having a single large compartment, the wagon was divided into four (or other number) parallel compartments each able to tip separately. An article in the journal *The Implement and Machinery Review* gives a good description:[1] "The chassis is of the same type as is used in the company's ordinary 5-ton wagon but, instead of a platform, cross rails are fitted on to the girder frame. On these rails the four tipping boxes are mounted, each box being capable of holding a ton of coal. The boxes are carried on wheels, and can be easily pushed to either side of the wagon; they tip of their own weight, and check chains are provided to prevent them falling off the frame. The Butterley Company, Ltd., Derby, have purchased three of this type of wagon, whilst amongst other colliery owners using it may be named the Cowpen Coal Company, Ltd., Blyth, and Locket's Merthyr Collieries, Ltd., Bute Docks, Cardiff."

Figure 123: Compartment Wagon
Compartment wagons were primarily aimed at colliery owners, coal agents and municipal authorities. They allowed small loads, perhaps of different materials, to tip independently. *(Mann Catalogue)*

One of the specialist machines produced by Mann's was the Gully Cleaner. The primary component of this machine was the vacuum tank to hold the liquors extracted from the road drains etc. The tank had a 1000-gallon capacity and was fitted to a standard tipping chassis. As the vacuum tank was removable, this enabled the vehicle to be used as a standard tipping wagon where necessary. In normal use, i.e. when filling the tank, the tank was held in the horizontal position. When emptying the contents, the rear manhole was swung open and the tank raised to an angle of approximately 45 degrees. This was sufficient to eject the liquid and also to flush out any solid matter.

To clean the gully, a steam ejector, fed from the boiler, was used to create a vacuum of 20 inches in the tank, which was achieved in 5 minutes. The ejector could be operated whilst the vehicle was travelling, so that the vacuum was ready when the wagon stopped. The suction pipe was fitted in the gully and the tank valve opened. The suction pipe was connected to the tank by a 4-inch flexible rubber pipe and was supported by a swivelling jib. The jib was counter balanced to make it easy for the operator to manoeuvre. A gauge indicated if the tank was full, and as an additional safeguard, a high-level float valve was fitted which broke the vacuum to prevent overfilling. To maximise the number of gullies dealt with, it was possible to drain off the settled water from the top of the tank into a street drain. This was done by using a hose connected via a valve fitted two-thirds up the tank. Additional fresh water tanks could be fitted to the vehicle for swilling down and re-sealing the gully siphons. The Mann literature suggests, "With this machine 9 seconds only is required for emptying the average street gully, containing 15 to 20 gallons of liquid. This enables 15 to 20 gullies to be emptied per hour."[2]

Some examples of Mann Gully Cleaners are listed below: [3]

Owner	Engine Number	Date (approx.)
Chertsey Urban District Council	742	1912
Metropolitan Borough of Stepney	1593	1922
London Borough of Hammersmith	1924	1924

Figure 124: Gully Cleaner
Mann's built gully cleaners in small numbers for municipal authorities. The wagon was based on a standard 5-ton (or latterly 6-ton) tipping chassis, to which was fixed a storage tank of 1000-gallon capacity. *(Mann Catalogue)*

Another special vehicle that could be supplied, using the standard steam tipping chassis, was the Street Watering Wagon. This vehicle was fitted with a 1500-gallon tank, and could spray a 20-foot wide strip at 5 m.p.h. covering 15,000 square yards. The water spray was provided by a centrifugal pump, however a lower cost version was available using an "American pattern of sprinkler head", this being fed by gravity from the tank; but this provided an inconsistent spray pattern as the tank emptied. The spray control valves were located adjacent to the driver. The water tank and associated equipment was demountable, allowing the wagon to be used for general haulage work. This was a great benefit as it allowed the vehicle to be fully utilised. The publicity material also relates, "We have given special attention to simplifying the operation of converting from the tipping wagon to the watering tanks so that the change shall be made in about half an hour to avoid waste of time."[4]

A terse but favourable letter from Mr. Chas Jones illustrates a satisfied customer:

Chas Jones Esq., Borough Engineer & Surveyor.
Ealing Corporation, Town Hall Ealing, London. W
January 11, 1909

To Messrs. Mann's Patent Steam Cart & Wagon Co. Ltd.
9, Fenchurch Avenue, London E,C.

Gentlemen,

Your favour of the 9th inst. to hand. In reply to same, although I am not in the habit of giving testimonials, I will do so in this case, because I have found that the 5-ton Steam Wagon that we had from you has fulfilled all that is claimed for it, both as regards its ordinary use, and also for street watering purposes. We have had it in use for three and a half years.

Yours faithfully (signed) CHAS JONES.

A pair of watering wagons was built in 1911 for the State of Patiala in India. The basis of the wagons was the newly introduced 5-ton chain-driven overtype, to which was fitted a 1000-gallon tank. When the vehicle was in motion, a chain-drive drove through bevel gears a pair of rotary sprinklers at the back of the wagon. These could be disengaged when required. When travelling at 5 m.p.h. the sprinklers spun at 1000 r.p.m. and the resulting fine spray covered a path of 60-foot width. For the purposes of filling the tank, a centrifugal pump was fitted, driven from an intermediate shaft by a belt on the flywheel. A steam-operated air ejector was also fitted for priming the pump.[5]

Some examples of Mann Street Watering Wagons are listed below: [6]

Owner	Engine Number	Date (approx.)
Cardiff Corporation	-	1904
Ealing Corporation	336	1905
Surbiton Urban District Council	400	1907
Kingston on Thames Corporation	649	1911
Patiala State, India (2 wagons) [7]	-	1911
Yeovil Corporation	1008	1915
Ealing Corporation	1074	1915
Tottenham Urban District Council	1472	1920
Metropolitan Borough of Hammersmith	1481	1920
Metropolitan Borough of Hammersmith	1482	1920

Figure 125: Street Watering Wagon Another speciality that Mann's built in small numbers for municipal authorities was the Street Watering Wagon. The wagon was based on a standard tipping chassis, to which was fixed a storage tank of 1500-gallon capacity. This particular vehicle was supplied to Surbiton Urban Council in 1907. *(Mann Catalogue)*

High Pressure Tar Sprayer

Yet another variation to the standard wagon was the High Pressure Tar Sprayer. This was fitted with a 1000-gallon rectangular tank, fitted with heating coils to keep the tar at a low viscosity. The spray equipment was of the Aitken type, invented by Thomas Aitken, of Cupar, Scotland. In May of 1907, Rees Jeffreys, then Secretary of the Roads Improvement Association organised a competition of tar spreading machines and the preparation of tar. The trial was carried out on the Hounslow-Staines road to the west of London. The 100-guinea prize was awarded to Thomas Aitken, of Cupar, for his "Aitken's Pneumatic Tar Sprayer". The device consisted of a double acting piston pump driven from the rear axle by roller chains. A dog clutch was fitted to disconnect the pump when not required. The pump did not directly pump the tar, rather it was used to compress air in a receiver at around 200 p.s.i. This air pressure forced the heated tar through distribution pipes to the spray nozzles at the rear of the vehicle. The high pressure arrangement was said to provide penetration of the tar into the road surface: "These nozzles give a fan shaped jet of tar broken up into an exceedingly fine spray which retains the velocity due to the pressure in the receiver and gives a very considerable penetration into the joints of a water-bound macadamised road when surface spraying." [8]

For very heavy tars used in the construction of new roads, the main tank could be fitted with a fire-box and flue to provide additional heating. The system was capable of spraying at a rate of 1,600 gallons per hour, and the controls were operated from the driver's position.

The bulk of these machines were supplied to the Aitken Tar Roads Syndicate Ltd., 29 St. Vincent Place, Glasgow, with the first in 1907. Over the next twenty-two years, Mann's Patent Steam Cart and Wagon Company supplied sixteen Tar Sprayers to Aitken, with the last being recorded as engine number 2003 supplied in 1929. One of these was exported to New Zealand in 1923. According to the journal *Motor Transport* this was built on a standard 5-ton chassis.[9]

Figure 126: High Pressure Tar Sprayer
Another special that Mann's produced was the High Pressure Tar Sprayer for road construction and repair. The spray equipment was invented by Thomas Aitken, of Cupar, Scotland. A 1,000-gallon rectangular tank was fitted with heating coils to keep the tar in a liquid state. *(Mann Catalogue)*

Steam Buses

Steam buses were not a primary product of Mann's Patent Steam Cart and Wagon Company, but they did build a small number. The few that were made were conversions of their standard steam vehicles. The predominant builders of steam buses was the National Steam Car Company and its predecessor, Clarkson Steam Motors, Chelmsford. They produced over two hundred steam buses up to 1919.[10] Mann's earliest example was despatched to India in 1905 and was described in the magazine *Commercial Motor* as, "... for carrying natives, baggage and goods. It was required to have all the room possible for the luggage, so the top portions of the skeleton sides were made with hinges to fall inwards to form seats, and the bottom portions to fall outwards to form foot-rests."[11] The first British application of a Mann wagon used as a bus was illustrated in the journal *Commercial Motor* of December 1906.[12] The machine was used to carry colliers from Doncaster to a pit that was being sunk several miles from the town. The bunker side is labelled WESTFIELD, COAL MERCHANTS, DONCASTER. This company were based at 1 York Road, Doncaster, and they also owned a Mann tractor U1971.[13]

Another example started life as a 5-ton wagon and was converted to a charabanc, probably during the First World War. This was operated for a number of years by G. W. Leggott & Sons, Clayton, Manchester.[14] The last known example was constructed at Pepper Road in 1922 and despatched to Africa. The main vehicle was based on a 5-ton wagon, whilst the bus trailer was constructed from a normal haulage trailer. According to Wilf Cole, a Mann employee, the whole bodywork was probably done in-house as the company had the capability.[15] Unfortunately no further details have survived. In the latter years of the company, there was a proposal for a coach, based on the Mann Express chassis, however there is no evidence that such a vehicle was ever constructed.

Figure 127: Steam Bus and Trailer
This vehicle is based on a standard 5-ton wagon and is probably the bus delivered to Africa in 1922. *(Mann Catalogue)*

Figure 128: Proposed coach based on the Mann Express chassis
By the mid-1920s the petrol-powered bus was becoming an established product and it is unlikely that a steam-powered bus would have found many customers. *(Mann Catalogue)*

Furniture Wagons

The furniture-moving wagon was a specialist type of vehicle that the company became involved with at an early stage. In 1905 the journal *Commercial Motor* reported, "Mann's Limited had recently built a steam wagon for the use of furniture removers,... The advantage of a steam-propelled furniture removal van over the horse-drawn pantechnicon are so obvious as to require no explanation. The transhipment of a full load of house furniture to another dwelling is to-day a long and tedious process, especially when horses have to draw the van the whole distance between the two points. It is quite possible for the owner of the self-propelled vehicle to make two journeys to every one done by horses, and this means an increase of business, not to mention the valuable advertisement gained by the appearance of the vehicles in the street." [16] Another feature of Mann's furniture removing wagons, observed by the publication *Engineering* was the use of supplementary springs. According to the journal, the main wheel springs, by which the total load, tare and paying was carried, were necessarily strong and stiff. To protect the delicate cargo, additional lighter springs were fitted between the chassis and the load-platform to damp out the road shocks before they reached the load-platform.[17]

The following testimonial from Mr. J. Hollin of Chepstow gives a fascinating and glowing report of his vehicle, and the service he received from Mann's:

J. Hollin Esq., Removal Contractor
The Wye Stores, Church Street, Chepstow
September 16, 1909

To Messrs. Mann's Ltd.

Dear Sirs,

Now that I have had time to test the new wagon I bought from you, I beg to congratulate you on the great improvement you have made in them since I had the first from you. I am very proud of it, as it is the best, strongest, and most up-to-date wagon on the market. It runs like a motor car; this is what all the people, including the police say; of course the old wagon had got rather noisy, it was built under the old act with split wheels. If you remember I was one of the first in the country to start Steam Hauling. Some of my friends said I had got a white elephant and it would not last two years, but when they saw it working day and night over our mountains, doing all kinds of work, carrying Coal, Lime, Stones, Furniture, etc,. for nearly eight years, they said it was a marvel. This old wagon has never been out of our yard for repair; all the repairs that have been done to it have been done by ourselves. If any thing was worn out, or went wrong during the day, when the wagon returned in the evening, I have wired you for parts required, and although you are about 200 miles away, I have received them by 6 a.m. next morning, in time to fix them and go on our day's work. This old wagon took five tons of Coal a journey of fourteen miles the last day we used her. I only sold her because I have not enough work for the two. There was nothing whatever done to the boiler, she was never re-tubed, there was only one tube leaking, the last day we used her. In my opinion yours is the best boiler made, this will prove it, and I would not change with any other wagon on the road. New one only uses half the fuel the old wagon did, and can do three times the distance without stopping for water. I expect this new wagon to run ten years, and I am sure I shall never regret buying the second Mann's Wagon.

Yours truly, (signed) J. HOLLINS.

Steel Plate Carrier

In 1907 a steel-plate carrier was made for Swan, Hunter and Wigham Richardson, Limited, the ship builders of Wallsend-on-Tyne. The machine was sufficiently low to carry large shell plates below the frame of the vessel, after which they were lifted into position by hydraulic jacks. The machine must have been very costly to manufacture as it shares very few components with the standard wagons being produced at the same period. The chassis is very heavily constructed with riveted box girder sections for the bulk of its length. Within the rear of this chassis was the undertype engine with long pipes carrying the steam from the front mounted boiler and back to the chimney. The return pipe can clearly be seen running along the side of the chassis. By necessity the chimney was horizontal, so as to avoid clashing with the load being carried on top of the machine. The boiler appears to be a conventional locomotive type with the firehole fitted to the firebox backplate, rather than the side entry arrangement normally associated with Mann boilers. Steering was achieved by a horizontal shaft, placed crosswise, and fitted with a steering wheel at each end. The driver was thus able to steer from either side, as the occasion demanded.[18] Similarly, the centrally located main steam valve or regulator was fitted with a double-ended operating lever that allowed the operator to control the wagon from either side of the vehicle. The subsequent history of this wagon is unknown.

Figure 129: Mann Furniture Wagon
Furniture wagons were built in small numbers for household removers. These wagons featured supplementary springs between the chassis and the load platform to protect the contents from jolts caused by the poor road surfaces of the day. *(Mann Catalogue)*

Figure 130: Steel Plate Carrier
This very robust looking steel-plate carrier was made in 1907 for Swan, Hunter and Wigham Richardson, Limited, the ship builders of Wallsend-on-Tyne. The original photograph shows a load around twice as long as the wagon, however this view has been trimmed to emphasise the wagon detail. *(Michael Walters collection)*

References

1 *The Implement and Machinery Review*, 1 November 1916, p774
2 Mann's Patent Steam Cart and Wagon Company, *Catalogue C*, p67
3 Duke, Alan, *Mann Engine List*, Road Locomotive Society, 1988
4 Mann's Patent Steam Cart and Wagon Company, *Catalogue C*, p69
5 *Commercial Motor*, 28 September 1911, p77
6 Duke, Alan, *Mann Engine List*, Road Locomotive Society, 1988
7 *Commercial Motor*, 28 September 1911, p77
8 Mann's Patent Steam Cart and Wagon Company, *Catalogue C*, p70
9 *Motor Transport*, 13 November 1922, p637
10 Lee, Charles E., "*Rise and Decline of the Steam-Driven Omnibus*" Lecture, Inst. C. E., 14 March 1951
11 *Commercial Motor*, 23 March 1905, Supplement, p6
12 *Commercial Motor*, 6 December 1906, p293
13 *Doncaster Gazette*, 10 September 1964
14 Stoyel, B. D., *Portfolio 18*, Road Locomotive Society, 1947
15 Wright, G. & Cole, W., *Portfolio number 18*, Road Locomotive Society, 1949
16 *Commercial Motor*, 28 September 1905, p41
17 *Engineering*, 25 June 1909, p852
18 *Commercial Motor*, 26 September 1907, p80

Chapter 8

Users of Mann's Carts and Wagons

The following information is largely based on the Alan Duke records held by the Road Locomotive Society. Because the actual records of Mann's Patent Steam Cart and Wagon Company have not survived, the data presented is based on the best available evidence and may be incomplete.

Breweries

Figure 131: Sam Smith's Brewery Wagon
This delivery wagon is in service with Sam Smith's Brewery, Tadcaster, North Yorkshire. The wagon is a 5-ton undertype. *(Leeds & District Traction Engine Club collection)*

One of the most successful and earliest applications of the Mann wagon was the brewery wagon. This was, in part, due to the two-stage suspension fitted to these vehicles. As well as the primary suspension on the wheels, a secondary set of springs was fitted underneath the load platform to further isolate the bottles from the poor road surfaces. The first identified example was delivered to J. W. Cameron's Brewery in 1901. In a testimonial they state: [1]

J. W. Cameron & Co. Ltd.
Lion Brewery, West Hartlepool
February 9, 1910

To Messrs. Mann's Patent Steam Cart & Wagon Co. Ltd., LEEDS.

Dear Sirs,
We purchased two of your steam wagons in 1901, a third in 1904, and two more in July 1908 and March 1909 respectively. Our experience of their running is satisfactory over long distances for which the wagons have been almost exclusively used. The later type of wagon is a material improvement on the original design: they are good hill climbers and are generally reliable.

(signed) p.pro J. W. CAMERON & Co. Ltd.
A. T. MORGAN, DIRECTOR

In a report on the 1909 Brewers' Exhibition, held at the Agricultural Hall, Islington, the commentator makes the following remarks about William Hancock's Brewery at Cardiff. "This is the ninth steam wagon which they have built for this firm, which fact, in itself, is an excellent testimony to the good running of this make of machine. This important brewing firm have told Messrs. Mann that hey have found the use of steam waggons in their business of considerable advantage to them, and have found waggons of Messrs. Mann's manufacture most satisfactory."[2]

The following list identifies some of the breweries using Mann wagons. Note that some wagons were not new when purchased by the brewery.

Albion Brewery (Leeds) Ltd.
Ashby's Staines Brewery Ltd.
Ashton Gate Brewery, Bristol
Aylesbury Brewery Co. Ltd.
Barclay Perkins, Southwark
Bentley's Yorkshire Breweries Ltd., Woodlesford
Buchan, Romney
J. W. Cameron & Co. Ltd., West Hartlepool
Crosswell's Cardiff Brewery Ltd.
Crowley, Alton
Eley's Stafford Brewery Ltd.
Forster's Bishop Middleham Brewery Co.
Hansard, Merthyr
Hey and Co., Bradford
Holt Brothers, Burnham
Hook Norton Brewery, Oxfordshire
Jennings, Cockermouth
Jones, Aberdare
Lamb Brewery, Frome
Mappin's Masbro' Old Brewery, Rotherham
McMullen & Son, The Brewery, Hertford
Mitchell, Toms, Chard
Morgan & Sons Ltd., Pontyclun
Morris & Co. Ampthill Brewery
Newcastle Breweries Ltd.
Ord, Battiscombe and Elwes, Somerton, Somerset
Phillips, Newport
Powley, Sunderland
Reffells, Bexley Brewery, Kent
Rhymney Brewery Co., Monmouthshire
Robinson Brothers (Brewers) Ltd., Houghton-le-Spring, Co. Durham
Samuel Smith's Brewery, Tadcaster
Welsh, Winchester
West Auckland Brewery, Co. Durham
William Hancock Co. Ltd., Cardiff
Winchester Brewery Co. Ltd.
Wolverhampton & Dudley Breweries

Figure 132: Bentley's Yorkshire Breweries Ltd., Woodlesford
This view, taken outside Bentley's Yorkshire Breweries illustrates on the right, a Mann 5-ton undertype wagon, and on the left, a pair of Yorkshire wagons. *(Leeds and District Traction Engine Club collection)*

Local Councils

The largest group of users of the Mann wagon, in all its varieties, was local councils. These machines were predominantly wagons, tipping wagons and roller wagons, although the more specialised types were also bought in small numbers, e.g. gully flushers and water carts.[3]

Aberdare Urban District Council
Abertillery Rural District Council
Acton Urban District Council, Middlesex
Alcester Rural District Council
Argyllshire County Council
Ashton under Lyne Corporation
Barry Urban District Council
Batley Corporation
Belfast Corporation
Blackburn Rural District Council
Bristol Corporation
Brixworth Rural District Council
Burgh of Aberdeen (Links and Parks Dept.)
Burnley Rural District Council
Cairo City Council, Egypt
Cardiff Corporation
Kingston upon Thames Corporation
Lancashire Rural District Council
Lancaster Corporation
Leeds Corporation
Liverpool Corporation
London Borough of Hammersmith
Long Ashton Rural District Council,
Loughborough Corporation
Lunesdale Rural District Council, Lancashire
Malton Rural District Council
Marsden Urban District Council
Merthyr Tydfil Corporation
Metropolitan Borough of Hammersmith
Metropolitan Borough of Hampstead
Metropolitan Borough of Lambeth
Metropolitan Borough of Stepney

Cardiganshire County Council
Cheltenham Corporation
Chepping Wycombe Corporation
Chertsey Urban District Council
Chesterfield Corporation
Chester-le-Street Rural District Council
Coventry Corporation
Croydon Corporation
Devonport Corporation
Doncaster Corporation (Gas Dept.)
Douglas Corporation, Isle of Man
Dumfriesshire County Council
Durham County Council
Ealing Corporation
East Ham Corporation
Eastleigh Rural District Council
Elgin (later Morayshire) County Council
Esher & The Dittons Urban District Council
Exeter Corporation
Fylde Rural District Council, Lancashire
Gateshead Corporation
Gloucester Corporation
Great Yarmouth Corporation
Hereford Corporation
Herefordshire County Council
Hornsey Corporation, Middlesex
Hucknall Urban District Council
Ilford Urban District Council
Ipswich Corporation
Itchen Urban District Council, Southampton
Kent County Council
Kerry County Council
Metropolitan Borough of Wandsworth
Monmouthshire County Council
Mountain Ash Urban District Council
Neath Rural District Council
North Riding County Council
Nuneaton Corporation
Oakham Rural District Council
Plymouth Corporation
Portsmouth Corporation
Rhondda Urban District Council
Ripon Rural District Council
Seisdon Rural District Council, Staffs
Settle Rural District Council
Shanghai Municipality, China
Southampton Corporation
Spilsby Rural District Council, Lindsey
Stanley Urban District Council
Surbiton Urban District Council, Surrey
Thirsk Rural District Council, North Riding
Tottenham Urban District Council
Tyrone County Council
Walthamstow Urban District Council
Wandsworth Corporation
Warwickshire County Council
Washington Urban District Council
West Riding County Council
Weston-Super-Mare Urban District Council
Wetherby Rural District Council
Wharfedale Rural District Council
Wimbledon Corporation, Surrey
Worcestershire County Council
Yeovil Corporation

Machines Exported

Unfortunately, the record of exported machines is particularly poor, and understates the company's achievements. The largest recipient country appears to be Australia, however other known destinations include: Africa, Austria, Canada, China, Egypt, Germany, India, Manila, New Zealand, Spain, South America and Switzerland. In a letter written in 1916, the Australian company, Gibson Battle & Co. Ltd., 535 Kent Street, Sydney, N.S.W., state that they supplied four Mann steam tipping carts, one 5-ton version to Alexandria Municipality, a second 5-ton version to Bathurst Municipality, and two to Port Adelaide Municipal Council; unfortunately no dates are given.[4] Gibson Battle were machinery dealers, amongst other things, and it does appear that they acted as agents for Mann. This is certainly possible as they also acted for J. & H. McLaren, of Leeds, and given James Mann's early links with McLaren it is likely that they came to some amicable arrangement.

Some examples of exported machines are listed below: [5]

Destination	Engine Number	Date (approx.)	Type
H. Reifenrath, Germany	28	1898	Roller 14-ton
Fraser & Neave, Singapore [6]	-	1903	Wagon
India	-	1905	Omnibus
Austria	-	1906	Timber wagon
Clayton Gas Co., Egypt	-	1907	Wagon 2-ton, fire extinguisher
Vienna, Austria**	-	1909	Wagon 5-ton
Harris, Scaife, Australia [7]	-	1909	Wagon 5-ton
Sydney, Australia [8]	51x	1909	Steam Cart
Shanghai Corporation, China [9]	-	1911	Roller Wagon
Cairo City Council, Egypt	665	1911	Roller Wagon
Patiala State, Delhi, India [10]	-	1911	Road Sprinkler (batch of 2)
Entumeni, Natal, South Africa[11]	-	1911	Agricultural Tractor
Canada	751	1912	Agricultural Tractor
New Zealand	-	1912	-
Vancouver, Canada [12]	-	1913	Wagons (batch of 6)
South America [13]	-	1913	5-ton wagon
DSFB Co. Ltd., Adelaide [14]	85x	1913	Steam Cart/Roller (batch of 8)
DSFB Co. Ltd., Australia	87x	1913	Wagon
H.M. India Office[15]	-	1913	Steam Cart (batch of 6)
Delhi, India[16]	-	1913	Direct Ploughing Tractor
Africa	-	1922	Omnibus
New Zealand	15xx	1923	Tar Sprayer
South Australian Government	159x	1923	Wagon (3 vehicles)
Australia	1673	1927	Wagon

** - supplied to Angol Gephulonlegessegck, Vienna [17]
x - indicates that this digit is not known

A German catalogue produced by John Fowler's Magdeburg branch, circa 1902, has recently been discovered. Entitled *Fowler's Dampf-Rollwagen und Dampf-Kippkarren, system Mann*, the contents illustrate and describe the Mann steam cart and steam lorry. It is clear from this evidence that Fowler's were acting as Mann's agents in Eastern Europe. Fowler's Magdeburg branch was established as a separate company in 1872, and eventually had branches in Prague, Vienna, Budapest and Kiev. These offices controlled the sales in the whole of Eastern Europe including Greece and Turkey. It is not known how long the arrangement between Mann and Fowler lasted, or how many Mann vehicles were sold through this operation, however, due to the First World War, the Magdeburg company closed in 1916.

Figure 133: Mann Wagon at the Instituto de la Patagonia, South America
This wagon was used for carrying bales of wool by the Sociedad Explotadora de Tierra del Fuego (SETF). This organisation was set up in 1893 as a sheep ranching enterprise in Patagonia, at its height, the company owned almost two-million sheep. *(Richard Morris)*

Figure 134: John Fowler catalogue illustrating Mann vehicle.
This illustration was included in a German catalogue produced by John Fowler's Magdeburg branch, circa 1902. It is clear from this evidence that Fowlers were acting as Mann's agents in Eastern Europe. (*Stefan Mattes collection*)

The largest individual user of Mann machines was the hauliers, G. W. Leggott & Son, Clayton, Manchester. Over the period 1913 to 1932 this company purchased twenty-three machines, although the majority were second hand. In the journal *The World's Carriers* a view of a new Mann Express wagon is shown to an order placed by G. W. Leggott, however no further evidence of this wagon is known.[18]

The quarry owners P. W. Spencer, Lothersdale, West Riding, owned nine machines purchased over the years 1911 to 1922. However an article in the magazine *Commercial Motor* suggests that they had been using Mann wagons for a much longer period, "The first machine, purchased about 18 years ago, is now at Lothersdale, and was working up to a short time ago. The second engine, about 17 years of age, is still in harness and running well at Giggleswick. The carriage of lime and limestone over difficult roads with stiff gradients is heavy work."[19] These wagons often featured in Mann publicity.

George Armitage & Sons Ltd. were a local brick maker with a quarry at Robin Hood, only three miles south of the Pepper Road works. They purchased nine wagons, mainly of the tipping variety between 1908 and 1929.

The last of the big individual users was George Hattersley & Sons Ltd., Keighley. Hattersley were famous manufacturers of textile machinery; one of their achievements was the construction in 1834 of the first power loom for weaving worsted cloth. They had owned fourteen wagons by the year 1917 and another five were purchased after this date. An article in the journal *Commercial Motor* gives some details on the Hattersley wagons and particularly

Figure 135: Hattersley Steam Lorry
This view of an early Mann steam lorry shows it loaded with textile machinery made by the Keighley firm of George Hattersley & Sons Ltd. Richard Longden Hattersley was a director of Mann's Patent Steam Cart and Wagon Company. *(John Middlemiss collection)*

vehicle U1335: "This engine had been working for seven years, carrying supplies to the works, principally pig iron and coke, and the firm has been using Mann vehicles for at least 18 years. To the knowledge of the present foreman, 14 engines have been purchased during 15 years, and in his words there had not been a "wrong-un" amongst them. The earlier machines had steel tyres, but of recent years rubber tyres have been adopted, a course which was found to lead to a considerable saving in the repair bills, added to the lives of the vehicles, and also contributed to the comfort of the drivers." [20] It is likely that the other Mann wagons were used for similar purposes and for the delivery of machinery to the many woollen mills in the West Riding. Richard Longden Hattersley, one of George Hattersley's sons, was a director and shareholder of Mann's Patent Steam Cart and Wagon Company.

References

1 Mann's Patent Steam Cart and Wagon Company, *Catalogue,* 1910, p59
2 *Motor Traction*, 16 October 1909, p315
3 Duke, Alan, *Mann Engine List*, Road Locomotive Society, 1988
4 Letter to Water Conservation & Irrigation Commission, Sydney, from Gibson Battle, 12 October 1916
5 Duke, Alan, *Mann Engine List*, Road Locomotive Society, 1988
6 *Commercial Motor*, 21 February 1907, p551
7 *Commercial Motor*, 30 September 1909, p77
8 *Commercial Motor*, 24 June 1909, p328A
9 *Commercial Motor*, 22 June 1911, p326
10 *Commercial Motor*, 28 September 1911, p77
11 *Commercial Motor*, 22 June 1911, p325
12 *Commercial Motor*, January 1913, p17 (Supplement)
13 *Commercial Motor*, January 1914, p8 (Supplement)
14 *Commercial Motor*, 3 July 1913, p427
15 *Commercial Motor*, January 1914, p8 (Supplement)
16 *Commercial Motor*, January 1914, p35 (Supplement)
17 *Commercial Motor*, 30 September 1909, p77
18 *The World's Carriers*, 16 February 1925
19 *Commercial Motor*, 6 December 1917, p317
20 *Commercial Motor*, 20 December 1917, p363

Chapter 9

Reminders of Mann's Patent Steam Cart and Wagon Company

In their 36 years of existence, Mann's produced nearly two thousand road vehicles, primarily steam wagons and carts. They were one of the principal suppliers of steam wagons, with a superb reputation for reliability and longevity. Unfortunately, Mann's did not make the transition to internal combustion powered vehicles and this sealed their fate. Nevertheless, their innovations were many, including the single eccentric valve gear and the overtype steam wagon.

Figure 136: Mann's Patent Steam Cart and Wagon Company, Blue Plaque
This commemorative plaque, on the Pepper Road Works, was organised by the Leeds & District Traction Engine Society. It was unveiled on 15 June 2003 to recognise the pioneering achievements of Mann's Patent Steam Cart and Wagon Company.

There are few surviving artefacts of Mann's Patent Steam Cart and Wagon Company and its predecessor Mann and Charlesworth. The original Canning Street works of Mann and Charlesworth no longer exists. The site on Dewsbury Road is now buried under the approach roads to the M621 motorway. The Pepper Road works occupied by Mann's Patent Steam Cart and Wagon Company does still exist, and externally these buildings are largely unaltered. In the summer of 2003 the Leeds & District Traction Engine Society in association with the Leeds Civic Trust unveiled a Blue Plaque commemorating the achievements of the company. There are also a number of vehicles preserved both in Britain and around the world, in Canada, Australia and South America. These physical reminders of Mann's Patent Steam Cart and Wagon Company will hopefully stand the test of time, and prevent future generations forgetting the pioneering achievements of the company who played an important role in establishing steam road transport in Britain and elsewhere.

Figure 137: The Pepper Road Works in 2004
This view of the Pepper Road Works in 2004 shows it in the ownership of PONTIFEX, a company manufacturing high-grade stainless steel pressure vessels for process industries. The external view of the building is largely unaltered from when it was opened in 1901. *(Malcolm Parsons)*

Figure 138: Preserved Mann Tractor
Roy Wakefield's superbly restored Brinkburn Lass, Mann 1386 of 1919, was present in Leeds at the Blue Plaque event. It spent its working life on the Fenwick and Brinkburn estates in Northumberland, where it was used in ploughing and sawmills.

Figure 139: Preserved Mann Wagons
The 2004 Bedfordshire Show at Old Warden Park is the setting for this superb photograph. On the left is 5-ton wagon 1120 of 1916, whilst on the right is 3-ton wagon 1365 of 1919, both magnificently restored. *(Paul Sharpe - www.sharpos-world.co.uk)*

Appendix 1

Land Registration, Canning Street, 7 June 1893

The following text is taken from deed book 19, page 766, held in the West Riding Registry of Deeds, Wakefield.

Memorial of an indenture for registration dated 7th day of June 1893.

The London and Midland Bank Limited having its offices situate at number 52 Cornhill in the City of London of the one part, and

James Hutchinson Mann and George Hutchinson Mann both of the City of Leeds, Mechanical Engineers of the other part.

All that parcel of land situate in the township of Hunslet in the City of Leeds aforesaid formerly part of lands called Dunwell Ings and measuring on the north side thereof (including one half of Smithson Street, nine yards wide) One hundred and thirty feet eight inches, on the South side (including one half of Smithson Street aforesaid) 135 feet, on the East side (including one half in width of Canning Street nine yards wide and Borough Street eight yards wide) One hundred and thirty four feet two inches, and on the west side (including as last aforesaid) One hundred and twenty seven feet eight inches be the same measurement respectively more or less and containing altogether including the halves of Canning Street, Smithson Street and Borough Street aforesaid so far as coextensive with said parcel of land Two thousand and twelve square yards be the same more or less, and bounded on the north by the middle of Canning Street aforesaid, on the south in part by the middle of Borough Street and in the remaining part by the hereditaments now or lately belonging to Mr Wood, on the east in part by Dewsbury Road and in the remaining part by the said hereditaments now or lately belonging to Mr Wood, and on the west by the middle of Smithson Street aforesaid.

Also all those workshops warehouses sheds and other buildings erected and standing on part of the said land and called Canning Street Works and which said parcel of land and premises formed Lot 89 on the sale plan of the Jack Lane Estate of John Charles Burton Borough of whom the same were purchased by Thomas Bell and were lately in the occupation of Tom Thompson and Abraham Wilson but now of Walter Foster. Also all the steam engine boiler shafting, going gear, piers and beams for a Goliath and other fixtures now on the premise, the property of the said bank.

Appendix 2

Land Registration, Pepper Road, 29 September 1900

The following text is taken from deed book 42, page 4, held in the West Riding Registry of Deeds, Wakefield.

Memorial of an indenture of conveyance for registration dated 29th day of September 1900.

Graham, Morton, and Company Limited (whose registered office was formerly situate at Amberley House, Norfolk Street, London WC, but is now situate at Black Bull Street in the City of Leeds) Engineers, hereinafter referred to as "the vendors" of the one part, and
Mann's Patent Steam Cart and Wagon Company Limited (whose registered office is situate at the Canning Works, Dewsbury Road in the City of Leeds) Engineers of the other part.

All that plot of land situate on the South easterly side of Pepper Road in Hunslet in Leeds aforesaid measuring in length from North west to South East on the North East side thereof Two hundred and seventy one feet ten inches, and on the South West side thereof Three hundred and two feet ten inches, and in breadth from the North East to South West on the North West side thereof (including the half in width of Cumberland Street thirty six feet wide on the South West) One hundred and forty seven feet and on the South East side thereof (including the aforesaid) One hundred and fifty three feet containing in the whole four thousand six hundred and ninety three square yards or thereabouts and bounded on or towards the North or North East by other property of the said Joshua Bower on or towards the South or South West by the middle of Cumberland Street on or towards the East or South East by property of the Middleton Estates and Colliery Company Limited and on or towards the West or North West by other property of the said Joshua Bower. And which said plot of land is more particularly delineated in the plan drawn on an Indenture dates the twentieth day of May One Thousand eight hundred and ninety eight and made between Joshua Bower of the one part and the Vendors of the other part...

Appendix 3

Patents of Mann's patent Steam Cart and Wagon Company and its predecessor

Number	Application	Title
13,958	20 July 1894	Improved Arrangements of Reversing Gear for Steam and other Engines
2571	6 February 1895	Improvements in Shaft or Automatic Expansion Governors for Steam Engines
11,578	14 June 1895	Improved Double Crank Shaft Bracket for Traction Engines and Road Rollers
13,236	14 June 1898	Improvements in or in connection with Road Traction Engines and Draught Road Vehicles adapted to be used therewith
19,786	5 November 1900	Improvements in or in connection with Road Traction Engines and Draught Road Vehicles adapted to be used therewith
21,085	22 November 1900	Improvements in or in connection with Steam Wagons or Vehicles for the Conveyance of Passengers and Goods on Common Roads
8654	27 April 1901	Improvements in or in connection with the Mounting and Transport of Field Artillery
25,998	20 December 1901	Improvements in or in connection with Steam Carts
21,044	27 September 1902	Improvements in or in connection with Road Locomotives and Trucks, Wagons or Carts forming part of the same or adapted to be used therewith
584	9 January 1904	An Improvement or Improvements in or relating to Lubricators
2109	28 January 1904	An Improved Construction of Wheel for Traction Engines, Road Locomotives and the like
1347	24 January 1905	Improved Method and Means for Filling Steam Carts, Wagons and the like
2207	4 February 1905	An Improvement in Self-propelled Road Vehicles, Heavy Motor Cars and the like
742	11 January 1906	Improvements in or relating to Means for Weighing, whilst Filling and on Delivery, Definite Separate Portions of the Load of Motor Propelled Vehicles
1539	20 January 1906	An Improvement in or relating to Pipe Joints
14,469	24 June 1907	Improvements in and in connection with Boilers for Steam Motor Vehicles
14,469A	24 June 1907	Improvements in and in connection with Means for Firing Boilers for Steam Motor Vehicles and for other purposes
173,698	18 January 1921	Improvements in or relating to Boilers of the Locomotive Fire-tube Type
175,851	30 December 1920	Improvements in or relating to Boilers of the Locomotive Fire-tube Type
193,316	12 April 1922	Improvements in or relating to Vertical Boilers
252,947	5 September 1925	Improvements in or relating to Tipping Gear for Motor Road Vehicles

Appendix 4

Mann and Charlesworth Price List circa 1897

MANN & CHARLESWORTH, Canning, Works, LEEDS.

TELEGRAPHIC ADDRESS: "CANNING, LEEDS."
TELEPHONE No. 1335.

A.B.C. CODE USED.

PRICE LIST.

PATENT TRACTION ENGINES.—Complete, with Two Speeds, Winding Drum, Differential Gear, Water Lifter, and Outfit.

Nominal Horse Power.	Single Cylinder Engine.	EXTRAS.							
		Tandem Compound.	Double Crank Compound.	Extra Tank.	Springs.	Injector.	Awning.	Crane.	Close Packed.
5 ...	£360	...	...	£14	£30	£7	£8	£45	£8
7 ...	410	£35	£55	16	35	8	10	50	9
8 ...	465	42	75	18	40	8	12	60	12
10 ...	530	50	100	20	45	10	15	70	15

TRACTION WAGONS.—With Wrought-Iron Wheels, Draw-bar, Brake, and Springs.
To carry **4 Tons, £63**; to carry **6 Tons, £73**; to carry **8 Tons, £83.**

TANDEM COMPOUND SELF-CONTAINED SEMI-PORTABLE ENGINES, with Patent Automatic Expansion Gear.

Nominal Horse Power.	Price.	Injector.	Feed Heater.	Packing.
9	£275	£8	£10	£8
12	315	8	15	10
16	380	10	15	14
20	450	10	20	18
25	560	15	25	20

SELF-CONTAINED HORIZONTAL ENGINES, with Automatic Expansion Gear.

Nominal Horse Power.	Tandem Compound.	Single Cylinder.	Feed Heater.	Foundation Bolts.	Packing.
6	...	£64	£10	£2 0s.	£3 0s.
9	£145	90	10	2 10	4 10
12	175	120	15	3 0	6 0
16	205	...	15	3 10	7 10
20	230	...	20	4 0	9 0
25	290	...	25	5 0	11 0

SELF-CONTAINED VERTICAL ENGINES AND BOILERS.

Nominal Horse Power.	Engine and Boiler Combined, with Base Plate & Pump	Lagging.	Travelling Wheels.	Packing.	Foundation Bolts.	Engine only.	Feed Pump.	Automatic Expansion Governor.	Separate Vertical Boiler.
3 ...	£75	£3 10s.	£9	£2 5s.	£0 10s.	£32	£2 0s.	£3	£36
4½ ...	96	4 0	12	2 10	0 15	42	2 10	4	47
6 ...	125	5 0	...	3 0	1 0	55	3 0	5	60
8 ...	157	6 0	...	3 5	1 5	67	3 10	6	80
10 ...	180	6 10	...	3 10	1 10	80	3 10	7	88

Prices for Patent Shaft Governors, Single Eccentric Reversing Gears, and Road Rollers free on application.

Subject to alteration without notice.

Appendix 5

Early British Road Traffic Legislation

One of the biggest influences on road vehicle design was not the technology itself but road legislation. In the Victorian period, motorised vehicles developed rapidly and as a result, legislation was introduced to govern such things as speed and loading. The rules became so restrictive that, for the manufacturer, greater freedom was often abroad where higher speeds were possible and, as a result, the most technically interesting locomotives were the ones exported. Nevertheless, the ingenious manufacturers were keen to exploit any change in the rules and thereby give them a market advantage.

Prior to 1861 there were no specific laws in Britain governing steam powered road vehicles. Nevertheless, ordinary "Common Law" applied to any vehicle and so drivers were not allowed to cause nuisance and were to respect other road users. The first British law specifically governing steam powered road vehicles was **The Locomotive Act 1861**. The particular clauses applying to the construction of motorised vehicles were:

S3. Locomotives propelled by steam or any other than animal power and not drawing any carriage to have tyres of wheels 3in. wide for the first 3 tons weight, plus 1in. for each additional ton; if drawing a wagon or carriage, tyres of Locomotives to be not less than 9in.; unless specially licensed, no Locomotive to exceed 7ft. in width or 12 tons in weight; and wheels to be cylindrical and smooth soled.

S8. Every Locomotive propelled by steam or any other than animal power to be used on any Turnpike or public highway shall be constructed on the principle of consuming, and so to consume its own smoke. Maximum penalty for infringement £5 per day.

S9. Locomotives to be in charge of two persons, or three if carriages or wagons attached; two lights to be carried on front of locomotive at night.

S11. Speed limit 10 m.p.h. in the country and 5 m.p.h. in towns.

Four years later a more restrictive set of rules was put in place, **The Locomotive Act 1865**. This was the notorious 'Red Flag Act', so named because of the introduction of clause S3, which replaced clause S9 in the 1861 act:

> S3. Every Locomotive propelled by Steam or any other than Animal Power on any Turnpike Road or public Highway shall be worked according to the following Rules and Regulations; viz.
>
> Firstly at least three persons shall be employed to drive or conduct such Locomotive, and if more than Two Waggons or Carriages be attached thereto, an additional Person shall be employed, who shall take charge of such Waggons or Carriages:
>
> Secondly, one of such Persons, while any Locomotive is in Motion, shall precede such Locomotive on Foot by not less than Sixty Yards, and shall carry a Red Flag constantly displayed, and shall warn the Riders and Drivers of Horses of the Approach of such Locomotives, and shall signal the Driver thereof when it shall be necessary to stop, and shall assist Horses, and Carriages drawn by Horses, passing the same:
>
> Thirdly, the Drivers of such Locomotives shall give as much Space as possible for the passing of other traffic:
>
> Fourthly, the Whistle of such Locomotives shall not be sounded for any Purpose whatever; nor shall the Cylinder Taps be opened within Sight of any Person riding, driving, leading, or in charge of a Horse upon the Road; nor shall the Steam be allowed to attain a Pressure such as to exceed the Limit fixed by the Safety Valve, so that no Steam shall blow off when the Locomotive is upon the Road:
>
> Fifthly, every such Locomotive shall be instantly stopped, on the Person preceding the same, or any

other Person with a Horse or Carriage drawn by a Horse, putting up his Hand as a Signal to require such Locomotive to be stopped:

Sixthly, any Person in charge of any such Locomotive shall provide Two efficient Lights to be affixed conspicuously, One at each Side on the Front of the same, between the Hours of One Hour after Sunset and One Hour before Sunrise.

S4. Subject and without Prejudice to the Regulations herein-after authorised to be made by Local Authorities, it shall not be lawful to drive any such Locomotive along any Turnpike Road or public Highway at a greater speed than Four Miles an Hour, or through any City Town, or Village at a greater speed than Two Miles an Hour; any Person acting contrary thereto shall for every such Offence, on summary Conviction thereto, forfeit any Sum not exceeding Ten Pounds.

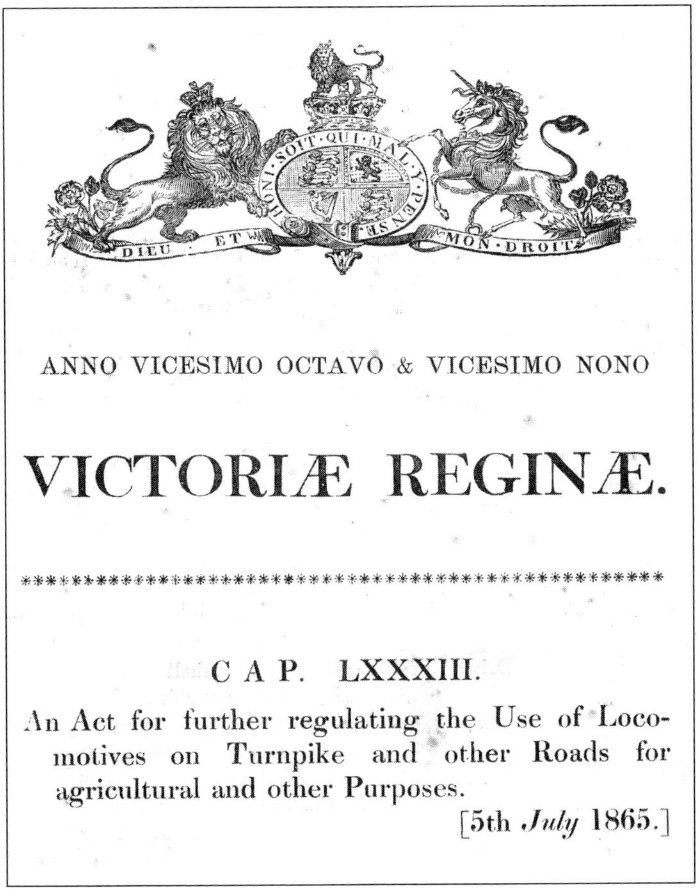

ANNO VICESIMO OCTAVO & VICESIMO NONO

VICTORIÆ REGINÆ.

****

C A P. LXXXIII.

An Act for further regulating the Use of Locomotives on Turnpike and other Roads for agricultural and other Purposes.

[5th *July* 1865.]

Figure 140: Cover of The Locomotive Act, 1865

These rigid controls remained in place for 13 years; however in 1873 a Select Committee on Locomotives on Roads was convened to examine the effect of the 1861 and 1865 Acts. After much deliberation they concluded, amongst other things, that the use of the Red Flag should be abandoned. The result of the Committee's efforts were put into effect by the **Highways and Locomotives (Amendment) Act 1878**, which is dated 16 August 1878. Curiously the amendments were specifically excluded from Scotland, Ireland and the Isle of Wight. The specific clauses affecting locomotive construction were as follows:

Section 28

1 A locomotive not drawing any carriage, and not exceeding in weight three tons, shall have the tires of the wheels thereof not less than three inches in width, with an additional inch for every ton or fraction of a ton above the first three tons.
2 A locomotive drawing any Waggon or carriage shall have the tires of the driving wheels thereof not less than two inches in width for every ton in weight of the locomotive unless the diameter of such wheels shall exceed five feet, when the width of the tires may be reduced in the same proportion as the diameter of the wheels is increased, but in such cases the width of such tires shall be not be less than fourteen inches.
3 A locomotive shall not exceed nine feet in width or fourteen tons in weight, except hereinafter provided.
4 The driving wheels of a locomotive shall be cylindrical and smooth-soled, or shod with diagonal cross-bars of not less than three inches in width nor more than three quarters of an inch in thickness, extending the full breadth of the tire, and the space intervening between each such cross-bar shall not exceed three inches.
With regard to the red flag requirement, i.e. the second clause of section 3 of **The Locomotive Act 1865**, this was reworded to read: "*Secondly, one of such persons, while the locomotive is in motion, shall precede by at least twenty yards the locomotive on foot, and shall in case of need assist horses and carriages drawn by horses, passing the same.*"
The requirement for consuming smoke was slightly modified to make it more realistic, thus: "*Every locomotive used on any turnpike road or highway shall be constructed on the principle of consuming its own smoke; and any person using any locomotive not so constructed, or not consuming, so far as practicable, its own smoke, shall be liable to a fine not exceeding five pounds for every day during which such locomotive is used on any such turnpike road or highway.*"

By the end of the nineteenth century, private motor cars were becoming more common but these were still subject to the same rules as locomotives. As a result of much canvassing, a new law was enacted defining a Light Locomotive. The new law was titled **Locomotives on Highways Act 1896.** In this document the important phrase was: "Any vehicle propelled by mechanical power if it is under three tons in weight, unladen, and is not used for the purpose of drawing more than one vehicle (such vehicle with its locomotive not to exceed in weight unladen four tons), and is so constructed that no smoke or visible vapour is emitted therefrom except from any temporary or accidental cause; and vehicles so exempted, whether locomotive or drawn by locomotives, are in this act referred to as light locomotives."

In addition, the following sections affected the engine construction;

3 Every light locomotive shall carry a bell or other instrument capable of giving audible and sufficient warning of the approach or position of the carriage.

4 No light locomotive shall travel along a public highway at a greater speed than fourteen miles an hour, or than any less speed that may be prescribed by regulation of the Local Government Board.

At the same period another Select Committee was set up to further consider the use of traction engines on roads. By this time it was estimated that 8,000 traction engines were in use in England and Wales, involving a capital outlay of £10 million and employing 30,000 to 40,000 men.[1] The outcome of the committee's deliberations was **The Locomotive Act 1898**. These rules largely affected the use of traction engines rather than their construction. In particular they addressed issues such as towing trailers (three only permitted), manning of engines, attendance when stationary, lighting at night.

The next piece of vehicle legislation was **The Motor Car Act 1903**. This was an amendment to the **Locomotives on Highways Act 1896** and was therefore only applicable to light locomotives. The principle change affecting the specification of vehicles was clause 9, which raised the speed limit to 20 miles per hour, or in restricted areas 10 miles per hour. The definition of a Motor Car or Light

Locomotive was still defined by its weight, i.e. to be less that 3 tons unladen or the combined weight of vehicle and trailer must be less than 4 tons.

A further refinement took place a year later, as defined by the **Heavy Motor Car Order 1904,** dated 27 December 1904. These new regulations came into force on 1 March 1905 and defined the heavy motor car as being a vehicle weighing more than two tons unladen but with a maximum unladen weight of five tons. Alternatively, six and a half tons were allowed for an unladen combination of heavy motor car and trailer. Curiously, Military Motor Cars were given special rights, for example, the maximum unladen weight was six tons, and the maximum unladen weight for a military motor car and trailer combination was eight tons. For all Heavy Motor Cars had to be fully sprung and for those weighing three tons or more, the maximum width of the vehicle was set at seven foot six inches. As well as these general points, there was also a lot of technical detail defined in the Order:

The tyres of each wheel of a heavy motor car had to be smooth and flat where they touched the ground, but the edges of the tyres could be bevelled or rounded at each edge to the extent of half an inch. The tyre could be constructed of separate plates, providing that nowhere the aggregate extent of the space or spaces in the course of a straight line drawn horizontally across the circumference of the wheel exceed an eighth of the width of the tyre. The width of the tyre was not less than five inches, but increased in a complicated calculation depending on load and wheel diameter. For pneumatic or soft tyres, a minimum wheel diameter of two foot was required.

The speed of the vehicle was restricted to eight miles per hour, but this was reduced to five miles per hour if the vehicle weighed in excess of three tons, or the registered axle weight exceeded six tons, or a trailer was being drawn. Furthermore, if the wheels were fitted with pneumatic or other soft tyres the speed limit was increased to twelve miles per hour, except if the registered axle weight exceeded six tons, then the maximum speed was eight miles per hour.

Finally, to comply with the rules the vehicle had to have painted on it, in one-inch high letters, the salient details of registration. The letters had to be legible and in contrast to the background colour of the vehicle. In addition, the regulations stated that the lettering had to be maintained to keep it legible. The information specified for display on the vehicle was as follows:

- The highest legal speed of the vehicle (M.P.H.), displayed on the left hand side (nearside) of the vehicle
- The registered axle weight of each axle – (A.W.) tons, displayed on the right hand side (offside) of the vehicle
- The registered weight, unladen (U.W.) tons, displayed on the right hand side (offside) of the vehicle

The unladen weight was defined in the regulations as, "the weight of a vehicle exclusive of the weight of any water, fuel, or accumulators, used for the purposes of propulsion". This was quite restrictive as the combined weight of fuel and water on a wagon was of the order one to one and a half tons.

In later years the **Roads Act, 1920**, increased the legal weight of an unladen vehicle from 5 to $7^1/_4$ tons, and allowed six-wheelers to carry 10 to 12 tons. Similarly, **The Finance Act, 1920,** and its later amendments, affected registration and licencing of vehicles. These acts did not affect the construction of vehicles but they affected the economics of heavy vehicles because of the heavy duties charged, and was one of the major influences in removing steam vehicles from public roads.

References

1 Lane, F. D., *Portfolio Number 40,* Road Locomotive Society

Appendix 6

Handbook of Instructions

This fascinating document, written around one hundred years ago, reflects changing attitudes to men, machines and materials. The use of asbestos and red-lead (lead oxide) for jointing material, both now restricted substances, was widespread. Similarly the suggestion that men should be given the "sack" for not cleaning their engines is out of step with current industrial practice. Similarly, advances in bearings and lubrication allow modern road vehicles to have long service intervals, and it is easy to forget that not long ago, machinery required daily lubrication, cleaning and examination.

Tel. Address: "CANNING," LEEDS. Tel. No. 27117.

MANN'S PATENT STEAM CART AND WAGON CO., Ltd.,

PEPPER ROAD WORKS, HUNSLET,

— LEEDS. —

LONDON OFFICE: 9. FENCHURCH AVENUE, E.C.
TEL. ADDRESS: "INTENSELY, FEN., LONDON."
TEL. NO. 12283 Central.

Handbook of Instructions

AND

USEFUL INFORMATION

FOR WORKING

Mann's Patent Steam Carts and Wagons.

PICKARD & REED, Printers, Malvern Road, Beeston Hill, Leeds.

Figure 141: Front Cover, Handbook of Instructions

Introduction

Before customers purchase one of our Patent Steam Carts or Wagons, we are able to demonstrate to them by an actual trial that they will take a certain load up a given gradient, and will travel at a certain speed for a given distance, with a definite amount of fuel, and that they are capable of being worked on bad roads.

They naturally ask - How long do we consider they will last, and what do we think they will cost a year in repairs? The answer to this is in a great measure conjectural, as so much depends upon the manner in which they are taken care of after they leave our hands, that we can only say they ought to last so many years, and only cost about so much per year in repairs, and it is in order to assist our friends in keeping within these limits that we publish this handbook of instructions and other useful information.

The principal reason why on undertaking a railway journey we can depend upon arriving at our destination without a breakdown is because a locomotive is never allowed to start on a journey without every part of it being in good working order, so far as can be ascertained by examination, whereas the majority of road engine owners and drivers appear to think that it is plenty soon enough to examine them after they have broken down. To be properly examined it is necessary that the engine should be clean.

We strongly advise our customers to have a good well-lighted shed to run them into at night, and to have them **cleaned and examined after every day's work**. Saturdays might with advantage be given to the man for washing out the boiler and tanks, packing glands, overhauling, adjusting, and thoroughly well cleaning the engine and oil bath, trimming lubricators, and doing any jobs necessary to keep them up to a high state of efficiency.

Where there are several engines we think it would be well to adopt locomotive practice, and have a man to come at night to clean the engines and get steam up ready to go out next morning.

The shed for a lurry should be 28 to 30 feet long, for a cart about 24 feet long, and for both at least 12 feet wide. If possible it should be lighted from roof, sides and ends, and should be provided with doors, a cowl and chimney for taking away the smoke when getting up steam, and with one or two ventilators in the roof. It should have a concrete floor, with a good fall for draining away the water; an adequate supply of water at a good pressure is necessary for washing out, or a force pump should be used similar to the one we illustrate. Gas lamps should be fixed for showing a good light on the parts necessary to be cleaned. A bench, vice, and suitable assortment of tools and appliances are also essential, and some strong roof timbers, for attaching a pair of chain blocks to, would occasionally be found useful.

We recommend our customers to employ competent and experienced drivers. Some makers of road engines state in their catalogues that "any intelligent labourer can drive their engines." They can drive ours so far as driving only is concerned, but owners will find out that there is something required beyond merely driving them along the road.

This (misnamed) economy of the "Intelligent Labourer Driver" (who is frequently rough and reckless) has taken such root in the minds of many traction engine owners that makers have been obliged to resort to unnecessary strength and heaviness in order to make the **engines suit the drivers**, whereas with these carts and lurries, which, although very strongly constructed, are by the Motor Cars Act limited to weight, it is necessary for the **drivers to suit the engines**. For instance, a man with hazy ideas as to the fitness of things, accustomed to exert all his strength in tightening up a 1 inch bolt, will frequently without thought do the same with a ½ inch one, which, although quite strong enough for its purpose, will either break off altogether, or be fractured in such a manner as to break off afterwards, causing delay, and then complain that the engine is not strong enough. When a number of engines are sent out, all of the same design and construction, doing similar work, and some cost considerably less in repairs than others, we can only account for it by being better taken care of, and in the hands of competent drivers.

For an engine to be kept in good order it is imperative that it should be kept **clean**. The driver's usual excuse for neglecting this is want of time, if this is so, give him time, and if this has not the desired effect, give him the "sack".

We state in our catalogues the loads that the engines are constructed to take; this is the maximum weight that should be put on to them on good roads, otherwise the cost of repairs to cart and lurry bodies, road wheels, and springs, will be increased. The engines themselves are powerful enough to haul these loads up very steep gradients, consequently on the level they have considerably more power than is required to pull the maximum load which the body is constructed to carry.

Instructions to Drivers

Cylinders

Open drain cocks before starting, in order to get rid of the water, especially in frosty weather, when engine has been standing for some time. Pull flywheel round by hand to see that all is free.

Auxiliary Starting Valve

This is useful for starting the engine when the high pressure crank is on the centre, also for letting high pressure steam into low pressure cylinder for assisting the engine to get out of a bad place, and climbing a **short** stiff gradient without changing the speed; this throws a considerable amount of strain on the engine and should not often be resorted to, as it is much better to put in the slow speed when anything like a steep hill is come across.

Reversing

This is effected by our Patent Single Eccentric Reversing Gear or by Link Motion, either of which can be notched up, and can thus be utilised as a brake, but for steep and long hills use the foot brake. Keep the band brake properly lined.

Clutch Gear

Always put a scotch under the road wheel when changing the gear, and do not merely depend upon holding the engine by tightening up the brake. With traction engines more serious accidents have occurred with them running away owing to not being properly scotched when changing speed than through any other cause.

Before putting the engine out of gear, or turning the flywheel, **always open the cylinder drain cocks**, to prevent the engine starting suddenly and perhaps injuring the driver.

Pump

Is bolted low down and is consequently flooded, therefore it may be relied upon even when the water in the tank is hot. Should it, however, refuse to pump, first see gland is properly packed, then examine pipes and couplings (not forgetting nozzle end of suction pipe in tank), also both pump valves and check valve on boiler side to see if they have stuck, or if there is anything lodged under them. **The hole in the boiler side should occasionally be cleaned out**, as with some kinds of water it scales up quickly.

Always carry spare pump valves in the tool box, and, if necessary, they can be inserted in a few minutes on the road.

Keep the water level more than half way up the gauge glass, and **regulate the pump so as to keep a constant supply of water** passing into the boiler. If the water is allowed to get too low, the fusible plug in the firebox top will be melted and the fire put out by the escaping steam. If this happens, put in a new plug. On no account put in any form of solid plug instead of the fusible one, or there is risk of serious injury to the boiler. If by accident the water gets dangerously low, run the front wheels up an incline to keep the water to the firebox end, and rake out the fire.

In frosty weather be careful to empty the pump and pipe connections before leaving the engine for the night, or they may be burst.

If, however, it gets frozen, thaw the pump and pipes by holding a shovel of fire under it, and then pull the engine completely round by hand to see that all is clear.

Injector

To work self-acting injectors first open the water and then the steam supply by means of the wheel valve. If there is any overflow, reduce the water supply by means of the regulating cock. The injector is then at work. If it should stop working when travelling over rough roads, it will restart automatically. Be sure the water pipe is perfectly air-tight. For self-acting injectors the water in the tank should not exceed 120^0 F.

If the injector will not act, unscrew union at steam pipe joint, and examine valve to see if small hole through it is blocked with dirt or grit.

If, for any reason, the injector refuses to work at the usual pressure let the steam pressure fall and go home on the slow speed. A very small pressure will get the engine home, as it may be raised temporarily to climb hills if necessary.

Adjusting Brasses

It is of the utmost importance that the bearings of the engine should be adjusted and tightened **immediately** they develop a slight knock. Do not wait until it becomes bad or mischief may commence, resulting in a broken shaft at some future time. Where the brasses are fitted "metal to metal", file a little off the edges till the bolts can be tightened up without nipping the shaft. When the brasses are fitted with "liners" made of a number of thin plates, as in the big ends of the connecting rod, commence by removing the thinnest plate, and as the wear continues, remove the thicker ones. If the removal of the next thinnest after the first makes the brass too tight, replace the thin one after removing the medium thick so as to get an intermediate adjustment. Be sure to replace all check nuts, split pins, etc. The crosshead bush is made big and long as the wear is so slight we find it cheaper to occasionally renew the plain bush than to devote time to adjustment. It also avoids the risk of the adjusting wedge slackening back. Be sure to renew the bush as soon as it becomes a little slack, and do not let it go on knocking.

Boiler

When using coke, keep a thick fire (if this is done the engine will travel a considerable distance without firing), and depend upon the dampers and injector or pump for keeping down steam. Do not, however, fill the firebox so full that the direct heat comes on the fire door ring. Clean grate bars often enough to prevent clinker obstructing the draught. The frequency for this depends upon the quality of the coke. **Welsh smokeless coal** causes less wear on the firebox than coke, and should be used with a thinner fire, and a considerably **larger orifice to the blast pipe** than is required for coke, or it will burn at a very extravagant rate. Do not let the ashes accumulate in the ashes pan, or they will burn it away, as well as the grate bars, besides obstructing the draught. Sweep tubes out every morning before starting, also clear smoke box from soot and dirt, which soon corrode away the bottom. A small hole in bottom drains away the water.

If the gas coke available is of very poor quality, or makes much clinker, mix it with a proportion of hard coke. Experiment will soon show how little hard coke will be satisfactory.

Wash boiler out once a week with a hosepipe having a good pressure of water (we make an efficient pump for this purpose; see back end of book). Poke out well with small mud rake, taking special care no scale or dirt is lodged fast between the stays, also rake out all mud round bottom on foundation ring. Break manhole joint so as to swill sides of firebox well down from the top, and take out plug in front tube plate to swill out barrel underneath the tubes.

Tallow plug and screw well home to prevent leakage, which soon damages thread and plates.

Make joints of mud doors with proper woven asbestos joint rings soaked in boiled oil.

If scale is seen to be forming on firebox and tubes use the boiler composition which we recommend for preventing it, as per instructions sent along with it. Directly tubes show signs of leaking they should be expanded at once, hence it is advisable to have an expander. At the firebox end it may be sufficient to drive the ferrules further in.

Exhaust Pipe

Alter the adjustable end of the blast nozzle below the chimney to suit the quality of fuel. Keep the hole as large as possible, so long as the boiler makes sufficient steam. If it is smaller than necessary, it handicaps the engine by reducing its power and it will not do as much work.

If the pipe becomes choked by sediment it will seriously reduce the hauling power, but it may be cleaned by heating in a fire and hammering it to loosen the scale. Do this thoroughly and do not leave half the scale in. The sediment is often caused by unsuitable oil.

Tanks

Wash tanks out frequently, as if mud is allowed to accumulate it may cause trouble by blocking the pump pipe, etc.

Taking Water On Roads

When a good supply of **clean** water is come across, it is advisable to fill up the tanks even when there is a considerable quantity in them, as it may prevent you being obliged to take up dirty water further on. When this is unavoidable, put nozzle end of suction pipe on a big stone or shovel and take every precaution against stirring up the mud. When water lifter refuses to act, tighten up all couplings and see that it is not drawing air.

Locking Gear For Steel Wheels

If when travelling on soft slippery ground one of the road wheels begins to revolve, while the one on the other side of the engine remains stationary, tighten the strap provided for locking the differential gear, but it will have to be loosened before the engine will turn a sharp corner.

Spuds

Before entering any really soft bad ground put on the **full set of spuds or bars**, and you are pretty certain of getting across without damage to road or engine. Many drivers have a bad habit of first trying to get across without, then when bogged, put about two spuds on each wheel, which then has to revolve half a revolution before the engine moves forward, all the time churning up the ground. This is repeated until it eventually gets across after considerably straining the engine and cutting up the road.

Gland Packing

We use graphited asbestos packing for cylinder glands, and chalk packing for the pump, and we keep all sizes in stock.

Joints

Steam chest, cylinder cover, etc. - Make these with special thin prepared asbestos sheet. Carry spare string asbestos, jointing material, and gland packing. If this is not at hand, use red lead cement and tar band for temporary jointing.

Lubrication Of Engines

Proper attention to lubrication is vital for either the overtype or the oilbath machines, and for both types we stock suitable blends specially prepared for our engines.

Do not grudge the oil, but on the other hand nothing is gained by wasting it. Experience will soon show how much wick should be used in the trimmings. For the big ends of the connecting rod the pipe must be nearly filled by the trimming, or the oil runs to waste through their rapid motion.

When the engine is standing, always lift the trimmings out of the pipes or the oil will run steadily to waste and use as much oil as when the engine is running.

For the cylinders use good quality thick cylinder oil, which we always keep in stock. Adjust the lubricator from time to time if necessary by means of the adjusting screw in the cover so as to keep a regular supply.

In the case of the oilbath type of engine, open the bath and examine the engine parts every day when it is new. Always fill the oilbath to the top of the level indicator on the engine side every day before starting. In the outfit we include a strainer, and at the end of each day this should be filled with oil run out of the plug in the bottom of the oil bath. The oil can then be strained back into the bath through one of the inspection lids in the cover, leaving the sediment in the strainer. Empty the bath every other week and fill with fresh oil. Always clean out the bath thoroughly to remove any grit which may have got in. You cannot expect good results if you do not do this. It would be as reasonable to put emery powder into the oil bath as to allow grit and dirt to accumulate, and if a user will not take this small amount of trouble, he does not deserve to get good results. A good machine is worth using well. Never use the oil over again without filtering it. Efficient filters may be obtained from us. Fill the grease cups (whether empty or not) before starting. Examine cups whenever opportunity offers on the road. Remember it is cheaper to lubricate than to spoil the bearings.

Besides filling lubricators the following, amongst other places, require to be well lubricated: fore carriage stud, sides of front axle where they rub against bracket; steel dies and slides of pin through front axle; steerage worm and quadrant, piston rods and slide spindles near glands (differential gear through pipe provided for that purpose); differential pinions; sliding ends of springs. In general, **wherever there is movement you must lubricate**.

Always carry spare pump valves, lubricators, jointing, etc., in tool box. **Do not leave them at home** or neglect ordering in time. Watch the gearing, tyres, brasses, etc., and order new ones when they are getting thin. Do not wait till the renewal is actually wanted, or you waste time in which the wagon might be working. Do not run the tyres so thin as to damage the rims of the wheels.

Oil, Grease, and General Stores

We have often found owners of steam wagons using unsuitable stores, and we therefore keep a stock of everything likely to be required. We stock the following:

- Engine Oil (special mixtures)
- Cylinder Oil
- Grease for Bearings
- Boiler Fluid for preventing scale
- Jointing, either in sheets or ready cut
- Gland Packing
- Waste
- Sponge Cloths
- Outfit and Tools (Buckets, Oil Cans, Oil Bottles, Spanners, Hammers, Files, Chisels, etc.)
- Oil Filters.

In conclusion, we recommend drivers to bear in mind that, although by Act of Parliament these Steam Carts and Wagons have just as much right on the road as a vehicle drawn by horses, there is, and will be for some time, a certain amount of prejudice against them, especially by people possessing horses and carriages, and it is advisable not only to keep a good look out in front, but **also behind**, and bring the engine to a standstill immediately the driver holds up his hand or a horse appears likely to become restive. Do all in your power to make things pleasant and give assistance, and thus minimise the objections they have against them. Just at present some of the police and other authorities are not very clear where the Light Locomotive or Motor Car Act ends and where the Traction Engine Act begins, and if stopped by them, always give a civil explanatory answer, and if they do not appear to be satisfied, ask them to kindly communicate with the owner or makers previous to taking any further steps in the matter, as it may be the means of saving them a considerable amount of trouble, and the owners from a vexatious and fruitless prosecution, as generally in these cases the summons is dismissed or withdrawn.

Appendix 7

Key Dates and Events

1860	Birth of James Hutchinson Mann
1893	Purchase of the Canning Works
1894	Formation of the company Mann and Charlesworth
1894	Single-Eccentric Reversing Gear patented
1898	Introduction of the Mann's Steam Cart
1899	Introduction of the Mann's Steam Lorry (5-ton)
1899	Formation of Mann's Patent Steam Cart and Wagon Company Limited
1900	Purchase of the Pepper Road site
1901	Silver medal awarded, Liverpool Trials
1901	Business transferred to the Pepper Road Works
1903	Introduction of the Colonial Steam Wagon
1905	Introduction of the 2-ton Undertype Wagon
1905	Revision of the 5-ton Undertype Wagon
1905	Introduction of the 5-ton Tractor (based on the steam cart)
1908	Introduction of the Fuel Hopper Wagon (2-ton)
1908	Introduction of the 5-ton Road Tractor (traction engine style)
1908	Introduction of the Patching Roller
1910	Introduction of the Direct Ploughing Tractor
1911	Introduction of the 3-ton and 5-ton Overtype Wagon
1915	Introduction of the low-cost Agricultural Tractor
1923	Introduction of the 3-speed, 4-ton and 6-ton Overtype Wagons
1924	Introduction of the Mann Express Wagon
1926	Company run by receiver
1927	Debts paid and business running normally
1929	Goodwill transferred to Atkinson Walker and Pepper Road Works sold
1932	Mann's Patent Steam Cart and Wagon Company Limited dissolved

Bibliography

Books

Aitken, T., *Road Making and Maintenance*, Griffin & Co. Ltd., London, 1907
Clark, R. H., *The Development of the English Traction Engine,* Goose & Son, 1960
Clark, R. H., *The Development of the English Steam Wagon,* Goose & Son, 1963
Kelly, M. A., *The Overtype Steam Road Waggon*, Goose & Son, 1971
Kelly, M. A., *The Undertype Steam Road Waggon*, Goose & Son, 1975
Kidner, R. W., *The Steam Lorry, Locomotion Papers No.3*, Oakwood Press, 1956
Lane, M. R., *The Story of the Britannia Ironworks*, Quiller Press, 1993
Lane, M. R., *The Story of the Steam Plough Works,* Northgate Publishing Co., 1980
Norris, W., *Modern Steam Road Wagons*, Longmans, Green and Co., 1906
Paterson, J., *The History and Development of Road Transport*, Pitman & Sons, 1927
Report of the Tractor Trials held at South Carlton Nr. Lincoln, S.M.M.T. 1919
Walker, J. W., *Yorkshire Pedigrees,* Harleian Society, 1944
Whitehead, R. A. & J. E., *Garrett Portable & Fixed Engines*, Tonbridge, 1997
Whitehead, R. A., *Garrett Traction & Ploughing Engines*, Tonbridge, 2004
Whyatt, H. G., *The Highway Engineers' Yearbook*, Pitman & Sons, 1924

Mann's Patent Steam Cart and Wagon Company Publications

Catalogues - Various
Illustrated list of Duplicate Parts – 5-ton Overtype Steam Wagon

Journals and Newspapers

Bradford Daily Telegraph
Bridlington Free Press
Commercial Motor
Doncaster Gazette
Engineering
Leeds Mercury
Journal of the Royal Agricultural Society of England
Proceedings of the Institute of Mechanical Engineers
Steaming
The Automotor and Horseless Vehicle Journal - later - *The Automotor Journal*
The Engineer
The Implement and Machinery Review
The Northern Star, Lismore, NSW, Australia
The Town and Country Journal, Sydney, Australia
The World's Carriers
Wakefield Express Newspaper
Yorkshire Evening Post

Archives

Armley Mills Industrial Museum, Leeds
Bradford Local Studies Library
Bridlington Local Studies Library
British Library, Boston Spa, Wetherby
Centre d'archives de Québec, Canada
Institution of Mechanical Engineers
Leeds Local History Library
Museum of English Rural Life, University of Reading
National Motor Museum, Beaulieu
Patents Information Unit, Leeds
Probate Registry, York
Public Record Office, London
Register of Births, Marriages & Deaths; Dewsbury, Hull, Leeds and Sheffield
Road Locomotive Society
Royal Agricultural Society of England
Society of Antiquaries of London
Society of Motor Manufacturers and Traders
The West Riding Registry of Deeds, Wakefield.
University of Leeds, Brotherton Library
Wakefield Local Studies Library
West Yorkshire Archive, Leeds and Wakefield
Yorkshire Agricultural Society, Harrogate
Yorkshire Archaeological Society, Leeds

Index